7-2-73

# THE SOUL, THE PILL AND THE FETUS

by
John Pelt

DORRANCE & COMPANY

Philadelphia

# CONTENTS

# PREFACE

When one considers the subjects of contraception and abortion, he is confronted immediately with a personal life and personal relations. Medical science in her accomplishments and endeavors to eliminate or alleviate the physical and mental suffering of the individual finds herself both challenged and aided by the interpreted principles of the Judeo-Christian Ethic, which adds a spiritual or moral dimension to man's nature.

Man from the beginning of creation was given the power to procreate, that is, to be in partnership with God in propagating his species. Life is both mysterious and sacred, and this is especially true in the case of man. In our contraceptive society and abortion reform law era, life is still mysterious and should be sacred, whether in the prevention of the union of two cells or in the termination of a pregnancy.

Man *possible* (sperm and or ovum) *potential* (union of the two cells), or *real* (at birth) deserves to be treated preferentially above any creature on earth because he was created in the image of God, and his relationship to God is unique.

Neither this work nor any other can answer the profound questions raised by Christians and non-Christians on the pros and cons of contraception and abortion. It is, however, the prayerful desire of the writer that the thoughts and research offered will prove of value to the Christian minister, physician, parishioner, or friend that must make decisions as he counsels individuals who must answer positively or negatively to the above issues.

Faith, revelation, reason, and experience must be coupled with the Holy Spirit in our quest for a better Christian understanding of the current subject. The issue is relevant in our age of changing morals and complex problems.

Situation ethics, an ally of existential theology, plays an important role in the changing attitudes toward existing laws on contraception and abortion. Rules are always subject to change and updating, but moral principles based on the Word of God are constant. The "pill" cannot dissolve the Scriptural injunction against illicit sexual behavior, nor can legalized abortion laws alter the Biblical principle of "reverence for life," since life is mysterious and sacred. Yet, we would hasten to add that the complex ethical problems confronting society and the individual cannot be easily brushed aside by an "either/or" answer. The Christian must wrestle with these important ethical and moral problems of our day. All the answers will never be given on the morality and ethics of contraception and abortion; however, by pondering the issues a greater respect for God, for man and life, can be experienced whereby sanctified reason will sway the will in the realm of these moral choices.

Perhaps it would not be out of order to say a few words about the circumstances surrounding the writing of this book. The writer has been in the pastoral ministry for seventeen years. The last nine years of these were in Glendale, California where he was pastor of the Glendale Vallejo Drive Seventh-day Adventist Church, which is adjacent to the Glendale Adventist General Hospital. Also, during the past nine years he served as a member of the board of directors in this hospital.

Many times the subject of contraception and abortion appeared, both in private counseling sessions and in discussion with various specialists and general practitioners in the field of medicine. He has struggled often with physicians and patients involved in the ethical and moral aspects of contraception and particularly of abortion. Especially in the realm of abortion, some decisions to terminate fetal life appeared as inevitable. Other decisions were borderline cases where either a "yes" or "no" answer appeared to be laden with uncertainty.

By no means have embalmed conclusions been arrived at concerning these ethical and moral dilemmas. However, case histories and research on this topic have deeply impressed the writer with a greater appreciation and reverence for life. This profound concern and respect for human life begins, in the writer's opinion, from the moment of conception, and to terminate this life at any stage of human development and growth is a terrible choice, even though at times it may be a necessary decision. It is the firm conviction of the writer that neither the soul surgeon nor the physician are adequately equipped to counsel or attempt either to save or terminate a life until they know the value of life.

Gratitude is expressed to the late Jaymes P. Morgan, Dr. Frderic W. Bush, Dr. Paul King Jewett, and Dr. Blenn Whitaker for their help and encouragement during the preparation of this book.

# INTRODUCTION

Prior to a study and investigation of the current subjects, Contraception and Abortion, it is fitting to consider the primary subject matter—"man." He is the latest and most important creature on earth. Both Christian and non-Christian anthropologists concur on this fact.

Man is presented in many different ways in the Bible, but always in relation to God. He must be discussed, in view of recent scientific discoveries, both biologically and psychologically. Current exegetes will be referred to as well as theologians and writers and spokesmen of various faiths.

The nature of man is pertinent to the subject of contraception and abortion. For example, when is one a person? At conception, fertilization, blastocyst, implantation, embryo? Or is one a person during subsequent fetal development, at birth, infancy, childhood? Furthermore, what about man's specific nature? Is he trichotomous (body, soul, and spirit) or dichotomous (body and soul)? What is the "Image of God" in man, and when does he receive it? Is man a composite unit or does he possess a mortal frame and some immortal entity?

It is important to establish a working model of man's nature as presented in Scripture in order to approach the current problems regarding contraception and abortion. The religious aspect of the problem cannot be ignored, as practically all ethical and legal codes of the western world are based upon Judeo-Christian ethics and principles. Man is properly viewed in Scripture in relation and communion with God. Jesus summarized man's whole moral duty when He answered the questioning scribe in Mark 12:30-31 "that we should love God and man." Only as we love God by virtue of the redeeming experience in

Christ can we truly love other human beings. Such love will produce respect and reverence for human life at every stage of development and growth.

Today a paradox seems to exist in man's great accomplishments, particularly in the area of science. Giant strides have been made in technology by the power and genius of human reason. Yet along with technology and automation, man who has accomplished so much is depreciated in many ways. Millions have perished by war, disease, and hunger. Since World War II, a great lack of "reverence for life" exists. Paul Tournier states that there are personality destroying social forces of our day, and despite counsel to the contrary, they treat this rational spiritual being as though he were an exploitable, disposable object. He is treated as though he were the means of an industrial, political, economic, or military end.[1]

In this book, it is the aim of the writer to refer to a number of specific professions dealing with man's total nature, particularly the field of theology and medicine, as well as law, and sociology. In all professions, human life as possible, potential, and as a mature being, demands concern and respect since man is created in the image of God. Man must not only be studied as object but he must be respected both as object and subject. He is much more than the complex arrangement of cells. He is a person with inalienable rights, and when, or at what point, these rights begin has not been conclusively established by any profession.

The total person concept as outlined in Scripture and attested to by medical science and many leading contemporary theologians should call forth a profound reverence and concern for life, especially in the area of abortion. This concern and reverence for human life should exist from the mysterious union of two cells throughout the entire life of a human being. In the field of anthropology and in Scripture, man is viewed as supreme in relation to every other creature on earth. The first section of this book deals with man in the realm of the above two references. Man must be studied both as subject and object prior to an investigation of contraception and abortion. Scientific anthropology can give us many insights concerning man, but only Scripture places the true value upon a human life. Thus, as a pre-requisite to a study and investigation of contraception and abortion, man in his totality must be considered.

## Notes to Introduction

1. Paul Tournier, "Man is Not a Thing," in *Are You Nobody*, ed. by Paul Tournier, et al. (Richmond: John Knox Press, 1967), p. 8.

# Chapter I

# THE TOTAL PERSON

## Man Considered Anthropologically

Man, anthropologically speaking, is the most recent and significant of all creatures on the earth. He soars with his reason oftentimes in an autonomous fashion. Scientists appear to have it in their power to alter the surface of the earth and to choose which type or types of species shall survive to populate and control the earth. In a few decades he has unlocked and harnessed many of nature's powers and secrets. To a limited degree he has escaped his temporal environment in his conquest of space. Less spectacular but by no means less significant and important are discoveries in the minutia of creation, such as the field of genetics. In this area of scientific activity, man via genetic control and surgery appears to be capable of structuring his species as he deems fit. This is true not only physically, but mentally as well in this age of advanced medical science.

To the general observer, it appears that man in the name of science is the greater miracle worker, that he can now play God! Parenthetically, we might add that every great civilization had its "Tower of Babel" as a tribute to the genius of man. Has man reached the zenith of his mental abilities? In its individual capacities and penetrations man's brain may have reached its organic limits.[1] This view would be difficult for most non-Christian anthropologists to accept since man's course to them is ever upward, not downward, nor even horizontal.

Man's understanding of himself as to his origin no doubt influences his attitude and behavior toward human life whether potential or real. It is true that the origin of man poses a number of problems, such as, did human organism descend from preexisting beings in the animal order? If so, how did this come about? The problems of anthropology are far more pressing to evangelical Christianity than those of geology or astronomy. Anthropologists have discussed at great length physical anthropology. Some stress the polygenetic origin of man, others lean toward monogenesis. Jean S. J. De Fraine states that a scientist would probably admit that the great majority of anthropologists accept monophyletism, the hypothesis claiming that the whole of mankind derives from one single animal stem.[2]

Modern science claims to have demonstrated the great antiquity of man, dating him back 500,000 years, or as the renowned anthropologist Dr. Leakey says, our nearest cousin dates back 20,000,000 years. Thus, there is a pure scientific view of the origin of man, also a philosophical view, and finally a religious view of man. The latter will be discussed under the topics "Man in Scripture" and "The Scriptural Use of the Total Person." It is not the purpose of this paper to discuss the problem of fossil man in relation to the Scriptural account of man's origin. However, in order to make relevant our study of contraception and abortion, it is important to understand as much as we can about man's origin and nature. Anthropologists deal with man's past, basing their conclusions on varied pieces of evidence. The evangelical Christian must view man, *his origin, and nature from a recorded past which is the inspired Scriptures.*

The unity of the human race finds accord among the anthropologists, both Christian and non-Christian. Anatomically, man's body is the same among all types of human beings, whether small or large, fair or dark. Physiologically, the human race is one. This unity is significant theologically in view of the imputation of Adam's sin to the entire human race. In view of the unity of the race, polygeneticism appears difficult apart from the Scriptural view of man's origin. Polygeneticism would be damaging to theology in that theology is concerned more with the proof that man is one, rather than the near or far antiquity of man.[3] Liberalism had no problem with the fossil man and the creation account since her theology needed no historical anthropology. In liberalism, man simply fell upward and became capable of a religious experience. Historical anthropology proved more of a problem to the neo-orthodox in that creation, original sin and the fall, and redemption are important in neo-orthodoxy. For example, Brunner attempts to resolve the problem by approaching the problem existentially. He views the Genesis account of creation as ancient myth. God shines forth as Creator, but the truth is not scientific but an existential one.[4]

The fact that most anthropologists lean toward monogenesis and place man at the head of all forms of earthly life supports indirectly the Biblical view of man. In other words, both in Scripture and in the science of anthropology, man stands alone and unique as a rational moral being. His beginning is unique. It is fitting that we begin immediately with the Scriptural view of the total person because man as we know him today is presented as a model, both to the medical scientist and to the theologian.

*Man in Scripture*

Traditionally, the ethical and moral judgments of the western Christian world originated and are derived from God. God Himself and His principles are revealed in the Bible, and these revealed principles have been available for centuries. God in Scripture is more than an "idea" or "product of history." He is not conceived through faith alone, but by faith, revelation, reason, and experience. He must be a priori; that is, God first, then man. Such a concept is necessary if we are to understand our origin, our nature, and to place a proper value upon human life. God is the Creator who set in motion inanimate matter; He created man and established a written moral code for his conduct and behavior; He is also Judge and Savior to the human race. God is the source of creation. Creation is not an extension of God. It is the product of His creative power.

The significance and importance of man is seen early in the creation account as outlined in Scripture. In the beginning man was given dominion over the earth and its creatures (cf. Genesis 1:28-30); however, he was not given control over the lives of fellow human beings. Today, man may perform his wonders in science, yet he must never control moral judgments. No doubt in these matters most scientists neither proclaim nor prefer moral detachment. None have memories so brief in these matters as to forget the Nazi scientists who experimented with human beings as if they were monkeys, rats, and guinea pigs. To them, the Jews were not really human beings. It was a disregard for the definition and worth of man anthropologically and Scripturally. Man's dominion over the creatures was never given to negate a reverence for life even among the brute creation. And this in no way is to imply a pantheistic view of creation. No life, even among the animal kingdom, was to be sacrificed for the selfish gain of the individual.

The psalmist voiced his opinion as to who and what is man. In Psalm 8:4-6 he asks the question: "What is man, that thou art mindful of him, and the son of man, that thou visitest him? For thou hast made him a little lower than the angels." The Psalmist recognizes the fact that man is more than a complex biological organism; he is not just a chemical machine. He is pictured in the phrase "Thou (God) visitest him" in communion relationship to God. Man was the crowning act or goal of God in His creative activity. In Gen. 1 and 2, there are distinctive features granted to him in creation. He does not appear in the creation narrative, for instance, as light does: "Let there be light" (Gen. 1:3), but *Elohim* said, "let us make man in our image" (Gen. 2:26a). Man alone in the creation account was copied after God, all other living creatures were after their kind and over them God gave man dominion. As to who man is, he is a being created by God and placed above all creation by virtue of the fact that he was in the image of God. The *Imago Dei* in man separates him from all other forms of created life. We will consider more fully the image of God in man in a later section. Thus, man was created above all the animal creation, but a little lower than the angels.

Man is of the same composition as the animal kingdom, a mammal, but vastly different! The Bible repeatedly points to these two different sides of man, namely, the fact that on one

8

side he is actually a mammal, and on the other, a real image of God.[5] In the Biblical narrative the stars, plants, and animals are only objects of the creative, "let there be!" Man is addressed in the second person singular as "thou." He is entrusted with a perfect character which he could and did abandon. Man at creation is possessed with a consciousness of self which is not true of the rest of the animal kingdom. It is true that they possess marvelous instincts, but they are not self-conscious nor capable of abstract reasoning. No wonder the writer of Psalm 139:14 said: "I will praise thee; for I am fearfully and wonderfully made."

The word "man" in Hebrew is 'adam. In Genesis 5:2, God employed this word to depict the father of the human race. The meaning of the word has been explained in different ways, depicting either his color from 'adam "to be red," or his appearance from an Arabic root which signifies "to shine," making Adam or 'adam the "brilliant one"; or his nature as to God's image, from 'dam, "likeness," or and most probably his origin, "the ground," from 'adamah, "the one of the soil."[6] Although 'adam denotes mankind in Scripture, it is used also to designate the first man who was created by God in His image. The Genesis author is undoubtedly pointing to a first man in time and space. However, the stress on "mankind" as a proper name is certainly significant. In fact, following the book of Genesis, Scripture is silent in specifically referring to the first man Adam with the exception perhaps of Romans 5, I Corinthians 15, and in I Timothy 2:13, 14. If there was a "last" Adam in history, there must have been a first one.

In Scripture, the fact exists that one day God created man as we know him today, with the exception of the effects of sin which was imputed to the race as a consequence of the sin of the first man, Adam. The biological aspects of the original sin have affected the total person. The imputation of sin and its transmission to the race involves more than some particle being carried and passed on through the genes and chromosomes. There are many things beyond apprehension in their mode, but definite in their reality. Sin is a condition of being as well as an

9

act involving the will. Even though the first man fell, he remains nevertheless, man, whom God created in His image.

Who man is according to the Bible can be explained easier than what man is. Whether we consider Adam, the first man, or his posterity, there is something unique and unaccountable about each man. He cannot be deduced from a microscopic examination of tissue or glands. With the arrival of each new person there is an "I-Thou" relationship. In Genesis 3:8-11, Adam was conscious of himself and God: "The Lord called unto Adam, and Adam heard the voice of God." In this narrative, Adam is revealed as a self-conscious moral being created in the image and likeness of God. He was capable of and did hold fellowship and communion with God. This union was broken by man's free choice, which is revealed by his disobedience and fall from grace.

The Bible says man is of divine origin. God, the transcendent Creator, created the universe by His word alone without the help of a demiurge. In Psalms 33:6, we are told: "By the word of the Lord were the heavens made." God remains forever the first and primitive source of all human dignity. Such is the religious teaching concerning the origin of man as presented also in Gen. 1:26-28.[7] In this passage, monogenesis is stressed as well as in Gen. 2:7, 18-24, Romans 5:12-19, and in Acts 17:26. The Bible in no way sanctions polygenesis regarding the origin of the race. Such a view appears to be totally untenable particularly in light of the above passages, and in the light of the transmission or imputation of original sin.

The unity of the race is evidenced in the collective meaning of the name 'adam; historically and physiologically all mankind is related. Also, according to the profound insight of Kierkegaard, Adam is both himself and his progeny.[8]

A true knowledge of man must be grounded in the acknowledgment of a revelation as offered in the Word of God. Only in relation to God can we understand man's origin, purpose, and destiny in life. Specifically in Christ, the second Adam, are we able to interpret and understand the first Adam as a singular

10

person in time and history as related in the creation narrative. We might add that the dignity of human life in all its history, from the moment of conception until death, is better appreciated as one studies the two Adams in Scripture. The first Adam experienced his fall in history. The second Adam, Jesus Christ, was also a man in time and history, making possible the restoration of the fallen first man and his posterity. The first Adam is not focused on at the moment of conception, birth, or even childhood. He is first revealed in Scripture as a mature physical and moral creature in God's image. Jesus Christ, the second Adam, in contrast is first revealed in His humanity at conception, at birth, childhood, and then as a mature person. He was not the acme of some evolutionary development, either physically or ethically. In Galatians 4:5, He was sent by God, "made of a woman." In the incarnation He became the unique Son of God, and this was not due to the mistaken notion that He inherited this quality from His mother, Mary. The uniqueness and sacredness of human life certainly is demonstrated to us in the person of Jesus Christ. From the moment of His conception, His human life was identified as such and of infinite value. In Luke 1:35, He is referred to as "that holy thing." By analogy, *man from conception is a human life, being created in the image of God*, even though the image has been marred by sin.

The ancients of the polytheistic Near East often conceived of man as being an extension of some pagan deity. The Christian view of man is that of contrast and distinction in relation to the creature and his Creator. Old Testament anthropology is closely bound up with the belief in the holy God, who is truly transcendent. As a result, there is a fundamental distinction between God and man. Man does not spring from God but is created (cf. Genesis 1) or formed by God out of the dust of the earth and made a living being by the breath (cf. Genesis 2:7). God gave Adam specifically and collectively the power to procreate, that is, to be a partner with God in the propagation of his species (cf. Genesis 1:28).

The true meaning of man, his dignity and intrinsic worth can

11

only be understood as he is related to God, the God of creation and redemption. On this point Isaiah 42:5 pictures the Creator and man: "Thus saith God the Lord, he that created the heavens, and stretched them out; he that spread forth the earth, and that which cometh out of it; *he that giveth breath unto the people upon it*, and spirit to them that walk therein." [Italics mine.] The passage implies that although man was created with the power to procreate, nevertheless God is by no means divorced in supplying the power to bring a new life into existence. Even though Adam's creation was more spectacular and unique, God is still man's Creator and source of life. He "giveth breath unto the people upon the earth."

Thus, we see man in Scripture, created in the image and likeness of God (Genesis 1:26), made a little lower than the angels and crowned with glory and honor, and given dominion over the earth (cf. Psalms 8:5, 6 and Hebrews 2:6-8). Man is the crown of creation and all things have been made with a purpose subordinate to his life and destiny.

## Different Theological Views of Man

This section will cover the leading views of man's nature as discussed by theologians and others. In the Old Testament the Hebrew writers were concrete and not abstract in their writings. This is especially true in their reference to the nature of man. The psychology of the Old Testament as well as the New presents man in many different ways. He is shown in varied contexts with many facets, yet these different aspects of his person are but manifestations of his unitive or total being. "The Hebrew conception of personality on its psychological side is distinctively that of a unity, not of a dualistic union of soul (or spirit) and body."[9] Berkouwer says of Barth's anthropology: "(he) . . . rejects the abstract and dualistic anthropology for which body and soul are two substances found together, two substances which, an immortal soul and mortal body, are intrinsically alien to each other."[10]

12

Present theological and psychological emphasis is almost altogether upon the fundamental wholeness of unity of man's being as against all philosophical attempts to divide it. Let us examine briefly the leading views as to man's nature.

There have been three leading theological views on the nature of man. The *first* is that he is trichotomous, i.e., that man is tripartite, composed of body, soul, and spirit. The concept no doubt originated from Plato's division of the person into body and soul and from Aristotle dividing the soul into an organic and intellectual aspect regarding man's being. Early Christian writers were influenced by Greek philosophy and confirmed their view by using I Thess. 5:23. "And the very God of peace sanctify you wholly; and ... your whole spirit, and soul and body be preserved blameless unto the coming of our Lord Jesus Christ." Scripture should be interpreted literally, figuratively or symbolically, or in its spiritual meaning. It is unfortunate that Greek philosophy has so profoundly influenced western Christian thought in the interpretation of Scripture because Greek metaphysic is chiefly dualistic, contrasting spirit and matter.[11] To the Greeks, matter and spirit were mutually exclusive; evil was imprisoned in matter and freed only at death; thus, matter was evil and the spirit good. The immortal soul was imprisoned by the body and freed at death.

> In Plato's impressive description of the death of Socrates, in the *Phaedo*, occurs perhaps the highest and most sublime doctrine ever presented on the immortality of the soul. ... We know the arguments he offers for the immortality of the soul. Our body is only an outer garment which, as long as we live, prevents our soul from moving freely and from living in conformity to its proper eternal essence.[12]

Oscar Cullman, commenting on Greek thought, stating further "The soul, confined within the body belongs to the eternal world. As long as we live our soul finds itself in a prison, that is, in a body essentially alien to it. Death in fact, is the great liberator.[13] The anthropology of the New Testament is not Greek as many

13

previously thought, but with Jewish conceptions. The idea of a trichotomy does not originate in Christendom, but in Greek philosophy.

The *second* theological view of man is that of a dichotomy, i.e., man is divided into two essential parts—body and soul (or spirit). A dichotomy has overtones from Greek philosophy. Plato taught that the body was perishable matter, but the soul existed in the heavenly world of pure form or idea before its incarnation in the human body. Thomas Aquinas was Aristotelian and developed the concept from Aristotle's "form and matter" that the individual soul was created in heaven and placed in the developing fetus at the time of quickening in the mother's womb. Contemporary theology usually rejects this view, holding to the body-soul unity of man as set forth in Hebrew thought: "And man became a living soul (being)" (Genesis 2:7). The Revised Standard Version of Scripture as well as the Jerusalem Bible translate "soul" as "being" in this passage. In the Old Testament there is no sign of this metaphysical, psychological, or ethical dualism; human nature is the created work of God, a unity of person.

The *third* theological view of man is that he is a unity, a whole, a total person. In the Old Testament, the Hebrew concept of man is that of the total person. He is not dissected into separate entities nor is he compartmentalized. He does not have a body, he is a body, he does not have a soul, he is a soul. E. L. Mascall writes:

> So strong was the conviction in Judaism that man is, to use the phrase of the late Dom Gregory Dix, an ensouled body rather than embodied soul, that the notion of the immortality of the soul played very little part in Jewish thought, all stress being laid upon the resurrection of the body.[14]

Many contemporary theologians are cognizant of the fact that the Bible views man in an impressive diversity; however, the unity of the whole man is never lost sight of in Biblical anthropology. In fact, his wholeness is brought out and accentuated over and over in Scripture. It appears clearly that Scripture does not view man even dualistically, nor is he a pluralistic being, but the whole man in his varied manifestations comes to the forefront in the inspired account.[15] Even in death the whole man is threatened. The fact that man was created from the dust of the earth and is called flesh is indicative of the fact that he is transitory.

Recent psychology agrees with the Scriptural view which emphasizes *the unity of man*. The science of psychology often uses various terms in the explanation of individual personality. However, these terms are not intended to compartmentalize the person; they are merely manifestations of the total person. When psychology speaks of regression, transference, sublimation, an aspect of the individual is merely described in relation to his behavior. Also in biology, both body and mind are but different aspects of the same thing.

A large number of Roman Catholic theologians are stressing the holistic man in their writings today. The authors of the new Dutch Catechism find difficulty in accepting the existence of spirit apart from matter. The Bible, according to this new catechism, never thinks of the soul as entirely divested of all corporeality. Here they are in accord with modern thought. What we are is so strongly linked up with our bodies that we cannot think of ourselves as an isolated "I" disconnected from our body.[16] Not only do many of the Dutch Roman Catholic theologians stress the total man concept, but many Germans of the same faith espouse the current view. These views are significant when we consider the centuries old view of the Catholic Church. She has taught for centuries that a new soul is created for each person at conception. This view is called Creationism.

Thus, man has been viewed as a trichotomy, dichotomy, and as an indivisible unit. It appears from science and leading contemporary theologians that the total person concept is the closest to the Scriptural view of man's nature. The idea that man is an indivisible unit, attested to in Scripture, makes life sacred and significant from the moment of conception. Such being the case, developing human life must be viewed with deeper reverence and respect than is currently expressed by many psychical and socio-economic spokesmen advocating radical changes regarding abortion laws. It is true that all the evidence is not yet in concerning the precise moment one becomes a person. From the standpoint of biological science it appears that scientists are making the union of two cells much more meaningful in light of recent discoveries in genetics. The full dignity of man, whether potential or mature, can only be appreciated with reverence and respect, as we look at man as viewed in Scripture. When man views himself from the standpoint of creation and redemption he is better able to place a value upon human life, regardless of its stage of development.

## Scriptural Use of the Total Person

### Hebrew Evidence

In the Old Testament, the Oriental, Semitic style of expression appears in contrast to Greek. The Hebrews did not write in an abstract but in a concrete manner. In Scripture, they view man in different ways, but always maintain his unity. We begin with the first book of the Pentateuch in our discussion of the terms body, soul, and spirit. As Edmund Hill remarked without apology in his comments on Gen. 1-11:

We start—at least I as a believer start, with an assumption which I am not going to try and justify now; it is that the whole Bible, including these chapters, is true, because it is inspired by the Spirit of God, it is the saving word of God to men, and God does not utter lies, or untruth, or mistakes, or deceit.[17]

The Hebrews in their psychology of man had no specific word for body, and the terms *nephesh* and *ruach* are translated in various ways as will be shown. In Gen. 2:7, the simple but mysterious formula for man is given. He stands uniquely on the horizon of creation, created by God from the elements of the earth. "It is impossible to attain to the profundity of Gen. 2:7; for this one verse is of such deep significance that interpretation can never exhaust it; it is the foundation of all true anthropology and psychology."[18] In Gen. 2:7, the Lord God "formed man of the dust of the ground," denoting the fact that man was mortal and transitory. Man is not truly man apart from God. Scripture immediately establishes anthropology in the God-man relationship. God "breathed into his nostrils and man became a living soul."

*Nephesh.*—The key phrase under consideration on the nature of man is the Hebrew word *nephesh*, translated "soul" in the KJV, but a better translation would be "man became a living being" as translated in the RSV. Man became (by virtue of God's creative act)"an animated body" and not as in Greek philosophy, "an immortal soul" enclosed in the body. Thus, man is formed from the elements of the earth and animated by the breath of life which comes from God. *Nephesh*, or "soul," is translated as soul, living being, life, self, person, desire, appetite, emotion, and passion. The significance in Gen. 2, whereby "man became a living being," is the fact that as far as matter is concerned man is merely material, but he has been called, created by God as a person who stands in connection with God. The term *nephesh* sums up the total person, his will, emotions, feelings, thoughts, desires, appetite, anatomy, and physiology, implying the total person. Thus, the conception of *nephesh* (mostly translated by soul) may quite often be taken in the sense of personality, the individuality, but never in the sense of an independent element in man which possesses eternal life in its own right. The *nephesh* is the vitality that animates the body and it is inconceivable that it should exist independently outside the body.

*Nephesh* is not a part of the person, it *is* the person, and in many instances is translated "person" (cf. Gen. 14:21; Num. 5:6;

17

Deut. 10:22; Ps. 3:2) or "self" (Lev. 11:43; I Kg. 19:4; Isa. 46:2). A person denotes relations, and man's first conscious moments in Gen. 2:7 reveals a unique relationship between man and his Creator. Apart from God there is no true *nephesh*; man became a "living being" only by God's breathing into him his own divine breath from his own mouth. The *nephesh* signifies that which is vital in man in the broadest sense, most significant the *nephesh* can die (cf. Num. 33:10), and thus the "living-being" relationship with God is broken.

Generally speaking, in contemporary Protestant and Catholic theology, the category of the "person" is strongly stressed. The *nephesh* is then simply the individual in his totality. After death the *nephesh* (soul or living being) ceases to exist, lingering only as long as the body is a body (Job. 14:22; Cf. II Kings 27:16-18; Amos. 2:1). The inhabitants of Sheol are never called souls. Parenthetically, we might add the term "soul" or *nephesh* is used freely by Old Testament writers. In its 754 uses it denotes the principle of life 282 times, the psychical aspect 249 times, and in a personal manner 223 times.[19] The foundation text (Gen. 2:7) sets the stage for the Christian view of man. The term "soul" in the passage is best translated "being" in order to convey from the beginning the unity of man in Scripture. Thus, the *nephesh* is the same dynamic element as the living being. It is the living being itself, the person. "Then the Lord God formed man of dust from the ground, and breathed into his nostrils the breath of life; and man became a *nephesh* (living being)" (Gen. 2:7). When the sacred writer wished to say "a living person," he simply said "a *nephesh*"; thus, when in Genesis 12:5 Abraham is shown journeying from the reign of the East to Canaan,he is said to have with him some *nephesh*, i.e., some people, some persons.[20] Therefore, the Hebrew presents man as a well-integrated unit of a psychical, physical, and spiritual combination.

*Ruach.*—The Hebrew word for "spirit" is *ruach*. The similar New Testament word is *pneuma*, and is used in all the ways in which the Hebrew *ruach* is used. The word *ruach* (spirit) is an onomatopoetic word, similar to *puach* and *naphach*, both of which mean to breath out through the mouth with a certain amount of violence, or even "to blow out."[21] Yet, *ruach*, like *nephesh*, is also used as a psychological term to denote a dominant disposition of the person or individual. *Nephesh* and *ruach*, to a large extent, are synonymous. A careful distinction must be made in the Old and New Testament whereby the use of *ruach* or *pneuma* is used in referring to the Holy Spirit or the Spirit of God. It appears that the Hebrew term *ruach* (spirit) spelled with a small "r" denotes primarily the divine energy, or life principle, that animates human beings, whereas the Hebrew word *nephesh* (soul) denotes primarily individuality or personality. *Ruach* is used 377 times in the Old Testament and most frequently is translated "spirit," "mind," or "breath" (cf. Gen. 8:1). In Jgs. 15:19, it denotes vitality; in Jos. 2:11, courage; in Jgs. 8:3, temper or anger; in Eze. 11:19, moral character; and in I Sa. 1:15, the seat of the emotions. This energizing spark of life, *ruach*, leaves the body and returns to God at death (cf. Ec. 12:7; Job. 34:14). There are a number of cases where the word *ruach* is used in similar ways, and they cover every type of disposition. H. Wheeler Robinson says *ruach* occurs 378 times in the Old Testament, denoting: (1) mind, natural or figurative, 131 times; (2) supernatural influences acting on man, 134 times; (3) the principle of life, 39 times; (4) the resultant physical life.[22] No clearer proof appears to be given that the term "dualism" is inappropriate and misleading in relation to Hebrew psychology; what we actually find is the explanation of the unity of personality. In Hebrew thought there is no room for the compartmentalizing of man.

Gerhard Von Rad, speaking on the life principle of man, states:

Life is possessed by man only in virtue of that breath of God; and this latter is in no sense inherently associated with

19

his body, and any withholding of this ephemeral gift would throw man back to a state of dead matter (Ps. civ. 29f.; Job XXIV. 14f).[23]

The new Dutch Catechism, well aware of these anthropological references in Scripture along with current scientific discoveries, comments on the "whole man": "Death is radical. It is not just the arms, legs, trunk and head that die. The whole earthly man dies. Here the deniers of immortality are right. Death is the end of the *whole man* as we have known him."[24] The unique unity of man in Scripture views him as a composite total person. Body and life merge with one another totally when God breathed into man's nostrils the breath of life. God breathes his spirit into the body of man. And this spirit is life and makes man alive. Dietrich Bonhoeffer says that the body is the existence-form of spirit, as spirit is the existence form of body.[25] In other words, they are not separate entities, but a union of matter and spirit (by God's Spirit) making the *nephesh* (soul) or total person. Man is an undivided unity created in the image of God.

*Body.*—The third key Scriptural reference to man anthropologically speaking is the word "body." The Hebrews have no definite word for "body." In Gen. 47:18, on the experience of the famine in Egypt, we read: "There is not aught left in the sight of my lord, but our *bodies*, and our lands" (italics mine). The Hebrew word here for body is *geviyah* from *gevah*. The first refers to a body whether dead or alive, the latter literally means "the back." In I Sam 31:12, we read: "All the valiant men arose, and went all night, and took the body of Saul and the bodies of his sons from the wall of Bethlehem, and came to Jabesh, and burnt them there." The reference naturally refers to the body as a corpse. In I Chron. 10:12, we read: "They arose, all the valiant men, and took away the bodies of his sons." Here the word for "bodies" is *guphah*, translated as "corpse" or "body" from *guph*, meaning "to hollow" or "arch."

The nearest Hebrew word perhaps to the Greek *soma* is *basar* (flesh). It is used with a psychical shade of meaning in 45 cases out of 266 in all in the Old Testament.[26] The Hebrew *leb* (heart), *nephesh* (soul-person), and *ruach* (spirit) are used to denote different aspects of the inner man. *Basar* refers to man's visible personality. The Greek equivalents in Paul's vocabulary are *psyche, pneuma,* and *sarx.* The emphasis in the Old Testament, whether the words "body" or "flesh" are used, is the unity of the personality, which is the main fact, and not the distinction of an immaterial and a material part, as in our modern usage. Thus, to the Hebrew, man was not a "body" and a "soul," but rather a "body-soul," a unit of vital power.

The absence of a specific term for "body" in Hebrew by no means negates the importance of the body as we conceive of it today. The translation of Enoch and Elijah in Gen. 5:24 and in II Kgs. 2:11 emphasizes, as does the New Testament, the importance and significance of the body in the Christian doctrine of man. God may also take a man to Himself, but here, too, both body and spirit are involved, man as a living being, as he exists here on earth (Enoch; Elijah).[27]

It is interesting to note in the Gen. 2 account of the creation narrative that no mention is made that God breathed into the body of the woman the breath of life. Some have used this passage, Gen. 2:21-23, in support of traducianism which states that the soul and body are derived. If we translate the term "soul" as "living being," or "person" in the Old Testament, particularly Gen. 2, there is no significance in the omission "breath of life" in relation to Gen. 2:7. In fact, we should refrain from translating this term as "soul" whenever possible.[28] No doubt God gave the principle of life to both Adam and Eve in the power to procreate. However, the details are lacking in the narrative whereby the duality of the sexes is given. Perhaps the genetic code so vital in procreation is intimated in Gen. 2:23 when Adam spoke of Eve as being "bone of my bones, and flesh of my flesh, because she was taken from man." Eve literally means the one who gives birth or the living one, although the name was given after the fall. The point is that the "body" is a characteristic element of Hebrew personality; about 80 different parts of the body are named in the Old Testament. By the creative act of God, "dust" became animated. A living, rational, moral being came into existence, a person created in the image of God. In the Old Testament, man began in a material manner and only has true humanity in relation to God. The significance of the "flesh" or "body" in the Hebrew economy as a unit may be interpreted also in their respect for the dead in the burial of the body as against cremation.

## Greek Evidence

*Psyche* (*soul*).—The Greek counterpart of *nephesh* or "soul" is *psyche*. The Old Testament was closed somewhere around 400 B.C. During the intertestamental period, Greek culture and language pervaded the civilized world. During this time, the Bible was translated into Greek (a version called the "Septuagint," the LXX). The Greek concept of the soul differed from the Hebrew usage of the term. Josephus, the famous historian, began to synthesize the Hebrew and Greek concept of the soul. This synthesis takes place after death, in the context of the individual's final destiny. Pure souls, he says, continue to exist after death. They attain a very holy place in heaven. Here, at the time when the change of *eros* takes place (the great long-awaited change, the eschatological age), the pure souls will again take possession of sanctified bodies.

Berkouwer says: "The whole man, according to the Old Testament as well as the New Testament is threatened by death.[29] We also meet the sharp criticism of dichotomy in H. Thielicke, who likewise stresses death strongly as judgment on the whole man, and who detects in the idea of immortality something of escapism, permitting the "real" man, the soul, to evade death; it is an effort to disarm death. Speaking of Dooyeweerd's concept of the soul, Berkouwer comments:

He (Dooyeweerd) formulated his own view quite sharply; all temporal existence, not merely one element in the fulness of man's being ends with death. Thus to the question of what activity remains for the soul separated from the body, the unqualified answer is obviously "nothing!"[30]

The New Testament writers wrote in a language which the Hellenized world understood; however, their Bible and background was Jewish. Paul views man in relation to God: Paul does not know the Greek-Hellenistic conception of the immortality of the soul, rather, *psyche* in Paul means primarily the Old Testament *nephesh*, rendered *psyche* in the LXX, which means vitality or life itself.[31] The use of "every soul" in the sense of "everyone," corresponds to the Old Testament idiom (cf. Rom. 2:9; 13:1). In this use, it is already apparent the *psyche*, too, can take on the meaning "person," or "self," like *nephesh*. Paul uses *psyche* altogether in the sense current in the Old Testament Jewish tradition, such as to designate human life or rather to denote man as a being. Paul does what the Old Testament writers did, that is, he uses a number of words which are merely representative of the total person, such as, *nous, pneuma, sarx, soma, kardia,* etc. When Paul speaks of the *pneuma* of man he does not mean some higher principle within him or some special intellectual or spiritual faculty of his, but simply his self.[32] In summary, Bultmann said that the various possibilities of regarding man, or the self, come to light in the use of the anthropological terms *soma, psyche,* and *pneuma.*[33] In the writings of the apostle Paul, one can replace the term *soma* (body) with the corresponding personal pronoun—with no damage done.

*Psyche* occurs 37 times in the New Testament and denotes in 16 cases physical life (cf. Matt. 2:20).[34] New Testament anthropology is an extension of continuation of Hebrew thought. The anthropology of the New Testament is not Greek, but is connected with Jewish conceptions. For the concepts of body, soul, flesh, and spirit (to name only these), the New Testament does indeed use the same words as the Greek philosopher, but the true meaning of the words are a continuation of Jewish thought and usage.

In summary, *psyche* or (soul) in the New Testament parallels the ancient Hebrew concept and use of *nephesh* or (soul) in the Old Testament. It means literally a life on earth in its external aspects; it is the earthly life itself, the seat of the inner life of man; it refers to feelings and emotions; it is the seat and center of life that transcends the earthly.

The word soul is currently used to express the deepest yearnings and feelings of the individual. Currently, some speak of "soul music," and "soul food"—terms denoting the deepest ties and feelings of the total person. Soul has, however, its deepest roots in the world of religion, and as Brunner said, the term soul was not discovered by science, but by religion, and the oldest doctrine about the soul, thousands of years before there was a science of the soul, was religious doctrine.[25] Plato took the term "soul" out of Orphic tradition into the realm of philosophy; Aristotle shifted the "soul" more to the empirical and scientific. Augustine, a Neo-platonist, baptized the term "soul" from a philosophical milieu into Christianity. Thomas Aquinas, though primarily of Augustine's view, followed Aristotle's form and matter concept and thus divides the soul, the soul being given to a fetus after viability. The distinctions commonly spoke of vegetative soul at the moment of conception, an animal soul at a later stage of embryonic development and a rational soul imparted as the moment of birth drew near.[36]

There is general agreement among theologians that man is an indivisible unit, body, soul, and spirit; not something that *has* a body, a soul, and a spirit. The Hebrew *nephesh* (soul) infers that it is the "life-principle" of the body (cf. Lev. 17:14), the total living *personal being* (cf. Gen. 2:7). The corresponding Greek term *psyche* (soul) also denotes life principle (cf. Acts. 20:10) as well as to denote the *total person* (cf. Rom. 11:3). In Acts 20, Paul had been preaching long when Eutychus fell three stories down and was killed. Paul went down and fell upon him, embracing him, he said: "Trouble not yourselves; for his *psyche* (life-principle) is in him." In Rom. 11:3, Paul is quoting Elijah's experience from I Kgs. 19:10, 14, stating: "I am left alone, and they seek my *psyche*, life" (cf. Rom. 16:4). Of a natural immortality of the soul, in the sense which our thought has inherited from Plato, he knows nothing.[37] The apostle uses *psyche* as a Jew with a Jewish background. The Dead Sea Scrolls illuminate the Old Testament influence upon the New Testament writers, especially Paul and John. It has often been said that the Dead Sea Scrolls add substantially to our knowledge of the Jewish background of Christianity. On this point, there is universal agreement. This is significant enough. It means, among other things, that both the Pauline and the Johannine literature can be understood in their Jewish background and that many of the odysseys of scholars some decades ago over the deep waters of Hellenistic philosophy and religion were more fascinating than they were rewarding.[38]

Paul does not use *psyche* alone to denote the individual self; he also employs other terms in describing man. An example is his use of "flesh." Kuhn comments on Rom. 7:17-20: "I am carnal, sold under sin," the characteristics of human existence is "flesh," and he interprets this "in me" as "in my flesh."[39] He could have said instead of "flesh," "in my body," "in my person," etc. "Flesh" is used ethically referring to the whole sinful person. Thus, Paul used various terms expressing the total person; however, this book is limited primarily to the Biblical usage of body, soul, and spirit.

*Pneuma (spirit).*—The New Testament *pneuma* is a continuation of the thought expressed by the Hebrew *ruach*. Again, this expression is a reference to the total person, a manifestation of the whole man. The basic meaning of *pneuma* paralleling *ruach* is: " 'Air in motion,' whether as the wind in nature or as the breath in a living thing."[40] In Rom. 8, Paul uses "spirit" over twenty times. In using the word, his real background is, first, the Old Testament, and second, the experience of primitive Christianity. By "spirit," Paul means the supernatural or divine element in human life, and his test for it is the presence of a love like the love of God in Christ.[41] This *pneuma* (spirit) is not an immortal entity within man. The error of idealism is that it

25

regards eternity as something which can be taken for granted, as part of the spiritual being of man, the result of his being somewhat divine.[42]

*Pneuma* can mean the person and take the place of a personal pronoun just as *soma* and *psyche* can. When Paul speaks of the *pneuma* of man he does not mean some higher principle within him or some special intellectual or spiritual faculty of his, but simply his self.[43] There is a difference between a wife and a virgin. We read in I Cor. 7:34: "The unmarried woman careth for the things of the Lord, that she may be holy both in body and in spirit." The phrase body and *pneuma* (spirit) is intended as a summary designation of the totality of a human being.

I Thess. 5:23 is not a text outlining a trichotomy as to Biblical anthropology, but stresses the fact that the total person is to be ready for Christ's second coming: "And I pray God your whole spirit, and soul and body be preserved blameless unto the coming of our Lord Jesus Christ." In distinction from *psyche, pneuma* seems also to mean the self regarded as conscious or aware. Thus, in Rom 8:16, we read: "The divine Spirit bears witness to our spirit that we are God's children," that is, He makes us conscious of it, and confers the knowledge of it upon us.

Thus, *pneuma* (spirit) is used by Paul much the same way as *ruach* (spirit) is in the Old Testament. Although the terms are used in various ways to describe man's nature and personality, they do not suggest a dichotomy or trichotomy. These are but indications that man is a "whole" consisting of these varied aspects. As suggested previously, Paul used *pneuma* with a higher and lower case, that is *Pneuma* in reference to a member of the Trinity, The Holy Spirit; and *pneuma*, as previously discussed, has a variety of meanings, but mainly as an aspect or expression of man's total person and personality. Even though the terms were "Greek" and fraught with philosophical connotations, Paul does not part from the Old Testament "unity of man" concept.[44] It is hardly conceivable that Paul would employ Greek mysticism in presenting the gospel to a people who were inspired by so many different gods.[45] It would be difficult to accept the idea that Paul's views were more Hellenic than Jewish. In Acts 15, at the first Christian Church Council, the apostle apparently concurred in the decision of the Council regarding certain Jewish distinctives (cf. Acts 15:19-22, 22:1-3). Therefore, his use of *pneuma* (spirit) in the New Testament is a continuation of the Old Testament usage of a term or terms referring to aspects or manifestations of the total person.

*Soma (body).*—The New Testament parallel to the Hebrew *geviyah* (body, corpse) and *basar* (flesh) is *soma* (body) and *sarx* (flesh). In an ethical sense Paul uses *sarx* (flesh) as the neutral house for sin. The passage in Rom. 8:1-5 most vividly illustrates the point. His argument is that the Law could not destroy the ascendancy of sin in the "flesh" even though it could win the homage of reason. He does not equate flesh with sin because Jesus himself, "the Word," became flesh (cf. Jn. 1:4). The apostle is cautious in his argument as he is well aware of the sinless nature of Christ. Thus, he uses the metaphorical expression in Rom. 8:3: "God sending his own Son in the *likeness* of sinful flesh, and for sin, condemned sin in the flesh" [italics mine]. He condemend "sin" but not the "flesh." A similar expression is: Christ condemned the sin, but not the sinner. Paul uses "flesh" in a twofold sense, first as a purely physical (or metaphysical) term, for the material element in human nature is morally indifferent, and second as a psychological and ethical term. C. H. Dodd, commenting on the passage, says that mankind was bound in the servitude of sin, established in the "flesh." Thus, the natural, flesh-and-blood life of man was the territory, so to speak of sin.[46] *Sarx* means, first of all, "flesh" as man's material corporeality; it is the animate flesh of man, active in its sensual manifestations and perceptible to the senses.[47] It is used also in reference to the total person. In fact, like *psyche* and *pneuma*, sarx can even be used to designate the person himself (cf. II. Cor. 7:5): "Our flesh had no rest"="I found no rest." In II Cor. 4:11, "flesh" is mortal and perishes with the end of physical life at death. In Gal. 2:20, we read: "The life which I now live in the

27

flesh I live by the faith of the Son of God." In other words, the
life I live as a man, day by day is his "in the flesh" meaning. In
the passage in Jn. 1:14, He (Jesus) "became flesh." The word
*sarx* (flesh) signifies human nature in and according to its
corporeal manifestation. He became flesh, but did not put on
flesh as clothing. Hence, as has been consistently revealed in
both the Old and New Testaments, these terms are manifestations of man's total nature or personality.

*Soma* (body) as used by Paul is one, if not his key anthropological expression. He cannot even view the future life apart
from the body. The *soma* is a vital aspect of the whole man. Even
Christians must die; outward death confronts them too, and this
dying will be a dying of the whole man and not merely of the
body. The whole man must pass through an experience of
annihilation which affects the whole man since the whole man is
a sinner.[48] Thus, Paul properly stressed the "bodily resurrection"
in I Cor. 15 in reference to the salvation and final glorification of
the total man—body, soul, and spirit. And this glorification of
man in his complete being aspect, minus sin and its effects and
consequences, is made possible by an "in Christ" relationship.
Apart from God, man is not truly man as Thielicke has written:
"In the view of the Bible, man is not to be seen at all as an
individual in isolation, but only as a child in relationship to his
father.[49] Man may be an upright "body" or "creature," yet the
ultimate and true significance and meaning for the "body" or
personality can only be fully realized in and through Christ.
"Flesh" and "blood" cannot inherit the kingdom of God; however, it is important to bear in mind the characteristic sense in
which Paul uses the term body, which is mostly brought out in I
Cor. 15: "It is not the structure of flesh and blood as such. The
flesh-and-blood structure may pass away, leaving not a vestige,
and yet the body remain self-identical. As it now partakes of the
perishable substance of 'flesh,' it may in the future partake of
the imperishable substance of 'glory' or splendour, and yet
remain the same 'body.' " Such is Paul's metaphysic.[50]

The body for Paul generally was the organized general self,

"for the body is not one member but many" (I Cor. 12:14). The apostle's analogy here is similar to his discussion of "body," "soul," and "spirit" and manifestations of the total personality. Commenting on I Cor 6:13-20 in vs. 14, Bultmann says:

... "And God raised the Lord and will also raise us up," the word "us" has taken the place of the expected phrase "our bodies," i.e., the equation "soma = self, person" hovers in the background. And when v 15 begins, "Do you not know that your bodies are members of Christ," "your bodies" means "you" (cf. 12:27, see above). But when it continues, "Shall I therefore take the members of Christ and make them members of a prostitute?" the other meaning of soma as the physical body sounds through again. And when according to v 16, he who joins himself to a prostitute becomes "one soma" with her, "soma" once more means physical body, even though the meaning tends toward the figurative in that it also means "unit," "one-ness."[51]

The result of all the foregoing is this: man, his person as a whole, can be denoted by *soma*. It may be significant that Paul never calls a corpse *soma*, though such usage is found both in profane Greek and in the LXX. The fact that man is *soma* (body) as an aspect of human existence caused Paul vigorously to defend the resurrection of the body to the Corinthians. It appears that the phrases "unity," "total," "whole," "indivisible unity," "corporate personality," "one," etc. run as common denominators in the views of leading contemporary theologians in their concept of Biblical anthropology. *Soma*, like *basar*, can refer to or denote the total person in both the Old and New Testament. The crowning revelation of the "holistic person" appears in Christ, at His incarnation, His life, death, burial, and resurrection in totality.

The decisive fact of importance regarding who and what man is, is that man is a whole consisting of *nephesh* (soul or person), *psyche* (soul or person), *ruach* (spirit-life principle), *pneuma* (spirit-life principle), *basar* (flesh-individual outwardly), *soma* (body, the person self). Man is an indivisible unity, not tripartite nor bipartite. He is one, total, holistic man created in the image of God. The New Testament references to anthropology are word images with an Old Testament (Jewish) background and not the philosophical milieu of Greek thought. The terms used describing man and his behavior are not abstract terms but concrete expressions always in conjunction with a total, unit, or holistic-man concept. Man is a complex, highly organized self by virtue of creation and redemption. All aspects of the total man are important; whether man is experimented with, or dealt with mentally, physically, or spiritually is of utmost importance. Any mistreatment of any aspect of man's nature will affect the whole. For example, the mind will sympathize with an injury of the body, and the reverse is true in relationship of the body to the mind. Man is not a compartmentalized creature, but a grand upright being from creation, marred by his moral fall, but restored freely through the plan of redemption in Christ Jesus. Whether redeemed or not, man is still a partial image of God. No wonder the psalmist, in awe and humility in his divinely illuminated consciousness of self and God, said: "I will praise thee; for I am fearfully and wonderfully made; marvelous are thy works; and that my soul (*nephesh*, total conscious self) knoweth right well" (Ps. 139:14).


## The Image of God and the Second Adam

A higher value, appreciation, and concern is placed upon human beings as one ponders the "image of God" concept in man. It was neither by accident nor by a long process of evolving that man became in the image of God. By the mysterious act of creation man appears immediately as a creature in the image of God. Whether we consider the singular or duality of sex, both were created in the image of God. The male prior to the female is difficult to harmonize with evolutionary science, but the purpose of this study is theological and not an attempt to correlate science and Scripture. This by no means infers that science and Scripture are mutually exclusive. The real issue, theologically, regarding Biblical anthropology, is, the willingness of man to say,"God gave us life; it did not originate in us nor our ancestors." Man alone was copied after his Creator; all other creatures were after their kind. There are many questions regarding what man was; the issue in this book is, "what man is."

He was created above the animals but a little lower than the angels (cf. Heb. 2:9). Passages in Scripture are limited in specific reference to man in the image or likeness of God. Theologians have discussed the "image of man" concept in both a broad and narrow sense. The "broader image" concept is that which defines man as a man, a person, an individual that is free and self-conscious, and a rational, moral, religious agent.[52] The meaning of the "image" in a broad sense includes the transcendent powers in man. Reason is learned in contrast to the hereditary instincts of the animal kingdom, although man, too, possesses instincts. With his moral faculties, man is able to aprove or disapprove of his neighbor's conduct. He has a penetrating sense of what is right and what is wrong. His religious faculty is alone and unique among all creation. "So although man has sprung from the earth and is a creature, like the animals with which he must share the earth, he stands wholly at God's side and is an independent, spiritual being; he as it were executes God's will.[53] He is aware of an "I-thou" relationship to his Creator. The very existence of sin is evidence of man's free will"; he has the ability to think and to do, and his choosing salvation through Christ is indicative of "free will" even though in a fallen state.

The Image in the narrower sense would be in the realm of a saving knowledge and relationship in Christ. For example, in Col. 3:10, we read: "and have put on the new man, that is renewed in knowledge after the image of him that created him." This knowledge we have in Christ, restoring the "marred image,"

31

is made possible by new light and dimension of understanding through the Holy Spirit. The "relationship" between man and God is a significant element of the "Imago Dei" before man's fall and in his renewed relationship in Christ.

The key Biblical references affirming the "image of God" in man are Gen. 1:26, 27; 5:1, 3; 9:6; I Cor. 11:7; Col. 3:10; and James 3:9. In Gen. 1:26, the Hebrew word for "image" is *selem*, which literally means "cut out," "resemblance," "shadow," or "likeness." The word for "likeness" is *demuth*, which means to "resemble," "be like," etc. The terms suggest the same thought and appear as synonyms. The word "likeness" is a continuation of "image." John Calvin says:

> The greater part, and nearly all, conceive that the word image is to be distinguished from likeness and the common distinction is, that image exists in substance, likeness in the accidents of anything. . . . As for myself, before I define the image of God, I would deny that it differs from his likeness.[54]

Since the plural (Elohim) is used in Gen. 1, this has led some to give the "image" a threefold meaning, as John R. Neilson has stated: "May not the words 'in our image,' mean, a threefold thing, as the blessed Trinity, Three in one and One in three."[55] Calvin believed that a portion of the image of God remained in fallen man. Calvin acknowledges that the image lies primarily in the understanding or in the heart, in the soul and its powers. To Calvin, the "image" consisted of "righteousness and true holiness," for though this is the chief part, it is not the whole of God's image. Calvin defines the original image (which fell) through its restoration in Christ. He intimates the image in total man by stating: "Thus the chief seat of the Divine image was in his mind and heart, where it was eminent; yet there was no part of him in which some scintillations of it did not shine forth."[56] This concept agrees with a number of contemporary theologians as Berkouwer informs us:

We can say that contemporary theologians rather generally lean more to this line of approach (i.e., the real, concrete meaning of the image), which is related to a strong consciousness of the integral unity of man, producing any opposition to any "division" of man into "spiritual" and "bodily" aspects.[57]

In Gen. 5:1, the use of "likeness of God" confirms the fact that "image" and "likeness" are synonymous, and in Gen. 5:3, the "likeness" and "image" are passed (at least in part) to the race. Man imitated his Creator in having dominion over the beasts, also through his intellect and will. The general concept has been that the image involved man's rational, moral, and spiritual side, more functional than ontological. The image of God in man includes these and more.

The total person concept as it relates to the "image" makes it appear plausible to include even the body as we understand it in our modern world. Certainly, the anthropomorphic aspect cannot be pressed into a pure human field of speculation. But Philip did say to Jesus: "Lord, shew us the Father, Jesus saith unto him, Have I been so long time with you, and yet hast thou not known me, Philip? He that hath seen me hath seen the father" (Jn. 14:8, 9). In all He (Christ) said, and did, and was, he was the express image of God's very person. He was the express image of the Father (cf. Heb. 1:1-3). The holistic concept is further strengthened in Christian theology when the importance of the "body" is stressed by Paul in the resurrection (cf. I Cor. 15 and I Thess. 4:13, 14). Von Rad suggests that the "image" and "likeness" include the entire person. The words *selem* and *demuth* denote correspondence and similarity referring to the whole of man, including the splendor of his bodily form. "Likeness" (*demuth*) helps to interpret *selem* (image).[58]

The juxtaposition of the two terms "image" and "likeness" refutes the idea of complex distinctions within the image. The "image in man" involves a resemblance to God in all aspects of the total man. The fall deeply marred and well nigh obliterated

33

the "divine image," also, man was no longer capable of face-to-face communion with God and he did not possess the power to resist sin. His moral fall was complete and a restoration could only be effected via Christ who was "the express image" of the Father (Father being an ethical and not a generic term) and came in the likeness of sinful flesh. Theologians use such texts as Eph. 4:24 and Col. 3:10 to illustrate how the "image" is restored or renewed. In Eph. 4:24, man is created anew, "in righteousness and holiness," but it was supernatural whereas Protestants held that the moral excellence of Adam was natural. The Roman Catholic Church understood the image to be only the rational, voluntary and freedom of the will aspect of man. Thus, the original sin is simply the loss of original righteousness. This concept immediately divides the unified nature of man whom God created perfect in his physical, mental, and spiritual aspects. "And God saw everything that he had made, and, behold, it was very good" (Gen. 1:31a). It appears much more consistent in view of the "total man" concept in Scripture that all of man was "in the likeness of God," including his rational nature and in his knowledge of "righteousness and holiness," which was not superadded. Man was created in the image of God "holistically," and not compartmentalized. As Brunner said: "Man's being as man is both in one, nature and grace."[59] Therefore, the Roman Catholic Scholastic view is untenable in dividing the "image," that is, in the fall man lost the image but retained the "likeness." The Lutherans think of the "image" more in terms of moral excellence. Barth was more Lutheran regarding the "image"; the fall was rational and metaphysical. Brunner was more Calvinistic, in that the point of contact for fallen man was via the "divine image."

Later theology interprets the divine image Christologically or eschatologically. Carl F. H. Henry states: "This orientation is formally commendable, since the God-man assuredly exhibits the divine intention for man and the glory of redeemed humanity will consist in full conformity to Christ's image."[60] He goes on to add that the danger is that "it diverts attention from the important question of man's primal origin—that is, from the creation and fall of the first Adam (q.v.)—because of a reluctance to challenge the modern evolutionary philosophy from the Genesis creation account."[61] Henry's point is well taken in view of the neo-orthodox view of revelation and inspiration. Also, in Rom. 5 and I Cor. 15: Christ as the second Adam makes relevant and pertinent the two Adams. The pendulum, however, could swing too much in one direction, whereas man the "image" is viewed from a purely naturalistic, rationalistic, anthropological concept, or Christologically and eschatologically. Schleiermacher actually gives up the fundamental Christian view of the origin of man, and substitutes for it an idealistic, evolutionary theory with a strongly naturalistic bent.

Many contemporary writers appear to stress "the relationship" aspect of man's nature in regards to the "Imago Dei." Brunner writes in his book, *God and Man*: "Through his relationship to God, through his being addressed by God and his obligation to answer, his responsibility, man is free. This is his creation in God's image, that he can answer God—or not answer."[62] Bonhoeffer suggests that freedom (image) is a relationship between two persons,[63] and Thielicke infers: "In view of the Bible, man is not to be seen at all as an individual in isolation, but only as a child in relationship to his father."[64] Certainly, relationship is an important aspect of man created in the image of God, but again the total must be included.

Modern theologians are right when they say the "true man" can only be understood through the revelation and person of Christ Jesus. Such is true, since the "divine image" in man was so marred by the fall. We would hasten to add that man is still a creature of God even in view of the trauma of Adam's fall. A "restored," "renewed" image experience in Christ gives to the individual a new spiritual experience and dimension and guarantees with promise a redeemed body at the return of Christ (cf. I Cor. 15:51-54; I Jn. 3:2; Phil. 3:20, 21). Christ became man[1] "God sent forth his Son made of a woman, made under the law" (Ga. 4:46). Further, the divine *kenosis* (divine emptying) is

35

staggering to the human mind (cf. Phil. 2:7) where the KJ says: "He took upon Him the form of a servant." This in no way implies that Jesus was only human rejecting all of His divinity. Karl Barth, in speaking of the mystery and revelation of Christ's humanity, states:

A man like us in space and time, who has all the properties of God and yet does not cease to be a human being and a creature too. The Creator Himself, without encroaching upon His deity, becomes, not a demi-god, not an angel, but very soberly, very really a man.[65]

The one who created man becomes man (cf. Col. 1:15-17). The Incarnation and Resurrection have challenged both reason and faith among Christian scholars since the events. Bultmann skips over the miraculous by demythologizing the New Testament. The emphasis by Bultmann and others center in the "witness" of the events. To many, the incarnation and resurrection of Christ are not objective events in history. However, space prohibits discussing more fully the many problems of Christology. We can say simply that Christ Jesus was truly the Son of God, the Son of man, He was God in the flesh (cf. I Jn. 4:2). He had two natures mysteriously blended into one.

Christ came as the second Adam to restore fully, through the plan of redemption, the "image of God" in man. The "divine image" though marred was passed on to all of Adam's posterity. The "divine image" restored in man is not given to all men, only to those who take advantage of the provision made for their individual salvation. As a man, or unit, He could understand and sympathize with man in all areas of man's behavior, since He was "tempted in all points like as we are" (Heb. 4:15). The unity of Christ's nature was stressed by Calvin:

Calvin is never interested in the divine nature or the human nature as abstract entities, as Luther, for instance, insisted on the presence of the flesh of Christ at the communion table to exert its life-giving power: but Calvin concerned himself with one Person of the Son, who operates and is present in all his works as mediator.[66]

Whenever Calvin comes to speak of the person of the Christ, he takes care to place emphasis simultaneously upon the unity of the God-man. We may never isolate a given deed or property of Christ from his divine or from his human nature. At stake here is the unity of the person. The Athanasian Creed states that Jesus Christ is one altogether, not by confusion of substance with substance, but by unity of person.[67] Commenting on Calvin, Francois Wendel says:

> Calvin even proceeds further in elaborating the analogy because he discovers in it something corresponding to the communication of properties in Christ. "Lastly, the properties of the soul are transferred to the body, and the property of the body to the soul; yet he that is composed of these two parts is more than one man. Such forms of expression signify that there is in man one person composed of two distinct parts; that there are two different natures united in him to constitute that one person."[68]

Calvin prefaced this analogy by saying: "If anything among men can be found to resemble so great a mystery, man himself appears to furnish the most apposite similitude."[69]

In man we have manifestations of the total person, and in Christ we see the unique union of two natures as revealed in Scripture. The fact that Christ in Heb. 1:3 is "the express image His person (God)," and became man, should elevate the true dignity of man, himself created in the image of God, though not the express image. Naturally, a respect for man can only be realized by the "restored image" made possible through Christ, the second Adam. From conception, as a microscopic cell, Jesus was called "the thing being born holy" (Lu. 1:35). Already, the Holy Spirit was identifying a minute cell as a person, the second Adam. Nothing human was unknown in Christ Jesus except sin.

His being totally human (as well as divine) made Him indispensable for our salvation. The restored image in Christ involves more than moral righteousness. In fact, the total restored image experience will come when our Lord returns and glorifies the body (cf. Rom 3:23). Thus, the image restored includes the total person.

One of the great purposes of the first advent of Christ was to reveal man. We must recognize our fallen condition in order to require supernatural help for our salvation. Yet, humanity can be relegated to a level whereby no "divine image" can be seen, like some theologians who have no high opinion of humanity even before the original sin. In the putting on of the "new man" made possible by Christ, the second Adam, "righteousness" and "true holiness" is restored in man (cf. Eph. 4:24). The divine *eikon* (image) and *homoiosis* (likeness) is restored by the birth, life, death, and resurrection of the One, "whence he ought by all means to become like His brothers" (literal translation, cf. Heb. 2:17). Righteousness and holiness restored, is the key to our understanding and love to God and man. Von Rad says that *sadaq* (righteousness) is the standard not only for man's relationship to his fellows, but even the standard for man's relationship to the animals and to his natural environment.[70]


## Summary of the Total Person

We have viewed man anthropologically and found him highly elevated as a moral creature above all creation and creatures. In medical science the emphasis by those in the healing arts is to make man whole. Biologically, man is a highly complex organism, yet in view of his complexity he is a biological unit. Psychologically and theologically, man is viewed as an indivisible unit by leading contemporary writers in these two fields. In both the Old and New Testament we found man to be holistic, not compartmentalized, but a total person. The Bible does not picture man as trichotomous nor dichotomous. It is true that various manifestations of his being are discussed in Scripture, such as body, soul, and spirit, yet these in no way suggest that man is a compartmentalized creature.

Theologically, the most profound Scriptural statement concerning man is that he was created in the image of God. Also in Scripture, and in the writings of many leading theologians, we observed that the image of God in man involved the total person. Previously, many theologians viewed man more from his rational, moral side. He was considered more ontological than functional. The crowning act of creation in the Genesis account was the creation of man. The narrator in Gen. 1:31 said: "And God saw everything that he had made, and, behold, it was very good." In Gen. 1:27, we read that "God created man and woman in His own image." This text is significant in view of the fact that Eve was created from the anatomy of Adam (cf. Gen. 2:21-24). Furthermore, the "image of God" in man is maintained via procreation following the fall of Adam (cf. Gen. 5:3), whereby Adam "begat a son in his own likeness, after his image." Both, in creation and procreation, man is a being in the image ofGod.

We also concluded from Scripture that Jesus Christ makes possible the restoration of the image which was marred by the fall. The total resoration of the image of God in man will come at the second coming of Christ when the body is glorified, and thus the total person is redeemed. This experience is given to the Christian by promise in Scripture. Such a view of man should make more meaningful the subject of contraception and abortion.

The significance of Biblical anthropology in relation to contraception and abortion is the fact that man, as created initially and in procreation, is an indivisible unit. In defining body, soul, and spirit in Scripture, we are better able to view the total person. The fact that man is created in the image of God, and an indivisible unit, makes the current issue of abortion a most serious problem to consider from the Christian view of man. Also, the subject of contraception is important in view of God granting man the power to procreate in His image, even though contraception is a Christian option.

In considering the total person, the fetus is most certainly a part of the total individual. The developing fetus is a potential human being. The "image of God" in man concept should call forth a profound reverence and respect for nascent life, or could we say, "reverence and respect for a developing image of God!" In Scripture we view man as the result of an act of direct and mediate creation by God. In either case, he is in the image of God.

The traducianist-creationist concept of the soul appears to complicate the abortion dilemma, which views are not supported by Scripture. The traducianist holds to the idea that the soul is derived from parents, whereas, the creationist teaches that the soul is bestowed at conception. The nature of man, as a total person, does simplify the problem of abortion whereby certain conditions and situations appear to warrant the termination of fetal life. Man from conception is not tripartite nor bipartite, but one developing unit.

When we consider the human being holistically, it appears that life from the moment of conception is more sacred than if he were viewed as a trichotomy or dichotomy. If either of the latter two views were held, therapeutic abortion would only involve the body, and the one or two mystic entities would escape the curette or medication. However, the body in Scripture is vital, as attested to by Paul's emphasis on the resurrection. Man in his totality must be considered by the Christian in his discussion and decision on the subject of contraception and abortion. Human life is mysterious and sacred, whether that life is possible, potential, or mature. The Scriptural view of man asserts that man is an indivisible unit from the beginning of his creation.

### Notes to Chapter 1

1. Pierre Teilhard de Chardin, *The Phenomenon of Man* (New York: Harper and Bros., 1959), p. 277.

2. Jean S. J. de Fraine, *The Bible and the Origin of Man* (New York: Desclee Company, 1962), p. 4.

3. Bernard Ramm, *The Christian View of Science and Scripture* (Grand Rapids: Wm. B. Eerdmans Publishing Co., 1966), p. 308.

4. Ibid., pp. 318, 319.

5. Helmuth Thielicke, *Man in God's World*, trans. John W. Doberstein (New York: Harper and Row, 1963), p. 87.

6. Cf. Samuel Bagster, *The Analytical Hebrew and Chaldee Lexicon* (New York: Harper and Bros., n.d.). Also, Francis Brown, S. R. Driver, and Charles Briggs, *A Hebrew and English Lexicon of the Old Testament* (Boston, New York, and Chicago: Houghton, Mifflin and Company, 1906), p. 9.

7. De Fraine, *The Bible and the Origin of Man*, p. 22.

8. Jean S. J. de Fraine, *Adam and the Family of Man*, trans. by Daniel Raible, C.P.P.S. (New York: Alba House, 1965), p. 152.

9. Wheeler Robinson, *The Christian Doctrine of Man* (Edinburgh: T. & T. Clark, 1913), p. 69.

10. G. C. Berkouwer, *Man: The Image of God* (Grand Rapids: Wm. B. Eerdman's Publishing Company, 1962), p. 94.

11. Robinson, *The Christian Doctrine of Man*, p. 153.

12. Oscar Cullmann, *Immortality of the Soul or Resurrection of the Dead?* (New York: The Macmillan Company, 1958), p. 20.

13. Ibid.

14. E. L. Mascall, *The Importance of Being Human* (New York: Columbia University Press, 1958), p. 25.

15. Berkouwer, *Man: The Image of God*, p. 201.

16. Hugh J. O'Connell, *Keeping Your Balance in the Modern Church* (Liquori, Missouri: Liquorian Pamphlets, Redemptorist Fathers, 1968), p. 163.

17. Edmund Hill, D. P., *The Truth of Genesis 1-11*. The Quarterly of the Catholic Biblical Association, Vol. XVIII, No. 43 (London: July, 1966). A paper given to the Catholic Society at Hull University, January 25, 1966.

18. Franz Delitzsch, *A System of Blilical Psychology* (Edinburgh: T. & T. Clark, n.d.), p. 90.

19. Robinson, *The Christian Doctrine of Man*, pp. 15, 16.

20. Albert Gelin, S. S., *The Concept of Man in the Bible*, trans. by David M. Murphy (London: Geoffrey Chapman, 1968), p. 14.

21. Norman H. Snaith, *The Distinctive Ideas of the Old Testament* (New York: Schocken Books, 1964), p. 143.

32. Robinson, *The Christian Doctrine of Man*, p. 21.

23. Gerhard Von Rad, *Old Testament Theology: The Theology of Israel's Historical Traditions*, trans. by D. M. G. Stalker (New York: Harper and Bros., 1962), p. 149.

41

24. *A New Catechism: Catholic Faith for Adults*, commissioned by the Hierarchy of Netherlands (New York: Herder and Herder, 1967), p. 9.

25. Dietrich Bonhoeffer, *Creation and Fall: Temptation* (New York: The Macmillan Company, 1966), p. 47.

26. Robinson, *The Christian Doctrine of Man*, p. 24.

27. T. H. Vriezen, *An Outline of Old Testament Theology* (Oxford: Basil Blackwell, 1958), p. 203.

28. Von Rad, *Old Testament Theology*, p. 153.

29. Berkouwer, *Man: The Image of God*, p. 256.

30. Ibid.

31. Rudolf Bultmann, *Theology of the New Testament* (New York: Charles Scribner's Sons, 1951), pp. 204, 205.

32. Ibid., p. 209.

33. Ibid.

34. Robinson, *The Christian Doctrine of Man*, p. 78.

35. Emil Brunner, *God and Man* (London: Student Christian Press, 1936), p. 136.

36. Paul King Jewett, "The Relation of the Soul to the Fetus," *Christianity Today*, XII (November, 1968), 18-19.

37. C. H. Dodd, *The Epistle of Paul to the Romans*, in *The Moffat New Testament Commentary* (New York: Harper and Bros., n.d.), p. 126.

38. Krister Stendahl, "Introduction" in *The Scrolls and the New Testament*, ed. by Krister Stendahl (New York: Harper and Bros., 1957), p. 5.

39. Karl Georg Kuhn, "New Light on Temptation, Sin, and Flesh in the New Testament," in ibid., p. 105.

40. Dodd, *The Epistle of Paul*, p. 117.

41. Ibid., p. 118.

42. Emil Brunner, *Man in Revolt: A Christian Anthropology* (Philadelphia: The Westminster Press, n.d.), p. 467.

43. Bultmann, *Theology of the New Testament*, p. 206.

44. In conjunction with this study, "unity of man" is in reference to the person or individual in contradistinction to the "unity of the race" in a generic sense, or common lot as a sinner.

45. Cf. Adolf Deissmann, *Paul, A Study in Social and Religious History* (New York: Harper Torchbooks, Harper and Bros., 1957), p. 147.

46. Dodd, *The Epistle of Paul*, p. 89.

47. Bultmann, *Theology of the New Testament*, p. 233.

48. Brunner, *Man in Revolt*, pp. 475, 476.

49. Thielicke, *Man in God's World*, p. 161.

50. Dodd, *The Epistle of Paul*, p. 90.

51. Bultmann, *Theology of the New Testament*, p. 195.

52. Paul K. Jewett, "The Divine Image," lecture given in class at the Fuller Theological Seminary in Pasadena, California, November, 1968.

53. Vriezen, *An Outline of Old Testament Theology*, p. 222.

54. John Calvin, *Commentaries on the First Book of Moses, Called Genesis*, I (Grand Rapids: Wm. B. Eerdman's Publishing Co., 1948), 93.

55. John Robertson Neilson, *Everlasting Punishment* (London: Skeffington & Son, 1897), p. 18.

56. Calvin, *Commentaries on the First Book of Moses*, p. 95.

57. Berkouwer, *Man: The Image of God*, p. 75.

58. Von Rad, *Old Testament Theology*, p. 145.

59. Brunner, *Man in Revolt*, p. 95.

60. Carl F. H. Henry, *Baker's Dictionary of Theology*, ed. by Everett F. Harrison (Grand Rapids: Baker Book House, 1960), p. 339.

61. Ibid., p. 399.

62. Brunner, *God and Man*, p. 155.

63. Bonhoeffer, *Creation and Fall*, p. 37.

64. Thielicke, *Man in God's World*, p. 161.

65. Karl Barth, *Dogmatics in Outline* (New York: Harper and Row, 1959), p. 84.

66. G. C. Berkouwer, *The Person of Christ* (Grand Rapids: Wm. B. Eerdman's Publishing Company, 1963), p. 287.

67. Francois Wendel, *Calvin: The Origins and Development of His Religious Thought* (New York: Harper and Row, 1963), p. 297.

68. Ibid., p. 298.

69. Ibid.

70. Von Rad, *Old Testament Theology*, p. 370.

## Chapter II

## CONTRACEPTION

### A General History of Contraception

This section is an investigation of "Contraception" historically and how it is related and relevant to the Christian today. The historical framework of the subject will be briefly covered, and the subject will be considered also in relation to the Roman Catholic faith from which most historical references are cited. This is due to the nature of church history in which the Roman Church has had the subject incorporated in her moral theology for centuries.

The Protestant viewpoint of the highly publicized "teaching" is to be considered with emphasis on the Protestant Evangelical Christian's view of contraception in the light of available Scripture, reason, experience, and Christian ethics. Such a topic demands the union of thought and observations from theologians, physicians, sociologists, psychologists, and the legal minds of society.

To the casual observer the subject may appear insignificant, and out-of-bounds even to the Christian minister or teacher. However, such a study touches upon the marriage relationship, extra-marital relations, the single person and sex, the origin and propagation of biological life of man, and the current population explosion.

Science, with her phenomenal discoveries and achievements, challenges the Christian to clarify and make relevant the principles of his faith and to discard those hindering traditions and customs in the society in which he lives. The most dramatic and publicized achievements in science, no doubt, are in the realm of space conquest, yet more important and pragmatic are discoveries in biology, the ovum, sperm, and the DNA factor in the field of genetics. Important as the control of our physical environment has been and can be, still the most important discoveries in this century will be those in the biological and psychological areas. Not because the physical scientists are going to lie down on the job, but rather because of the fantastic implications of our new outlook in biology.[1] Thus, as the vastness of creation captures man's mind and challenges him to explore space, also, the minuteness of creation is subject to critical scientific investigation. In space technology, man seeks an environment or life apart from his own and this order; in biological science, the emphasis is on *bios* (life) as it relates to man and his environment on this planet.

Whether man conquers space or the cell and its mysterious components, he should be guided by Christ, His Spirit, and His Word directly and indirectly. Thus, contraception with all its implications cannot be shut up in a purely "Victorian" or "Puritan" closet; the subject involves the "total man" and the entire "fabric" of society.

The subject is most certainly pertinent in view of the past agenda of Vatican II and legislative actions since 1950 in the United States and other countries. Also, the medical, theological, ethical, legal, and social discussions and publications have occupied large portions of the news media. The contraceptive society is here; therefore, the Christian minister and teacher is duty bound to be informed and to share the timeless moral principles of Christ and His Word with a changed and changing society. Such a study involves the Biblical view of man. Also, the moral and spiritual nature of man come into focus when one considers life, potential and real, in man's every day life and procreative sphere.

Contraception is simply the prevention of conception. This may be accomplished by mechanical devices, drugs, the rhythm method whereby an ovum will not be fertilized, and continence. Extra-Biblical sources offer some statements on the subject, viz., the Babylonian Talmud, Egyptian papyrus, the Jewish Talmud,

Greek, Roman, and the apostolic and post-Nicene writers; however, the bulk of historical reference material comes to us from the writers of the Roman Catholic Church. The Biblical references, both direct and indirect, will be covered in the next chapter. Contraception and abortion are inseparable in many ancient references. However, the latter will also be covered separately in more detail than contraception due to the fact that the two are separate and vastly different. In the male sperm and the female ovum, the *possibility* of human life exists in relation to contraception; however, with the union of the sperm and the ovum (conception) the *potential* human being exists.

The classic work by John Noonan on the history of contraception is without peer. Even though we Protestants differ with the Roman Catholic Church on a number of points of faith and behavior, we are bound to respect the objective and thorough work done by these modern scholars on this subject who freely discuss with pen and voice the pros and cons of vital theological, moral, and ethical issues unique to their faith and history. Noonan uncovers and documents the practice of contraception prior to the Christian era by almost 2,000 years. The existence of contraceptive technique in the pre-Christian Mediterranean world is well established. The oldest documents referring to the subject come from Egypt, so states Noonan:

> The oldest surviving documents are from Egypt. Five different papyri, all dating from between 1900 and 1100 B.C., provide recipes for contraceptive preparations to be used in the vulva . . . pulverized crocodile dung in fermented mucilage; honey and sodium carbonate to be sprinkled in the vulva. . . .[2]

As to the Hebrew's knowledge and use of contraceptive means, practically all writers on the subject refer to the early practice of coitus interruptus in Genesis 38:8-10, the story of Onan. By employing this reference and the Babylonian Talmud, Noonan concludes that the Jewish communities were familiar with various

47

means of contraception, such, as post-coital ejection, occlusive pessaries, sterilizing potions, and sterilizing surgery.[3]

Oftentimes commentators on Scripture, especially the Old Testament, are quick to point out the inferior role of women in the Hebrew economy. Despite the lesser station of the wife, the Jewish concept of marriage, by Christian standards, was never surpassed in antiquity by that of any other culture.[4] The ancients were not oblivious to the sacredness of life or potential human life.

The Babylonian Talmud substantiates this concept of marriage and procreation where it specifies that the judgment of death is deserved by a male who "emits semen in vain." This legacy of a high esteem for human life in general and marriage in particular, since the time of the prophets, is always noticeable in the stream of human history.[5]

From the viewpoint of medicine, sterilizing potions should prove of interest. In the course of history over a hundred different plants have been reported to contain substances affecting human fertility. Noonan adds that reports of such plants come from every continent in the world. The most successful instance of experimental tests of a "root potion" have been performed on a desert plant, Lithospermum ruderale, used by the Shoshone Indians of Nevada as a contraceptive.[6] The ancient Greeks also had insights into the phenomenon of biology and pharmacology. Two individuals wrote on animals and natural history in the fourth century B.C. and the first century A.D. The first was Aristotle and the other was Pliny the Elder (A.D. 23-79). The work by Aristotle, *History of Animals*, was highly regarded as a scientific work until the seventeenth century. No doubt Thomas Aquinas, the great Roman Catholic medieval theologian, followed Aristotelian thought, especially in regards to form and matter, in his observations on contraception. In procreation, the male supplies the form and the female the matter. The Greeks and Romans were acquainted with gynecology from the time of the school of Hippocrates in the fifth century B.C. "Potions are the first form of contraceptive mentioned by any of the classical writers, and the type most often mentioned. In the Hippocratic writings a potion is the only contraceptive described."[7]

Thus, oral contraceptives are not original with this generation of medical science. Today, the chemical formula is more highly developed and sophisticated than Dioscordes' mentioned potion, whereby the bark of white poplar was taken with the kidney of a mule (1:109).[8] If for no other than psychological reasons, such a potion whereby the ingredients were known would have its influence on the female recipient's reproductive organs and the pituitary gland.

Noonan states that the interesting aspect in the scientific works of Graeco-Roman authors is that coitus interruptus is not mentioned.[9] In the Graeco-Roman world, superstition and magic were also employed to affect the female reproductive system.

In the Christian era of the empire of Rome, there seems to have been no new inhibition to the dissemination of contraceptive techniques. However, in the Canons of the 318 Holy Fathers assembled in the city of Nice, they clearly condemn castration— an extreme form of contraception. In Canon One it is stated:

> If anyone in sickness has been subjected to physicians to a surgical operation, or if he has been castrated by barbarians, let him remain among the clergy; but if anyone in sound health has castrated himself, it behooves that such a one, if (already) enrolled among the clergy, should cease (from his ministry), and that from henceforth no such person should "be promoted."[10]

Not only did the council deal with the clergyman, but the layman as well. Canon XXIV states: "If a layman mutilate himself, let him be excommunicated for three years, as practicing against his own life."[11] Here the possibility and potential of procreation is brought clearly into focus.

The early Christians adopted the Jewish stoic rules and a

definite condemnation of contraception. This over reaction was called forth by the movement known as "Gnosticism." "*Gnosis*" is a good Greek word meaning "knowledge." They (the gnostics) claimed to have a special knowledge superseding special revelation, i.e., the Word of God. (Some existential theologians might well profit by reviewing this movement and era of church history.) Virtually without exception, the Gnostics challenged marriage as a child-bearing institution.[12]

John Noonan points out:

> In the second century there was a Christian "left" and a Christian "right." The left denied the existence of moral rules for Christians and contended that a Christian could reject marriage and procreation as unnecessary restrictions on his liberty. The right taught the total abstinence from sexual behaviour was the only conduct appropriate for the true follower of Christ.[13]

Abortion and Infanticide come into view during the infancy of the Christian Church; however, the subject of abortion will be considered in a subsequent chapter. The Didache, the Epistle of Barnabas, Clement of Alexandria, Soranos, Lactantius, *et al*, speak against contraception, yet space prohibits the recording of their remarks.

Jerome, in a passage denouncing teenage dress and abortion, takes a bold stand against contraception in "(Letter 22, to Eustochium 13, CSEL 54:160-161) ... There, in unmistakable language, contraception was described as a form of homicide.[14] But it was the work of Augustine on the subject of contraception that has influenced its history through the centuries in the Christian Church. Philosophically, Augustine was Neo-platonic, weaving many of Plato's concepts into the Christian faith. Augustine reacted against the Manichees who some said were allies or an extension of Gnosticism. His reaction followed that of John Chrysostom; however, Augustine himself had been a pupil of the Manichees. He spoke for the church defending procreation and marriage.

Augustine's concept of artificial contraceptives is quite clear in his work, *Marriage and Concupiscence.*

Sometimes this lustful cruelty, or cruel lust, come to this, that they even procure poisons of sterility (Sterilitatis venena), and if these do not work, extinguish and destroy the fetus in some way in the womb, preferring that their offspring die before it lives or if it is already alive in the womb to kill it before it is born. Assuredly if both husband and wife are like this, they are not married, and if they were like this from the beginning they come together not joined in matrimony but in seduction. If both are not like this I dare to say that either the wife is in a fashion the harlot of her husband or he is an adulterer with his own wife.[15]

The next great voice and pen on the subject following Augustine was Thomas Aquinas. Aquinas was Aristotelian in thought whereas Augustine was Platonic. His theological mentality, based upon Aristotelian thought, was argued from the premise of man's rational apparatus which in turn opened the door for a serious challenge to Augustine's conclusions. Yet, both condemned the use of contraceptives.

Luther switched from the scholastic concept of marriage to emphasize the need of love in the marriage relationship. Nowhere does Calvin treat in a definitive way the control of human reproduction. The bull Effraenatam, on October 29, 1588, decreed all abortion and contraception by potion or poison were to be treated as murder.[16] From about 1750 to the present time, as has been stated, there has been a general spread of birth control practice. The first book on the subject of birth control written in America was Robert Dale Owen's *Moral Philosophy,* published in 1831.

The next big change came about in this century as to the sale of contraceptive devices. In 1936, the United States Court of Appeals permitted contraceptive devices to be dispensed by medical agencies and physicians.[17]

A large number of churches have changed their views on the

subject, especially during the past thirty-five to forty years. Also, scholars of note who have taken a position against an absolute prohibition of contraception include Karl Barth, Emil Brunner, Jacques Ellul, Reinhold Niebuhr, and Helmuth Thielicke. All in contact with current news media are aware of the importance attached to contraception during the recent Second Vatican Council in 1964. A great percentage of the content of religious news service during the past two years has dealt with contraception and abortion. The ethicists have covered the subject oftentimes with *agape* (love) as the sole criterion for one's behavior in relation to the opposite sex.

We may conclude from this brief history that the Roman Catholic Church has rejected officially the practice of birth control per se. On the other hand, Protestants, since the Reformation, have defined marriage sufficient to encompass the use of contraception in the total marriage relationship.

## Roman Catholic and Protestant
## Views of Contraception

From Augustine until the eighteenth century A.D., sexual relations in marriage was based primarily on procreation and the education of children in the Roman Catholic Church. Strange as it may appear, the pill has incited Roman Catholic moral theologians to reexamine or rediscover God's original purpose in the total marriage covenant and experience. F. H. Drinkwater observes the contraception issue from the viewpoint of Roman Catholic moral theology in the following manner:

By far the most burning moral-theology question today is that of birth control. On this the attitude of the moralists has been changing during the last fifty years, but only slowly and reluctantly. Gradually the old dread of sex, originating perhaps as a reaction against pagan sex-worship with its frenzied lusts and cruelties, and dominating Christian feeling through patristic and medieval time, has been withering away to be replaced by a fresh vision, or shall we say rediscovery, of God's original purpose in creation, when God saw all that he had made and found it very good.[18]

Augustine condemned contraception in his work entitled *Marriage and Concupiscence*, calling it "poisons of sterility."[19] Thomas Aquinas condemned contraceptives as being unnatural. He defined an unnatural act in coitus when insemination is made impossible.

John T. Noonan lists traditional arguments against nature which he considers invalid:

1. Contraception is against nature. It frustrates the natural purpose of the sexual act and is therefore irrational because man may not act against his nature.
2. Contraception is against the primary purpose of marriage which is the procreation of children.
3. Contraception is against the teaching of the Bible. In particular it is against God's command to man to multiply (Genesis 1:28). It was punished by sudden death in the case of Onan, who practiced coitus interruptus (Genesis 38:8-10).[20]

The Catholic Church for centuries condemned contraception on the basis of Natural Law and the interpretation of the Onan incident. Natural Law is an ambiguous term and can be fitted to any number of issues in conduct and behavior. The Roman Catholic Church has deduced Natural Law from Romans 2, whereas the historic Protestant position has been to order his life in conduct and behavior as outlined in the Word of God with its objective counsel and admonition. Natural Law is too abstract, too metaphysical to be a practical guide in the twentieth century. For instance, in Drinkwater's evaluation of Natural Law:

"The Natural Law is surely an unfortunate term," said a Catholic woman, educated, thoughtful, to the present writer recently. . . . For me, the word "natural" in this connection has the meaning primarily of "knowable by the natural light of reason" . . . for some people it seems to refer to whatever moral conclusions may be deductible from the nature of anything created.[21]

He goes on to say that popular conscience, as we all know, is liable to go astray in such moral refinements on account of sentiment or misplaced compassion, the heart proving stronger than the head. Or there can be mistaken applications by the professional moral reasoners.[22] A book was written recently by a Protestant pastor in France to defend the "Christian pacifist" position, and it completely rejects the Natural Law as a criterion for conduct. "Scripture is all he will admit, and as for non-Christians, or secular government, they must follow the Decalogue as best they can.[23]

The rhythm concession granted to adherents of the Roman Catholic Church by Pope Pius XI on December 21, 1930 in his *Casti Connubii*, appears to the writer as a disguised form of contraception, for certainly, procreation is hoped to be avoided in the rhythm method. Rosemary Ruether, theologian and mother of three children, explains the anxiety of a member of the Catholic Church:

> The inadequacies and tensions caused by rhythm were too inadequate to be endured for long, it meant being the unwitting slave of biological fecundity. In fact rhythm turned out to be "a sexual version of the Chinese water torture."[24]

The pill has certainly put Rome in a precarious position in that the authority of the Church is being challenged in view of her dogmatizing tradition. No item so small has ever received such discussion and publicity in secular circles as well as various religious faiths.

Another factor which produced a most intriguing discussion not only among Christians but among all civilized people was the coming to market of the first contraceptive pill—hesperidin. This pill was first merchandised in the early 1950s, was followed by another pill in 1953—progesterone, which was more effective than hesperidin. Progesterone regulated the menstrual cycle, which in turn allowed for the practice of the rhythm method with greater confidence.

To the surprise of many, Pope Paul VI, in his encyclical letter on the 25th of July (1968) on the feast of St. James the Apostle, reiterated the traditional Roman Catholic view on contraception. "The Church, calling men back to the observance of the norms of the natural law, as interpreted by their constant doctrine, teaches that each and every marriage act (quilibet matrimonii usus) must remain open to the transmission of life."[25] Again, the encyclical reconfirmed the rhythm method to avoid conception.

Lloyd A. Kalland interprets this statement:

> If then, there are serious motives to space out births, which derive from the physical or psychological conditions of husband and wife, or from external conditions, the Church teaches that it is then licit to take into account the natural rhythm immanent in the generative functions, for the use of marriage, in the infecund periods only, and in this way to regulate birth without ending the moral principles which have been recalled earlier.[26]

The Roman Catholic moral theologians, at least some, have sought to conform to the Church's stand on Natural Law by sanctioning the use of anovulants, such as progesterone. It was regarded solely (by theologians) as an anovulant, that is, as an agent preventing conception by preventing ovulation. Noonan raises the question: If it was lawful to suppress ovulation to achieve a regularity necessary for successfully sterile intercourse, why was it not lawful to suppress ovulation without appeal to rhythm? If pregnancy could be prevented by pill plus rhythm, why not the pill alone? The Roman Catholic Church finds herself struggling against the embalmed traditions of the past in her stress of Natural Law above the statements of Scripture which offer no condemnation against contraception when one considers the total person in marriage.

There is no precise "Protestant View" on the subject of contraception. Calvin seemed to follow the old Catholic doctrine, and Luther held an Augustinian view of sexuality that did not encourage change. However, a number of evangelical conservative theologians offer excellent moral and ethical guidelines on the subject of contraception. They discuss the purpose of marriage in its totality. Sterilization, artificial insemination, and contraception and the single girl are all covered from the viewpoint of Scripture, reason, and experience. Far more pressing than the problem of contraception is abortion, a topic which is vital to Christians and non-Christians. This subject will be covered later.

### Scripture and Contraception

The word "contraception" is not found in either the Old Testament or the New Testament. Therefore, many would hasten to ask: "How can the exegete and theologian support or refute the practice of contraception with scriptural authority?" Yet, when one considers the total person and the unity of the marriage relationship, Scripture does offer counsel pertaining to the subject. One common denominator in Scripture in relation to marriage is "unity." Jesus states in Matthew 19:4, 6: "Have you not read that he who made them from the beginning made them male and female? What, therefore, God has joined together, let no man put asunder." The logion connects the order of creation with the order of redemption. We find in Genesis 1:26, 27: "And God said, let us make man in our image, in the image of God created he him; male and female created he them." Keil and Delitzsch, in commenting on this passage, state:

The distinction drawn between אתו (in the image of God created He him) and אתם (as man and woman created He them) must not be overlooked. The word [them] which indicates that God created the man and woman as two human beings, completely overthrows the idea that man was at first androgynous.[27]

Here a new element is introduced in the information given about the creation of man by mentioning differences in sex. The two words "male" and "female" are translations of Hebrew adjectives that indicate the sex of the two individuals. The blessing of fertility pronounced over the animals (v. 22) implies that they must have been created likewise with sexual differences; however, the fact is not mentioned. Perhaps it is because that only in man does the duality of sex express itself in the sacred institution of marriage. "And God blessed them," and "God saw everything that he had made and behold it was very good." Gen. 1:28, 31. The creation of woman from Adam's rib in Gen. 2:21 ff. suggests the fact that man and woman belong together. In Genesis 2:18, the need extends not only to the biological but to the psychological realm as well.

Helmuth Thielicke, in *The Ethics of Sex*, states:

In the first account of creation there is no indication whatsoever of any distinction of rank between man and woman (Gen. 1:26-28). The threefold reference to God's "creating" in verse 27 leaves no room for any distinction of value. Both, man and woman, are equally immediate to the Creator and his act. Furthermore, both together receive (v. 28) the blessing as well as the command to subdue the earth (1:28f).[28]

Mary Daly, in quoting the poet Claudel, states:

It has been said that the earthly calling of woman is in no way destructive of her supernatural autonomy; but, inversely, in recognizing this, the Catholic feels authorized to maintain in this world the prerogatives of the male. Venerating woman in God, men treat her in this world as a servant, even holding that the more one demands complete submission of her, the more surely one will advance her along the road of her salvation.[29]

Mary Daly views women in the Old Testament as subjugated and inferior beings. It is true that the cultural milieu of the Old Testament found women of the East subordinate to the male. However, in Scripture, the Lord created them both and said that they were very good. They were created for God and each other and are equal before our Creator and Redeemer.

In the Hebrew economy no population explosion existed; large families were needed for economic reasons in an agricultural environment. Today, we find the reverse in population and our economy. In Old Testament times, practically everybody married. In fact, the Old Testament has no word for "bachelor" at all.

In the Bible, marriage is used as a symbol for the relationship of God to his people. "For thy Maker is thine husband; the Lord of hosts in his name, For the Lord hath called thee as a woman, a wife of youth" (Isaiah 54:5, 6). The order of creation and the order of redemption converge in the symbol of marriage. As the Christian life is to be one in Christ, thus the marriage relationship is to be a total union of two lives. "Have ye not read, that he which made them at the beginning made them male and female, for this cause shall a man leave father and mother, and shall cleave to his wife; and they twain shall be one flesh? Wherefore, they are no more twain, but one flesh," Matthew 19:4-6. Therefore, it would appear that in Christian marriage, contraception would not be forbidden by Scripture when one considers the total person and the entire marriage relationship, including physical intimacies apart from procreation. We read in Genesis 2:18: "And the Lord said: 'It is not good that the man should be alone; I will make an help meet for him,'" and in Genesis 2:24: "They shall be one flesh." Adam was attracted to his wife. They see each other as male and female. They recognize both their differences and their oneness, their masculinity and femininity, which both differentiate and unite them. Differentiation and unity—male and female yet one flesh is what human life is all about.[30] Certainly, the Song of Solomon endeavors to place sex in a holy frame. When we consider the total person, both *agape* and *eros* are guided by the Holy Spirit and sanctified reason. Psychology and sociology are underscoring what the Bible has told us from the beginning: sexuality is not a partial concept; it is total.

The text that has been most widely used by Roman Catholic theologians and Canonists to refute the practice of contraception is Genesis 38:8-10, which reads:

> Then Judah said to Onan: "Go in to your brother's wife and perform the duty of a brother-in-law to her, and raise up offspring for your brother." . . . when he went in unto his brother's wife, he spilled it on the ground, lest that he should give seed to his brother. And the thing which he did displeased the Lord: wherefore he slew him also.

The context clearly indicates that Onan's sin lay in his selfish unwillingness to honor his levirate duty. The institution of levirate is from Lat. *levir* = brother.[31]

A number of Roman Catholic writers and exegetes reject the centuries old and embalmed interpretations of the Onan text. Drinkwater states:

> There ought to have been continual discussion of Casti Connubii during the past thirty-five years, on the new insights into the psychology of married love, on the *up-to-date exegesis of the Onan text*, on the scientific improvements in contraceptives, on the truth about the safe period, and lately about the pill; but above all, on the true bearings of the natural law. Instead, there has been a whole generation of frozen silence, the silence of intellectual death, or at least of paralysis.[32]

and Noonan:

> The argument from Genesis was not used by a good many theologians, including St. Jerome. . . . It was not used by all twentieth-century theologians. The term "onanism" was not itself an exegesis; it was merely the conventional term for the sin of contraception. The difference of exegetical opinion was clear in the early twentieth century. De Smet wrote, "From the text and context it seems that the criticism of the sacred author is less directly and formally attached to the spilling of the seed than to the frustration of the levirate law which Onan intended to achieve." (Les Fioncailles et le mariage 2.1.3.1.1, anex 2, N. 5.)[33]

Bruce K. Waltke comments on Lev. 15:16-18 and Lev. 20:10-21. The first reads:

> And if a man has an emission of semen, he shall bathe his whole body in water and be unclean until the evening. And every garment and every skin on which the semen comes shall be washed with water, and be unclean until the evening. If a man lies with a woman and has an emission of semen they shall bathe with water and be unclean until the evening.

Interpreting the passage he says:

> The cogent point is that the emission of semen apart from coitus is not regarded as a sinful act. Because no sacrifice is demanded, Barclay says: "No moral fault is implied in connection with these impurities. So the laws are ceremonial."[34]

The second passage lists sexual crimes punishable by death. All these involve intercourse with a person apart from the marriage relationship. Again, there is no reference to withdrawal as a sexual abuse.

The New Testament does not single out contraception in its

broad coverage of Christian principles of conduct in the realm of sex. However, the New Testament writers are quite clear in speaking directly against illegitimate sexual relationships.[35]

In Ephesians 5:21-31, Paul discusses the total person in marriage. The unity of husband and wife is reiterated from the Old Testament in Genesis 2:24, whereas they become one flesh. No contingencies exist apart from *agape* in Christ, and *eros* in temperance and Spirit guided reason when individuals are one in Christ both by creation and redemption.

The absence of divine counsel in the realm of contraception would indicate that Scripture in both the Old Testament and New Testament does not condemn contraception per se. The marriage relationship involves more than procreation when one considers the total man. In Hebrews 13:4a we read: "Marriage is honorable in *all*, and the *bed undefiled*" [italics mine]. Calvin takes *pasin* (all) as masculine, and explains that marriage is not to be denied to any class of men, as to priests. Others explain that marriage is not to be avoided on ascetic grounds by any one.[36] Also, "in all" would suggest the total person in marriage in addition to procreation.

The passage in I Tim. 4:3, "Forbidding to marry," could very well refer to "celibacy," which was condemned by Paul along with other wrongs in his catalogue of sins. However, the phrase "honorable in all" appears to be best compared to Paul's remarks on marriage in I Cor. 7:1-9. There the overall issue is the question of getting married at all, and the physical relationship is a matter of mutual agreement.

Therefore, it would appear from Scripture that God sets forth marriage for the total person, and each are to respond to the other in *eros* and *agape* within the bounds of creation and redemption, in the light of Scripture, sanctified reason, and experience. The word of God offers no condemnation against contraception within the framework of the above in the marriage experience. The pill issue, involving the single person, revolves around two key premises held by modern ethicists. One emphasizes "love" as the sole guide to determine the Christian's behavior in any situation. The other emphasizes "love" and "rule" as guides to govern behavior in a situation. Contraception apart from marriage is without a doubt an issue to be considered by the Christian. The next section will be given to this subject.

## Contraception Apart from Marriage

Today, thousands of coeds and other single persons are taking birth control pills or the morning-after-pill to prevent or terminate a pregnancy. The morning-after-pill prohibits the new life from attaching itself to the uterine wall. Such a pill could fall into the abortifacient category; however, with this pill there is no way of knowing whether or not the sperm and ovum had ever united to form the mysterious genesis of a potential person. The Christian has ample Scriptural evidence forbidding illicit sex acts, yet for the Christian minister and physician to apply the principle absolutely, appears impractical in an age and generation whereby subcultures do exist as well as serious mental defects.

Thus, the clergy and the physician are confronted today with questions and decisions which challenge the objectivity of Scripture. The autonomy of man looms up to question scriptural authority or to employ a hermeneutic which bypasses "a thus saith the Lord." Both err oftentimes by sanctioning moral and ethical decisions, or counsel from the viewpoint of the individual and the situation. Fletcher stresses *agape* in moral and ethical choices. He says that love is a monolithic and jealous standard, a univalent form. It shoulders aside all other lesser goods. Christian situation ethics reduces love from a statutory system of rules to the love canon alone.[37] Further, he says: Jesus and Paul replaced the precepts of Torah with the living principles of *agape, agape* being good will at work in partnership with reason.[38] A psychologist in Miami says that sex is not even a moral question. We should not ask "Is it right or wrong?" he says, but "Is it feasible?" He goes on to state that his view is fast becoming the view of many Protestant church leaders. The preachers, he says, no longer wag their fingers at the young folk because they surrender to biological urges and do some experimenting. They don't yell "Stop!" "What's wrong!"[39] Situationists are saying that we are never to appeal to rules. Instead we are to tell what we should do in a particular situation. God then asks what is the loving or most loving thing to do in it.[40] Paul Ramsey, commenting on Christian ethics, reveals the true *agape* approach in a situation by stating: " 'Men should deal with one another as God deals with them' (cf. Ecc. 2:39). Neither in a secular context is it possible to formulate the ethical question as what am I to do?"[41]

With the perfection and dispension of the pill, premarital relations have been looked upon more favorably by the situationists. The pill not only has changed the lives of many single people, but a storm has arisen in the Roman Catholic Church so intense as to shake her very foundations. Apart from the theological challenges and questions, the Vatican has come under fire over a Vatican-owned pharmaceutical house. Ramsey states:

Pope Paul's encyclical condemning contraception has given rise to a birth pill explosion here on the papal doorstep. Awkward as this may be for Vatican officials, they soon will be riding on the horns of another dilemma with the revelation that a Vatican-owned pharmaceutical house has been producing and is marketing oral birth control capsules. L'Istituto Farmacologico Serona, which has its main offices in Milan and its plant a few miles outside the city, is a thriving drug company with a capitalization of $1.4 million. ... Most Italian doctors have no qualms about prescribing the use of these capsules to cure gynecological ailments. ... Since sacred scripture neither condemns nor recommends contraception, many Italian Catholics prefer to make their own decisions about it. In any event, they like to refer

to the current controversy as "the bitter pill of Pope Paul."[42]
Thus, the problem of sexual ethics confronts the church, the pharmacist, the physician, the sociologist, and the Christian minister. Whereas the Roman Catholic Church faces the contraception problem in marriage and outside of marriage, Protestants face the right or wrong aspect of contraception for the single person.

Orville S. Walters views the physician with one of several attitudes in his prescribing contraceptives: (1) the broadly permissive, (2) the neutralist, (3) reluctant sanction, (4) the situationist, and (5) the historic Christian position.[43] As to the broadly permissive, Orville S. Walters states:

> Freud prepared the way for the Kinsey report, according to Lionel Trilling. . . . Trilling commented upon the permissive influence of the report, while Reinhold Niebuhr described the permarital promiscuity that Kinsey advocated as "moral anarchism." . . . In the same vein, one might say that Kinsey prepared the way for the Playboy Philosophy and many of the expressions of sexual permissiveness in today's world.[44]

Sex must not roam over the country with no bridle, whereby no moral territory is out of bounds or off limits. Aside from the question of decency and morality, promiscuity is bad because it is harmful to the young woman. It works against her interests. Human nature being what it is, the demonstration that a course of action is harmful is more likely to be effective than the argument that it is indecent or immoral.[45] In contrast, Fletcher says:

> The triple terrors of infection, conception, and detection, which once seared people into "Christian" sex relations (marital monopoly), have pretty well become obsolete through medicine and urbanism. There is less and less cause, on the basis of situation ethics, for the opinion that people should abide by, or pretend to, an ideal or standard that is not their own.[46]

He goes on to cite the case of the whore in the Greek movie, "Never on Sunday," who aids the young sailor to function sexually whereby he gains his self-respect and psychic freedom. To the single Christian, the question would not be to gain respect but to lose respect by disobedience to Christ.

Orville S. Walters sums up an argument against premarital coition:

> Girls and boys of this generation need help in detecting and rejecting ... the ... subtly persuasive, fraudulent national propaganda of the new sexual morality. ... Four thousand years of Judeo-Christian wisdom cannot be dismissed lightly. There are still valid and urgent reasons for saving sex for the right time, place, and person, within the sanctions of a concerned society.[47]

The gospel prophet Isaiah prophetically referring to Jesus, says in Isaiah 7:15b, "that he may learn to refuse the evil and choose the good." One must be cognizant of the fact that we live in a sinful order and as long as sin exists there are negative and positive choices in and for Christ.

The physician cannot ignore his responsibility in counseling and prescribing contraceptive medication to the single person. "The single person seeking contraceptive advice requires concerned counseling by the physician. If he provides contraceptive agents, he participates in the intent of their use. Sexual intercourse is rightly confined to marriage. Therefore, fornication, adultery, and prostitution with or without contraception are not a Christian option.[48] The Christian physician must deal with patients in totality and not in part.

Illicit sexual relations between the single man and woman is never the total experience ordained by God in sexual relations. It is admitted by the majority of sexologists that full personal realization is found, when there is a sexual relation, only in complete and real love, with its carnal and psychological components fully respected. Marriage alone can allow the fulfillment of these conditions, even though it does not always realize them, because it, and it alone, involves the total giving of self and total possession of a partner, at the same time without any restriction.

Sex relations outside the marriage circle violate God's plan for man to procreate and propagate his race. We read in Genesis 2:28: "Be fruitful and multiply and replenish the earth." It is a violation of the total union which God ordained to exist between husband and wife. The two can never become one via a physical union which union itself is incomplete as a part of the total marriage experience. Monogamy is not selfish monopoly by one person over another; it is simply the plan outlined by God. Premarital relations paves the way for gross infidelity in marriage which may become a subtle form of polygamy. Far too many people, promiscuous in the realm of sex, desire only erotic liberties minus responsibilities. Even in a divinely ordained marriage, along with the privileges of marriage are the unavoidable responsibilities. Premarital sex usually negates responsibility.

The Christian physician along with all Christians are their "brother's keeper." He cannot afford to be neutral or reluctantly sanction sex violations. We hasten to add that even the Christian physician faces a choice of lesser evil whereby he prescribes birth control pills to one in a subcultural environment. But even so, he should outline the ideal moral norm as revealed in Christ and His law, and must also live with the reality of the situation.

Today, the counsel for and against contraception is primarily centered around the single girl. The pill was developed for the female. History and tradition attest to the fact that the woman has been primarily responsible for her virginity. Medical science, moving in a practical direction, developed a pill to affect ovulation. The female manufactures approximately one egg per month, whereby the male manufactures billions of sperm cells each month. It is said that one thimble full of male sperm would be sufficient to repopulate the entire earth! Thus, medical science being pragmatic, developed the pill for the woman.

In view of this it is still proper that the single male be equally informed and admonished in the realm of moral sexual behavior and responsibility.

To comply with an unmarried girl's request for contraceptives is not simply to transfer the ethical decision to her; it is to take part in the decision. Considerable professional authority is bound up in the role of a doctor. Every prescription he gives is considered to reflect what he feels is best for the patient, and the patient's acceptance of a prescription implies confidence in the doctor's ability to make a wise choice. The doctor is paid to make choices for his patients, and he cannot avoid responsibility for the course he recommends.[49]

The Christian physician must rely on the timeless principles outlined in Scripture as his guide and point of reference to point individuals to Christ and away from sin. Every game has rules, thus it is also in the game of life. The Ten Commandments do offer guidelines for moral conduct and cannot be ignored without impunity. In fact, the whole salvation issue is obedience to God's will through Christ. But the Bishop of Woolwich says:

The sanctions of Sinai have lost their terrors, and people no longer accept the authority of Jesus even as a great moral teacher. Robbed of its supernatural supports, men find it difficult to take seriously a code of living that confessedly depended on them. "Why shouldn't I?" or "What's wrong with it?" are questions which in our generation press for an answer. And supranaturalists reason—that God or Christ pronounced it "a sin"—have force, and even meaning, for none but a diminishing religious remnant.[50]

In our age of sex revolution, the student of Scripture and history can readily see that man is not capable of charting his own course and setting up his own rules of moral conduct. The prophet Jeremiah says: "O Lord, I know that the way of man is not in himself; it is not in man that walketh to direct his steps" (Jeremiah 10:23). The situationists have merely projected existential theology against Scripture as being objective and authoritative. These they say lie subjectively within man and his reason; thus, authority shifts from special revelation, the Word of God, to the individual. The condition can best be summed up in

Judges 21:25: "In those days there was no king in Israel: every man did that which was right in his own eyes." The day of situation ethics in this era of the Judges proved to be one of the darkest periods of Israelite history.

Love and rule in ethics are akin to the law and the gospel in Scripture. They are not mutually exclusive, but are compatible and complimentary. Fletcher's contradistinct approach challenges even the moral law which is a transcript of God's character. The moral law is a great standard; Christ is the means of attaining that standard. But Fletcher maintains that situational factors are so primary that we may even say circumstances alter rules and principles. The notion that there are immutable laws of heaven is idolatrous and a demonic pretension. To him, the situationist, there are no rules at all. Love will not share its authority with any other laws, either natural or supernatural. The individual in a situation is not acting in isolation whether in the realm of sex or other areas. He must consider God, revelation, and the moral conscience of society as well as his own.

However, there is another side of the moral coin. Gardner believes situationism will prove to be transitory. Bennett says that the Christian must recognize the situation. Kennedy speaks of valid tradition as giving votes to the most obscure of all classes, our ancestors. Tradition asks us not to neglect a good man's opinion, even if he is our father. We will have the dead at our councils.[52]

Men as well as women are to exercise moral restraint in the face of temptation. The young woman may avoid conception as the result of a pill prescribed by a physician; she may immunize her womb to a pregnancy, but she is violating the command and will of God. Here we are naturally dealing with the enlightened person; that is, the person who knows what is right and wrong.

The woman or young lady is never symbolized as the church in Scripture apart from purity. The wise man said: "Who can find a virtuous woman? for her price is far above rubies. The heart of her husband doth safely trust in her" (Proverbs 31:10,11). Jesus in His sermon on the mount magnifies the far-reaching claims of the moral law. In Matthew 5:27 ff., He deals with adultery and fornication in its embryonic stages emphasizing the fact that illicit sexual behavior is a violation of the moral law and a sin against the body. Paul is most implicit on the subject in I Cor. 7:2: "Nevertheless, to avoid fornication, let every man have his own wife, and let every woman have her own husband." And in v. 8, 9, "I say therefore to the unmarried and widows, it is good for them if they abide even as I. But if they cannot contain, let them marry: for it is better to marry than to burn." Some commentators misinterpret Paul's expression in v. 6: "But I speak this by permission and not of commandment." Here the apostle is not giving counsel which is uninspired, he is simply stating that the Lord gave no express commandment against marriage, but in the eschatological framework and tension of Christianity in the first century A.D., he said: "It is best to be as I am." It is also possible that he is addressing some who would be uniquely committed to the service of the kingdom of God as our Lord intimates in Matthew 19:12b: "And there be eunuchs, which have made themselves eunuchs for the kingdom of heaven's sake." The apostle nowhere sanctions sexual relations outside the marriage covenant.

The issue in Scripture is not contraception with the single male or female, which is merely symptomatic of a moral problem in sexual behavior. The real crux of the issue is in the sinful use of sex as mentioned in Romans 13:13. "Let us walk honestly, as in the day; not in rioting and drunkedness, not chambering [illicit sexual acts]."

The minister, the physician, ethicist, psychologist, and sociologist may understand and be redemptive toward those caught in a situation, but he has no right to abrogate or negate the divine injunction against illicit sexual behavior. No physician may have an opinion of himself that transcends the human. However high he may have risen, the doctor has not ceased to be a man, subject to divine and human laws, written and unwritten, which should be sacred for him because his powers are greater. If he fails to observe them, it is first and foremost with his own conscience that he must reckon.

Scripture does not condemn contraception per se with the

single person, whether male or female. However, the New Testament writers in trumpet tones condemn unequivocally sexual intimacies outside the marriage circle. The Christian ethic is based upon the Word of God. The single person should preserve his or her sexual powers and privileges until they are united as one in the divinely ordained marriage union. When the New Testament writers catalogue sins in the last days they most specifically and generally include illicit sexual behavior among the serious offenses in the sight of God. Both male and female are admonished in Scripture to obey God's commands and to claim His promises. The single person refuses premarital relations simply because God forbids such; secondly, he or she claims God's promise that only in the marriage union do two people become one and the full blessing of sex can be realized.

The single person who never marries is encouraged in Scripture to let sanctified reason control all the faculties of the body. *Eros* is to be kept in check by the power of the Spirit within the mind. The great apostle says: "Know ye not that ye are the temple of God, and that the Spirit of God dwelleth in you?" (I Cor. 3:16); also, "Know ye not that your bodies are the members of Christ? Shall I then take the members of Christ, and make them the members of an harlot? God forbid" (I Cor. 5:15). Finally, Paul states in I Cor. 9:27: "But I keep under my body, and bring it into subjection: lest that by any means, when I have preached to others, I myself should be a castaway." The Greek verb "bruise" is a more accurate translation than the KJV "keep." Paul's use of the phrase is literally translated: "But I bruise my body," that is, he employs a term used in the Grecian sport of boxing, to render a devastating blow to strike his old nature that looms up to assume mastery over the body.

Contraception is not condemned in Scripture, but premarital or illicit sexual behavior is. Therefore, contraceptive devices and medications are not issues with the true Christian. The whole case as to the pill and the single person may be laid to rest for the Christian from the inspired statements of Scripture on the subject. The Bible simply, clearly, and unequivocally forbids premarital sex. But the Christian physician and minister must deal with the problem on an individual basis, especially whereby a person engaging in illicit sexual acts is bound to a subcultural environment. The Christian church has been confronted with kindred moral problems in heathen countries where converts were involved in polygamous situations. The "ideal" must ever be held before such individuals, but the "real" situation demands education, love, and understanding in order that individuals may be led to a higher place of moral perfection in Christ. Contraception is not ideal apart from the marriage experience. However, it may be a lesser-of-evils choice for the Christian physician prescribing a contraceptive for a patient ensnared in a subcultural environment. Along with the prescription, the Christian physician must offer counsel of concern for the moral behavior of his patient. A prescription to prevent conception among single persons is always a choice of lesser evil. Yet it may well be the only option afforded the Christian physician in a unique situation, such as a subcultural or amoral society.

The evangelical Christian cannot treat lightly the subject of contraception. Even though the evangelical Protestant differs with the Roman Catholic Church on her stand against contraception in the marriage relationship, many do share in her concern over the sacredness of life and the divine gift of procreation to propagate like species. It is also a heavenly sanction to rear children and share in their training for the school of the hereafter. However, as one examines the "total man" and his role in the "entire" marriage relationship, the sexual union of two partners is a part of the many aspects of the marriage experience. The Word of God offers no counsel against contraception being employed in marriage. I would hasten to add that the use of contraceptives in no way gives license for the Christian to run with no bridle upon his sexual desires. Like food and drink, sex is a legitimate desire of the body at the right time and proper place.

It is true that a multitude of problems are annexed to the apparent blessings of medical science. The removal of the fear of pregnancy, the irresponsibility of single persons guilty of promiscuity, the increase of venereal diseases, and the premature drain on the life forces of the young should call the Christian minister to a responsible role in dealing with this "blessing" which has become a curse to many. Sweden is called the "Contraceptive Society" by J. Robert Moskin, and is filled with "new morality stories" and case histories. He states:

> Ninety-three per cent of all Swedes accept sex regularity between persons who are engaged or "going steady." Ninety-eight per cent of the married population had intercourse before marriage . . . only nine per cent of those under thirty *did not have intercourse before marriage.*[53]

Sex, along with science, has become a god to millions of people in this decade of change. It was given and ordained for use in the will of God, but it is not to be cheapened and abused by mechanical contraceptive devices or medications. This blessing of medical science should not become an asset to sinful lusts.

God created mankind with the duality of sex, to produce off-spring to His glory, to unite man and woman in a tie or bond more sacred and close than any other experience apart from the living experience in Christ. Contraception is a blessing in this age of population explosion and the eonomic challenge of urban living. The blessing can become a bitter curse if the life and teachings of Christ in His Word are not followed in all aspects of our living, especially in the realm of sex which God said was very good. No device, whether mental, mechanical, or chemical must cheapen what God created and blessed. Contraceptive measures are afforded to the Christian as an option. Contraception has proven to be a positive benefit in view of the above reasons; also, in consideration of the health of a wife, and especially in view of possible genetic defects.

## Artificial Insemination

Opposite the contraception and abortion issue is the question of artificial insemination. The desire for artificial insemination is brought about by a husband being sterile or unable to impregnate his wife due to impotency or other factors either physical or psychic. Secondly, the experience may be requested due to the pollution of the genetic pool whereby a couple desire as near perfect a child as possible with the co-operation of medical science. The great medical and moral change of attitudes toward this issue was recently expressed by Professor George P. Smith, writing in the *Family Law Quarterly*:

" . . . said a 1968 California Court decision holding a husband liable for the support of the child if he allows his wife to be artificially inseminated marks a distinct change in judicial attitudes toward insemination. The decision holds, Smith said, that the term 'father' must be construed broadly . . . and, under no circumstances, (can it) be tied to a rigid definition of a biologic or natural father.[54]

Smith, who is an assistant professor and assistant dean at the State University of New York at Buffalo School of Law, went on to say that as recently as the 1950's, courts held artificial insemination "is illegitimate and the very act itself is adulterous."[55]

Along with some of these sudden changes in attitudes are some frightening thoughts as to genetic control, such as, who determines the ideal man or woman? God forbid that some modern Hitler make the decision as to I.Q., color of eyes, and hair. Artificial insemination on the basis of genetic control is not fool proof or without certain risk. Dr. Leroy Augenstein says that all have some defective genes. On the average, from 5 to 10. If these were matched up with a partner there is one chance in four a catastrophe is going to result.[56] Fortunately most do not match up. Nevertheless, the potential danger even in selecting genes exists. The paradox of medical science is evident in cases of diabetes. The discovery of insulin, in other words, insures that the number of people in the population with genes for diabetes will increase. Augenstein goes on to add that if our present medical practice continues, within 75 to 150 years one out of ten children born will be seriously defective in one way or another.[57] Such a future outlook causes many, no doubt, to look with favor on artificial insemination. The individuals planning on marriage with defective genes may not have to decide as to whether or not they will have children. For instance, in Denmark, a list of defects have been drawn up, and if an individual has one of them they are required to be sterilized before a marriage license is issued. The question arises as to whether the individual or the state should decide in such cases. Yet, the unborn and society must be heard in these delicate and important decisions.

The theological issue regarding artificial insemination centers around the "one flesh" or "unity in marriage" experience. Married couples who find it impossible to conceive through natural intercourse sometimes achieve impregnation via three types of artificial insemination:

1. Use of semen from the husband, commonly referred to as A.I.H.
2. Insemination with semen from a donor who is usually anonymous and with whom the recipient has no contact (A.I.O.).
3. Insemination with semen from the husband and semen from a donor who is again usually anonymous (C.A.I.)[58]

Any of the above methods is unnatural. Reaction to artificial insemination has been very heated with individuals either for or against, with very little indication of a middle of the road attitude. It appears to the writer that artificial insemination in relation to the above types (2) and (3) are to be rejected by the Christian on the basis that two, not three, should form the sacred marriage union. This thought was reiterated by Jesus in Matthew 19:5-6, which says that: "Two shall become one ... what God

74

therefore has joined together, let no man put asunder." The psychological influence cannot be ignored. What will be the husband's reaction to this other person who, after all, has been substituted for himself and has done what he could not? Such an experience in the marriage relationship appears to relegate deep love between two individuals to a process. The dehumanizing and depersonalizing of the persons appear unavoidable in this context of a Christian marriage.

Artificial insemination, whereby the husband is the donor, would be impossible to classify as a moral violation. However, that it is unnatural cannot be denied. Adoption would appear to be a better solution to a couple who cannot have children in view of the expense, psychological reactions, and theological considerations. Some things are lawful, but not expedient. Insemination may be a substitute for the total marriage experience. Even technical medical skills in specialized areas cannot afford not to take into account the total person. If we wish to summarize this opposition between technical knowledge on the one hand, and philosophy and theology on the other, we can say that it bears chiefly on three points. Firstly, the specialist looks only to one part of the reality—and deliberately does so, because such limitation is the condition of his success; since, for him, man is considered merely from the viewpoint of one of his functions, one of his activities, one of his states, neither the philosopher nor the theologian can hold that either must confine himself to such limitations to judge a human action correctly. One point of view only is admissible for the philosopher or the theologian: that of the totality.[59]

In a marriage union whereby two people fail to become "one flesh" physically and psychically, even homologous insemination (semen of the husband) under exceptional circumstances is not without risk. It would be a noble gesture for two people unable to have children naturally to adopt children in a world filled with unwanted children. Even with a homologous insemination the biological process of procreation is removed from the psychophysical totality of the marital fellowship. Whether theologians, physicians, or jurists, there is certainly no unanimity on the subject as Thielicke stated:

> The positions hitherto taken with respect to the question of artificial insemination—no matter whether they come from doctors and lawyers, from Catholic or Protestant theologians —exhibit a confusing diversity. This confusion of opinions can be reduced to some kind of statistical order only to the extent that we can say on the medical side there are advocates both of homologous and heterologous insemination, whereas homologous insemination finds fairly unanimous acceptance on the part of jurists and divided recognition on the part of theologians, and heterologous insemination is very generally rejected by the jurists and radically rejected by the theologians.[60]

Thus, even homologous insemination is far from ideal in view of the psychophysical totality of the marital fellowship. Recently, an obstetrician friend of mine told me that most of the patients who had solicited his medical advice and skill for insemination revealed psychological problems. The polar unity (Gen. 1:27) of husband and wife as "one flesh" (Gen. 2:23-24) does not encourage insemination. Naturally, the Christian minister, frowning on artificial insemination, would offer such counsel to a couple by inference and opinion and not as an expressed Scriptural command.

The case against heterologous insemination does offer a much more serious problem to the theologian. It appears to be dignified adultery whereby the violation of the "one flesh" concept exists. A third party, even as an anonymous donor, invades the mysterious marriage circle formed by two. Such dehumanizes and depersonalizes the individual. Some proud human stallion could conceivably father thousands of children without responsibility. As we previously stated, a thimbleful of male sperm is sufficient to populate the entire earth. Apart from the moral infringement on the marriage covenant, other dangers and problems exist with heterologous insemination. Thielicke relates a Danish report which describes a particular case of artificial insemination and its tragic results:

The father of the artificially procreated child is an unknown semen donor. The transmission was undertaken at the request of the married couple since the sterility of the husband would not permit the begetting of children. And yet even during the pregnancy there developed in the husband a hate-complex toward the unborn child, which, as the very well-known gynecologist who was acting in the case expressed it, had become for him "a symbol of his own weakness." This led to tension in the marriage which ended in divorce. The child has now come into the world utterly unwanted and fatherless. The physician, who had recommended the artificial insemination to the couple, says that after this experience he will never again advise this method.[61]

The writer had occasion a few years ago to counsel with a couple emotionally disturbed over their child who was the result of heterologous insemination. The husband deeply resented the child and brutally took out his hostility on the innocent victim. That which is engendered as a blessing of medical science can very well become a curse. The I-thou relationship is most vital to a total marriage relationship and naturally canot exist in insemination.

Apart from the ethical objections whereby a psychophysical unity of the sex relationship is dissolved and personhood is subordinated to a purely biological process, there is danger of incest on the medical side, especially with anonymous donors. Also, the function of the "spermator" would appear objectionable with a pathological divorce between the physiological and the personal dimension of the sex realm.[62]

In summary, artificial insemination appears to be freighted with too many questions and objections as a course to pursue by a couple desiring a child. No risk is worth taking if the marriage relationship is jeopardized: "If one member suffers, all suffer together" (I Cor. 12:26). Adoption is a better plan for a couple who cannot have children of their own. At least the child is on equal footing with the adopted father and mother as far as parents are concerned. Yet there is no moral violation in a marriage whereby the husband is the donor.

## Notes to Chapter II

1. Leroy Augenstein, *Come, Let Us Play God* (New York: Harper and Row, 1969), p. 141.

2. John T. Noonan, Jr., *Contraception: A History of Its Treatment by the Catholic Theologians and Canonists* (Cambridge: Harvard University Press, 1966), p. 1.

3. Ibid., p. 11.

4. Lloyd A. Kalland, "Views and Position of the Christian Church— An Historical Review," in *Birth Control and the Christian*, ed. by Walter O. Spitzer and Carlyle T. Saylor (Wheaton: Tyndale House Publishers, 1969), p. 419.

5. Ibid.

6. Noonan, *Contraception: A History*, pp. 11-12.

7. Ibid., p. 13.

8. Ibid., p. 14.

9. Ibid., p. 17.

10. Henry Wace and Philip Schaff, *The Seven Ecumenical Councils: Nicene and Post-Nicene Fathers*, XIV (New York: Charles Scribner's Sons, 1900), 8.

11. Ibid., p. 595.

12. Noonan, *Contraception: A History*, p. 57. For further details, the reader is referred to Noonan's Chart, p. 57, of the word cited for a comparison of the far "left," "center," and "right" as to Gnostic sexual behavior during the first and second centuries A.D.

13. John T. Noonan, Jr., *The Church and Contraception* (New York: Paulist Press Deus Books, 1967), p. 29.

14. Noonan, *Contraception: A History*, p. 101.

15. Kalland, "Views and Position," p. 431.

16. Noonan, *Contraception: A History*, p. 362.

17. *U.S. vs. One Package*, December 30, 1936. See Ernest R. Groves, *Marriage* (2nd ed. revised; New York: Host, 1947).

18. F. H. Drinkwater, *Birth Control and Natural Law* (Baltimore-

Dublin: Billing and Sons, Ltd., Guildford and London, for Helicon Press, Inc., 1965), pp. 28-29.

19. Kalland, "Views and Position," p. 431.

20. Noonan, *The Church and Contraception*, pp. 2-3.

21. Drinkwater, *Birth Control and Natural Law*, p. 7.

22. Ibid., pp. 13-14.

23. Ibid., pp. 8-9.

24. Mary Daly, *The Church and the Second Sex* (New York: Harper and Row, 1968), p. 91.

25. Kalland, "Views and Position," p. 463.

26. Ibid.

27. C. F. Keil and F. Delitzsch, *Biblical Commentary on the Old Testament*, trans. by James Martin, Vol. I: *The Pentateuch* (Grand Rapids: Wm. E. Eerdman's Publishing Co., n.d.), pp. 64, 65.

28. Helmuth Thielicke, *The Ethics of Sex*, trans. by John W. Doberstein (New York: Harper and Row, 1964), p. 3.

29. Daly, *The Church and the Second Sex*, p. 17.

30. David Allan Hubbard, "Old Testament Light on the Meaning of Marriage." This article originally appeared as "Love and Marriage" in the *Covenant Companion*, January 1 and 15, 1969.

31. Bruce K. Waltke, "Old Testament Texts Bearing on the Problem of the Control of Human Reproduction," in *Birth Control and the Christian*, p. 18.

32. Drinkwater, *Birth Control and Natural Law*, p. 62.

33. Noonan, *Contraception: A History*, p. 528.

34. Waltke, "Old Testament," p. 19.

35. Cf. Matthew 5:32 ff., I Corinthians 6:13 ff., Rom. 1:29, and Revelation 14:8, 17:1 ff.

36. Marvin R. Vincent, *Word Studies in the New Testament*, IV (Grand Rapids: Wm. B. Eerdmans Publishing Co., reprinted 1957), 562.

37. Joseph Fletcher, *Situation Ethics, The New Morality*, paperback (Philadelphia: The Westminster Press, n.d.), p. 69.

38. Ibid.

39. Lou Woodrum, *The Rebellious Planet* (Grand Rapids: Zondervan Publishing House, 1965), p. 35.

40. Paul Ramsey, *Deeds and Rules in Christian Ethics* (New York: Charles Scribner's Sons, 1967), p. 3.

41. Ibid., p. 81.

42. Nino Lo Bello, "Vatican Has Interest in the Pill," *Sacramento Bee*, March 23, 1969.

43. Orville S. Walters, "Contraceptives and the Single Person," in *Birth Control and the Christian*, p. 225.

44. Ibid., p. 226.

45. *Vassar and the Non-Virgins*, p. 4, quoted in Walters, "Contraceptives and the Single Person," pp. 226-27.

46. Fletcher, *Situation Ethics*, p. 80.

47. "What are the Psychological Effects of Premarital Intercourse?" quoted in Walters, "Contraceptives and the Single Person," p. 227.

48. "A Protestant Affirmation on the Control of Human Reproduction," *Christianity Today*, XIII (November 8, 1968), 19.

49. Walters, "Contraceptives and the Single Person," p. 228.

50. John A. T. Robinson, *Honest to God* (Philadelphia: Westminster Press, 1963), II, 109-110.

51. Walters, "Contraceptives and the Single Person," p. 231.

52. Robert Moskin, "Sweden: The Contraceptive Society," *Reader's Digest*, April, 1969.

53. George P. Smith, "Changes in Legal Attitudes on Insemination Told," *The Los Angeles Daily Journal*, March 19, 1969.

54. Ibid.

55. Leroy Augenstein, *Come, Let Us Play God*, p. 31.

56. Ibid., p. 31.

57. Oliver J. Steiner, "Artificial Insemination: Moral and Legal Implications," in *Birth Control and the Christian*, pp. 569-70.

58. Rev. Père K. Lalrere, *Artificial Insemination and the Moral Law. New Problems in Medical Ethics*, ed. and trans. by Dom Peter Flood. No. 1. Artificial Insemination, Death (Techny, Illinois: Divine Word Publications, 1962), p. 33.

59. Thielicke, *The Ethics of Sex*, p. 249. Note: since the publication of Thielicke's book, jurists' opinions have changed in this country. Cf. quotation by Prof. George P. Smith, p. 40.

60. Ibid.

61. Ibid., p. 265.

# Chapter III

# ABORTION

For many years, Protestant Christians in general have favored therapeutic abortions only when the life of the mother was endangered or at stake. Recently, many Christians, in view of social and medical science, have extended their views regarding therapeutic abortions, giving such reasons for abortion as rape, incest, the risk of a malformed fetus (a kindred medical decision would be euthanasia), social and economic reasons, and on psychiatric grounds.

The legal tradition has been uniform for decades concerning state laws prohibiting abortion. The exception has generally been that a mother's life must be jeopardized before a therapeutic abortion is permissible. In fact, a violation of state abortion laws constituted and still constitutes a felony or criminal offense in most states. This very penalty appears indicative of the fact that past legislators and specialists in jurisprudence respected and sought to protect nascent life as a person.

Today, medicine, law, sociology, politics, and the church are all involved in the current storm over the ethics and morality of therapeutic abortions. Those for and against abortions arrive at their opinions and conclusions based upon their concept of the fetus as a person, potential person, or merely a biological growth as a part of the mother or mother-to-be.

There are many who consider abortion in sharp contrast to contraception, and rightly so, from a Christian point of view. The latter, contraception, is the prevention of procreation, whereas abortion is the termination of a human life or a potential person. Man was created an indivisible unit in the image of God, and was given the power to procreate in a "one-flesh" marriage experience. In view of this and of recent genetic discoveries, the Christian should view the problem of abortion and its alternatives in a most serious manner. In fact, the issue cannot be correctly viewed apart from a Christian view of man, as expressed in Scripture.

No dogmatic answers can be given even from a Christian viewpoint in regards to therapeutic abortions. However, even the puzzling exceptions and alternatives are freighted with moral and ethical dilemmas. At best, we may study the problem, consider the options, and suggest guidelines in conclusion.

The danger always exists of going too far in one direction or the other concerning ethical and moral issues. Theologians make their way as a sailing ship which has to tack back and forth with and against the wind. It does not follow the straight line like a steamer, and any particular generation is either to the right or to the left of center. Its genius lies in having within itself the check against its own excesses. So, often theologians have gone so far, they know they have passed the main point and must come back. Then in their enthusiasm they will probably go too far in the other direction and sooner or later will have to come back again.[1] However, the decision to terminate fetal life in no way should be a vacillating one. Sound ethical and moral guidelines should be established to guide medical and moral surgeons in exceptional cases.

The world is a place of limits, and neither ethics nor theology can ever be made a simple matter of saying "yes." Every time a man says "yes" to one thing, he has to say "no" to something else. In medical ethics, as well as in theological ethics, a "yes" and "no" must exist inasmuch as we live in a sinful order.

The danger in the current abortion discussion is that some advocating radical reforms will not only do away with the letter of the law but the principle as well. Exceptional abortion situations should not be the sole norm for rejecting completely the traditional Christian view on the subject. The opposite danger is to become embalmed in a fixed tradition whereby the mind is closed to the question of abortion under any circumstances.

Abortion is without doubt one of the most burning ethical and moral issues of the century confronting medicine, theology, and sociology. It could very well be that the outcome of the current abortion issue could have a significant influence in determining not only who should live, but also who should die! Therefore, it is imperative that the Christian wrestle with the issue, even though clear-cut answers cannot be given in every situation concerning abortion dilemmas.

## History of Abortion

Abortion, like contraception, has a history. It is most often discussed in ancient writings along with contraception. References to nascent life and the attitude of parents toward infants, both direct and indirect, are found in Scripture during the Hebrew Economy and in extra-Biblical sources as well. Historical references to abortion almost disappear after the 4th Century A.D. because of the influence of Christianity. With the advent of Christianity, all abortions were considered undesirable, if not criminal, and this was especially true of those done for socio-economic reasons. A gradual discussion of the subject commenced in the 18th Century A.D., leading to wide publicity and discussion today.

Abortion is not new, although records of the practice are somewhat limited. References to abortion are made by most civilizations.

It was no doubt an ancient practice. The records of almost every civilization indicate knowledge of abortifacient agents and abortive techniques. Among the more primitive people, the more extreme methods were gruesome and remain so among certain groups today. One tribe encouraged large red ants to bite the woman's body and occasionally the insects were taken internally.[2]

The early Hebrews knew abortive techniques although they strongly disapproved of the practice. The Greeks, on the other hand, advocated abortion in order to control population size and insure good social and economic conditions among the people. Hippocrates advised abortion in certain situations but, as a general rule, condemned the practice because it so often resulted in the mother's injury or death.

In Exodus 21:22, 25, the passage refers to a pregnant woman losing her child as the result of the striving together of two men. In context, this passage deals with penalties inflicted against the person. The word "fruit" in the KJV is *yeled* in Hebrew, definitely referring to a child. The LXX also translates the passage in vs. 22, *paidion* (child) instead of "fruit."[3] The significance of the passage in Exodus 21 certainly stresses a profound respect for nascent life; and as to infanticide among the Hebrews, nowhere in the Old Testament do we find the view that one might dispose of one's children. In Lev. 20:2, the death penalty was inflicted upon any who gave their *zara* (seed, children) to Molech. In Lev. 18:21, none of Israel's seed (children) were to be sacrificed to Molech. Thus, the Hebrews were taught of God to respect nascent and infant life.

During the time of the Roman Empire, a low estimate of human life existed. The conventional Roman attitude on fetal and infant life was strikingly callous. Seneca refers to the drowning of abnormal or weak children at birth as a commonplace Roman phenomenon and as a reasonable kind of action.[4] Parents exposed their children with apparently no laws protecting the rights of the children. Concerning the Jews during this time, Noonan quotes Tacitus: " '... it is remarkable that they do not kill children who are born after the father has made his will, that is, children born when the parents no longer want offspring as heirs' (Histories 5:5)."[5]

Government interest seemed to favor the upper class of society as far as reproduction was concerned. In Rome, at the beginning of the Christian era, abortion and infanticide were common and widely accepted practices of long standing. Roman abortion arose from luxurious and dissipated living amongst wealthy and the powerful, inspired by idleness, love of comfort and female vanity.[6] Laws were adopted at one time or another to check the practice, but their success was limited until Christianity became powerful in the pagan Roman Empire. Most measures against dealers in abortifacient potions and aphrodisiacs were apparently designed simply to shield adult health rather than preserve fetal life against attack. Other laws punishing women who underwent abortions without the husband's consent were intended as protection for the rights of the deprived father rather than the child. In general, the Roman attitude toward fetal and infant life merited the description, "strikingly callous."

### Christian Attitudes on Abortion

Philo states that there was a group of parents who practiced infanticide, strangling, and drowning, and who exposed infants in desert areas to wild beasts. Justin claimed that these persons were killers of men. Moreover, in the Apology we read that Christians were forbidden to destroy even the fetus (9.8).[7]

Also in the *Didache*, or the teaching of the twelve, this practice was looked upon as identical with the killers of children (5.2). And in the *Letter to Barnabas* (early second century) we read, "Thou shalt not kill the fetus by an abortion or commit infanticide" (19.5). The same interpretation was made by Tertullian, Cyprian, and others.

The attitude appeared to be the same in the Eastern and Western churches during the infancy of the Christian church. In the Eastern church, in the basic legislation which was the Canons of Saint Basil, there was a condemnation without qualification of all women who committed abortion, whatever the state or development of the fetus. In the West, Jerome also condemned this practice. This means that for all intents and purposes, the life-giving process was viewed as identical to life itself and it was equally wrong to kill a fetus as it was to take the life of a child.[8]

The Christian opposition to abortion during the first few centuries A.D. was indicative of the believers' reverence and respect for nascent life. Up until the destruction of Jerusalem in 70 A.D., Christianity was accepted by the Roman Government as a form of Judaism. After that, Christianity was viewed by the

Romans as antagonistic to the Empire. During the 2nd and 3rd centuries A.D., as has been previously shown, a number of Christian writers took a bold stand against abortion. Others deserving mention in the 2nd century were Athenagoras and Clement of Alexandria, who attacked abortion with zeal. Two apocryphal but orthodox works, the *Apocalypse of Peter* and the *Apocalypse of Paul*, testified to the popular Christian abhorrence of abortion.[9] During the pagan persecutions of Decian (250 A.D.) to Diocletian (305 A.D.), little was written by Christian writers against abortion.

In the 4th century, Jerome and Augustine condemned abortion. In the Western church, St. Jerome described the mother who sought an abortion as a parricide. Augustine wrote on abortion and was quoted by Pope Pius XI in his encyclical Casti Connubii:

"Sometimes this lustful cruelty, or cruel lust,come to this, that they even procure poisons of sterility, and if these do not work extinguish and destroy the fetus in some way in the womb, preferring that their offspring die before it lives, or if it was already alive in the womb to kill it before it was born. Assuredly if both husband and wife are like this, they are not married, and if they were like this from the beginning they come together not joined in matrimony but in seduction."[10]

Augustine's view of abortion prevailed in the Western Christian world virtually unchallenged for centuries.

Not only did religious writers refer to abortion, but classical Roman writers also condemned the practice. Ovid sternly denounced abortion, stating: "Ah, women, why will you thrust and pierce with instrument, and give dire poisons to your children yet unborn."[11] Juvenal, a more strict moralist, spoke of women using arts and drugs to insure her barrenness and who killed men yet unborn.

It is interesting to note that the means of attaining an ancient abortion are similar to those used to perform therapeutic abortions today, viz, the curette and drugs. The instruments and drugs are mentioned, but causes for abortion are seldom mentioned in the historical records or by authorities interpreting history, apart from socioeconomic reasons. Certainly, rape and incest (two key reasons for therapeutic abortion to be legalized today) existed then. However, medical science was primitive in the areas of genetics, organic science, psychological insight, and understanding of various diseases affecting fetal growth and development.

The opinion of the early Christian writers appears to be unanimous in favor of the fetus regardless of the existing circumstances. Statutory rape could possibly be implied in Jerome's letter (22) to Eustochium (13). He " . . . urges a young teenage girl to remain a virgin, stating that others will drink sterility and murder a man not yet born, and yet others will use poisons to commit abortions—these are parricides."[12]

The question of fetal animation arose early in church history. Aristotle had taught that the fetus becomes human forty days after conception if the fetus was male, eighty days after conception if the fetus was female. Some have held that a similar view underlines the prescription in Lev. 12:1-5, that a woman must spend forty days in becoming purified if she has given birth to a boy, eighty days if she has given birth to a girl. Aristotle's ensoulment concept was that the soul enters the fetus not at the moment of conception but later. His theory was introduced into the Roman world by Galen, a Greek physician in the court of the Emperor Severus, and in one form or another came to be universally accepted.

Terms such as "unformed" and "formed" described the respective stage of fetal development. Jerome distinguished between an unformed and formed stage. Philo followed one of the divergent theories of Exodus 21:22, adopting the Septuagint version: "life for life" if the embryo is "formed."

Jerome's translation of the Old Testament followed the Hebrew in Exodus 21:22, and opened the possibility of treating the fetus as at no point of development human. Another view was expressed by Tertullian: "... that the embryo, after conception, has a soul, and that it is man (homo) when it attains its final form (Tertullian, *The Soul*, 25.2, 37.2)."[13] The prevailing Christian view seemed to be that of the Septuagint, distinguishing between the unformed and formed. Questions were raised and differences of opinion did exist as to the nature of the fetus in relation to Exodus 21. Augustine comments on the time when abortion wold be homicide:

> "Here the question of the soul is usually raised: Whether what is not formed can be understood to have no soul, and whether for that reason it is not homicide, because one cannot be deprived of a soul if one has not received a soul. The argument goes on to say, 'But if it has been formed, he shall give soul for soul'... if the embryo is still unformed, but yet in some way ensouled while unformed... the law does not provide that the act pertains to homicide, because still there cannot be said to be a live soul in a body that lacks sensation, if it is in flesh not yet formed and thus not yet endowed with senses (on Exodus 21:80, C Sel 282:147)."[14]

Augustine, Jerome, and Aquinas accepted the theory of the non-animated and animated fetus. The same distinction was introduced into church law in the twelfth century by Gratian, who made it the basis for assessing penalties for abortion. Early in the seventeenth century, however, scientists began to speculate that the human soul was infused immediately after conception. Fairly soon this became a commonly accepted position among theologians. It remains so at the present day, although reputable defenders can be found for both points of view. Thus, a contemporary argument for the "infusion" of the soul at a point prior to conception is based on the "necessary soul-body relationship."[15]

Helmuth Thielicke, commenting on the Catholic theory of the animation of the fetus, says:

Does it occur "creationistically" through individual divine acts of creation (so Clement of Alexandria and Lactantius) or "generationalistically" through parental propagation and transmission of the soul, which makes the child's soul an "offshoot" (tradux) of parental souls (so Tertullian and Appollinaris)? Likewise there must be an answer to the question when the animation of the fetus occurs and thus when an intervention in the germinating life becomes a "murder of the innocent." The solution to this question was partially influenced, especially in scholasticism by ideas that stem from Aristotle, namely, that the male fetus acquires a soul after forty days but the female fetus after eighty days. Thus the doctrine that there is such a thing as a foetus animatus and a foetus inanimatus had to be specifically rejected.[16]

Thus, controversy exists in history over the inanimate and animate, the unformed and formed in relation to abortion even in the Roman Catholic Church, though her opinion on abortion appears fixed today. Lloyd Kalland records a portion of the bull *Effraenatam* issued by Sixtus V:

"All abortion and all contraception by potion or poison were to be treated as murder. The ultimate ecclesiastical penalty of excommunication was invoked, and, to make the penalty even more stringent, only the Holy See could release the excommunication unless the sinner were in *articulo mortis*."[17]

The contribution of Sextus V, however, was shortlived because Gregory XIV repealed all the penalties established by Sixtus except those which applied to abortion of the ensouled 40-day fetus. The point of issue, as today, is when does the fetus become human? The issue is confused when the term soul is used in the context of Greek thought, whereas the soul is considered a separate entity. The Roman Catholic position is that one becomes a person at conception, as stated in the New Catholic Encyclopedia:

"... Modern studies in embryology reveal that at the moment sperm and ovum unite and the two pronuclei fuse, an orderly process of development begins with a definiteness governed by the pattern of the DNA molecule. The new individual is characterized by the resulting unique constellation of genes and chromosomes before the zygote divides for the first time. This organization is not only intricate and vital, it is specifically human. The chromosomes contain determiners for specifically human eyes and considers the living body from the one cell stage onward to be a human individual, not some general plant or animal that will become human in 40 or 80 days."[18]

The Roman Catholic view on the origin of the soul is that of Creationism. According to the creationist theory, God creates a new soul for each person at the moment of conception or birth and immediately unites it with the body. This union (soul and body) takes place at conception in Roman Catholic theology. Even in modern Catholic statements, the theory of animation asserts itself insofar as they seek to determine the precise period of time within which the impregnation or conception occurs (forty-eight hours), and which represents the time interval within which in special cases (rape) a pregnancy may be manipulated by means of irrigations and injections.

Until recently, such views prevailed in traditional Christian thought, but during the past two decades, Christian attitudes toward abortion have changed somewhat. In 1958 the Anglican Church's Lambeth Conference, while declaring that Christians reject abortion in the strongest terms, nevertheless went on to make room for the practice at the dictate of strict and undeniable medical practice. Also, the National Council of Churches stated in 1961 that the destruction of fetal life is permitted when the health or life of the mother is at stake.

Not only are churches involved in the current abortion issue, but attorneys, physicians, ethicists, and individual clergymen as well. In the area of law, we find that laws regulating sexual behavior have no peer at stirring up intense emotional reaction when the element of life itself is involved. The reaction is compounded and intensified. Abortion is perhaps the only·problem in which attitudes toward sexual activity itself and toward life and being are in seething turmoil. The American Law Institute has recommended new penal code sections on abortion.

The medical profession, or segments of it, wishes liberalization of abortion laws, so that decisions to perform dilation and currettage or other medical operations can be made as any other medical determination might be.[19]

Dr. Alan F. Guttmacher, the president of the Planned Parenthood-World Population Federation of America, said recently: "Abortion, readily available on demand, is the only birth control measure that has actually been shown to reduce dramatically the rate of population growth."[20] Such a statement by a medical authority should cause real concern by all who view human life as sacred at any form of development.

The American College of Obstetricians and Gynecologists' recent statement on therapeutic abortion suggests these new guidelines:

1. When continuation of the pregnancy may threaten the life of the woman or seriously impair her health. In determining whether or not there is such a risk to health, account may be taken of the patient's total environment, actual or reasonably foreseeable.
2. When pregnancy has resulted from rape or incest: in this case the same medical criteria should be employed in the evolution of the patient.
3. When continuation of the pregnancy is likely to result in the birth of a child with grave physical deformation or mental retardation.[21]

Not all physicians concur in the above. Some are much more conservative toward the abortion issue. Dr. Bernard J. Hanley, in an address to the Pacific Coast Obstetrical and Gynecological

91

Society, offered strong objections to a liberal abortion position, stating that the moral principles that govern direct therapeutic abortion and render it morally unjustifiable are two: The Divine Creator's Commandment, "Thou shalt not kill," and second, the principle of ethics that prohibits the doing of an evil deed to produce a good result.[22]

Ethicists have and are currently speaking on the issue. In fact, a storm over ethics has arisen particularly with the publication of Joseph Fletcher's book, *Situation Ethics: The New Morality.* In his book, he advocates abortion from a liberal point of view on the subject. Fletcher comments on the case of the woman in Arizona who a few years ago had taken thalidomide with the possibility of delivering a defective baby. She had asked the court to back her doctor and his hospital in terminating the pregnancy, and it refused. He said that her husband took her to Sweden, where love has more control of law, and there she was aborted. God be thanked, since the embryo was hideously deformed. But nobody could know for sure. It was a brave and responsible and right decision, even if the embryo had been all right. It was a *Kairos*, a fullness of time, a moment of decision.[23]

The American Public Health Association has gone on record suggesting an extremely liberal view on the need for abortion reform laws, recently voting that all women should have the right to safe legal abortions.[24]

The subject has been dormant for centuries due to traditional Christian influence and lack of medical knowledge and skill. But today, especially during the past decade, the abortion issue is most prominent not only among professionals, but among most individuals and families of our society. This current decade, as far as extant references are concerned, has already revealed more written material on the subject than the records show of all previous history.

It is important that man in his totality be considered in fetal growth and development prior to a decision for induced abortions. However, before we view the fetus more in detail, let us examine the widespread practice of abortion.

## The Widespread Practice of Abortion

It is readily understandable that therapeutic abortion has become increasingly popular in view of the population explosion of the past few decades. In a world full of dangers, one danger is coming to be feared more than any other. That danger is over-population. The world today contains about 3.5 billion people. That is double the population of 50 years ago. By the year 2000, according to projections made by the United Nations, the world's population will be about 6 billion. That means that in the next 31 years the world will acquire 2.5 billion additional people—an increase of more people than existed on this earth only 20 years ago. How to feed these added billions of people is only part of the problem that such a startling population explosion presents.

Japan pioneered the abortion reform era in 1948. Since that time abortion by qualified doctors gets major credit for reducing the birth rate in Japan to a modest 1 percent gain per year—one of the lowest in the world. Definitely, abortion in Japan is a contraceptive measure, a means of population control.[25]

The Japanese Eugenic Protection Law of 1948 authorized compulsory sterilization in some cases, and in 1952 this law was amended to make abortion easier. Practically any woman who so desires can now have her pregnancy terminated. Abortion is permitted up until the eighth month of pregnancy.[26] Estimates put the yearly abortions in Japan, both registered and unregistered, at a minimum of 2.3 million and perhaps substantially higher. This "open season" on the unborn fetus leaves one with mixed feelings, particularly where some pregnancies are terminated as late as the eighth month. Such a decision is all the more significant in view of the fact that many premature babies survive, grow up, and mature as normal persons, even though they are born, in some cases, two and one-half months early. In view of such, infanticide comes more and more into focus. The Japanese Minister of Welfare has referred to abortion as an "evil practice" which is eroding the physical and moral health of our nation. Also, the Japanese magazine, *Josei Jishin*, in March,

1962, gave a touching description of the run-of-the-mill abortion in Japanese social life:

> A steel forceps mangles and extracts a murkey mass of bloody tissue. There it lies now, soft and quivering. But in it are hands and feet, even eyes and a nose well formed. Wash if you will. But washing won't help. That tiny bleeding object dyed in red is a human being, no doubt about it. It whimpers now with a voice like a little kitten. It is tossed into a dark corner by itself. The cries become faint; now it is dead. Its life was short, but a few moments. Another artificial termination of pregnancy has been completed.
>
> But this child had a father and a mother. A young lady is sleeping under heavy sedatives. Beside her pillow waits a young man; he is whistling, not knowing what else to do with himself.
>
> The two now tread the darkened hospital corridor in slippered feet. Her face is white as ashes. Now they have emerged into the sunlight outside. Neither one turns to look back. They hadn't even bothered to inquire whether it was a boy or a girl.[27]

Some writers and authorities in Japan feel that the liberal abortion approach not only has resulted in many maternal illnesses, but the family and social life in general have suffered also. Dr. Ryutaro Komiya of the Tokyo University School of Economics has stated that there is scarcely any causal relation between birth control (including abortion) and the present economic prosperity of Japan.[28]

Even though the French Penal Code prohibits therapeutic abortions, France, like the United States, finds herself in the midst of this revolutionary aspect of a changing soiety. Criminal abortion was originally considered as a purely individual offense; now it tends to be accepted and looked upon more by the legislator as a social crime. The effects of abortion among French women is similar to the effects on Japanese women as previously reported. The social assurance department has published some significant figures which show that, of 1,000 women aborted, 610 have more or less prolonged complications as a result.[29] Abortion is forbidden in France; however, official figures show that there are about 250,000 to 600,000 induced abortions annually. Unofficial sources put this figure at a total of a million.[30]

Sweden has been a leading western European country in abortion reform, and also a leader in the current sexual revolution. In 1734, Sweden made induced abortion a capital crime or offense. In 1938, a new law was enacted, establishing sociomedical, humanitarian, and eugenic grounds for abortion. In 1946, the law was liberalized even more by an amendment permitting abortion when there is a likelihood of "foreseeable maternal weaknesses." Shaw goes on to say: In 1939, Sweden recorded 107,305 live births and 4,563 legal abortions. The opinion prevails among many that criminal abortions increased along side legal abortions in Sweden.

Shaw points out:

A Swedish delegate to a planned parenthood conference in Tokyo in 1955 said the number of criminal abortions had registered "a steady increase since the law came into force" and added: "This increase is due to the fact that the possibility of terminating pregnancy has become a common topic of conversation, with the result that the idea of abortion is generally accepted among our people."[31]

The idea seems to prevail in Sweden that it is a woman's prerogative to obtain an abortion and the potentiality of the fetus or its rights are not primarily considered. This opinion parallels that of American Public Health Association's recommendation of 1969 that any woman should have the right to an abortion.

Abortion laws have been liberalized in Communist countries. In Hungary, Radio Budapest reported in January, 1963, that an abortion was performed every three minutes. In 1964, the abortion rate was 91 per 1,000 married women aged fifteen to forty-nine; it was also 140 percent of the live birthrate—that is, abortions exceeded births by forty percent. Also, in Hungary, there is an increasing trend toward induced abortion among young, unmarried women. Nearly 7,000 (two percent) of the unmarried women under the age of twenty sought induced abortion in 1964.[32]

Since the 1956 uprising in Hungary up until 1966, there have been one million and a half legal abortions in Hungary. Shaw compares these figures to the United States population. In proportion, "this would have meant 28.5 million abortions in the same period."[33] These startling statistics could have been real had this country authorized abortion on demand. Like Japan, Hungary's aborted women and subsequent offspring have experienced serious health problems.

The Soviet Union experimented with abortion from 1917 to 1936. Thielicke refers to this period:

Here we refer to the decree of the Commissariate of Public Health, 1920, which along with the sanctioning of abortion contained the strict provision that the abortion must be performed only by approved physicians and also provided for free hospitalization. A further decree of the year 1924, necessitated by the overcrowding of hospitals with abortion cases, defined the degrees of priority. The definitions clearly indicate the pragmatic point of view: Women who are engaged in production are given first consideration. The results were devastating: In 1921 there were twenty-one abortions for every hundred births, and in 1926 they had reached ninety in every hundred births! The laws were therefore changed and all abortion was subjected to rigorous punishment.[34]

Even the utilitarian approach by the Soviet Union failed to produce the desired end results. The so-called justifiable means looms up as an actual judgment in history. The assembly line to the abortoriums was checked, but since November, 1955, the lines again have lengthened. Therefore, the Soviet abortion rate is extremely high, among the highest in the world. Estimates of the annual abortion total range between 2,000,000 and nearly 6,000,000.[35] Like Japan, abortion in the Soviet Union appears to be employed primarily as a contraceptive measure. Yet, even the most liberal situationist distinguishes clearly between Contraception and Abortion.

In the United States, the practice of abortion is rapidly increasing. A practicing psychiatrist and a practicing lawyer have stated in the pages of the American Bar Association Journal that "approximately 1,000,000 or more illegal abortions are performed in the United States each year with 5,000 to 10,000 deaths as a direct consequence.[36] In spite of the rigid laws that applied until recently throughout the United States, some authorities estimate there are from 700,000 to 2,000,000 abortions annually.[37]

Thus, the world-wide trend is definitely a more liberal approach toward abortion. Yet statistics warn us that the means employed to accomplish a good end is not the answer to the abortion dilemma. The records of nations leading the world in abortions on demand, and the often traumatic social, psychological, and physical results should warn others to move cautiously in this area of uncertainty.


## The Fetus

### Biological Growth?

The Christian's view on therapeutic abortion is generally governed by his understanding as to when one becomes a person, and his definition of a human fetus. Some view the human fetus as nothing more than a small glob of living tissue, a mere biological growth, as a part of the mother and not a unique entity. This concept of the fetus depreciates the origin of individual human life as a primordial person which bears the image of God in some sense.

Dr. Thomas S. Szasz, a psychiatrist, wrote in 1966 that no laws should exist or be enacted regulating abortion. Such an operation, to Szasz, would be no different than that of surgery for cosmetic purposes. The only requirement would be the woman's desire to have an abortion performed and the willingness of a physician to perform the operation.[38] This attitude or position is in sharp contrast to those who view the fetus as a person, or as a potential person.

It is true that fetal tissue is similar to that of certain animals. The real crux of the issue is that human fetal tissue, if undisturbed, will develop into a human being as we know him today. It is the human being aspect of the fetus from fertilized egg, to blastocyst, to embryo, to fetus, to the premature and infant stage, that has called forth a reverence and concern for human life regardless of the developmental stage. The fetus is not just a biological growth, it is not simply an animal fetus since the genetic makeup of man is not identical with that of any other animal. The fact that the fetus has legal rights in practically every state is indicative that from conception, especially implantation, the fetus, or potential person, has certain rights. It has the right not to be aborted, except under unusual circumstances. An unconceived child is hypothetical, but this is not the case relative to a developing fetus. When conception has been ascertained, a new potential person begins life.

There are a number of medical authorities and others who view the fetus in a purely biological manner. This by no means resolves the abortion issue in the Christian's view of man. The theologian adds the image of God dimension to his understanding of the nature of man. The great danger of viewing man only from the standpoint of biological science, lies in the fact that man could control his species without impunity if he were to view the fetus as mere object and not as subject and object. Dr. Leroy Augenstein, a biophysicist at Michigan State University, pinpoints the possible far-reaching influence of the current abortion issue. He states that the abortion dilemma is only "the currently visible fraction of the very large iceberg dealing with the control of quality of human life."[39]

A view of the human fetus as merely a biological growth could very well determine the manner in which we will handle or mishandle a number of other pressing ethical and moral problems, such as gene manipulation, spare parts for organ transplants, new drugs, and mind control. If the fetus is only a growth, naturally, it would not qualify for the protection which it now has. If the fetus is viewed as medical science views a tumor, then it is natural that no moral surgeon need be heard concerning the rights of the fetus. A mother and two or three medical jurists would decide the case of the living human fetus.

It appears to the writer that a view of the fetus as a mere biological growth is totally untenable from the Christian point of view of the nature of man; also, such a view is freighted with danger, inasmuch as a reverence and respect for developing human life would not exist. The image of God concept, as revealed in the total person, calls for a profound respect and reverence for human life, from the moment of conception or implantation to the conclusion of the earthly life of the individual person.

### Potential Person

Conception itself is a fantastic phenomenon, which is the beginning of the potential person. The mathematical odds of fertilization of the ovum by the one particular spermatozoon out of 200,000,000 to 600,000,000 spermatozoa available in a normal insemination are obviously astronomical. In each of these minute cells is a genetic package of DNA—the genetic thread of life. These packages contain within its body the entire endowment that heredity may pass on to a possible child. Biologists are discovering more and more the amazing facts of life at the moment two cells unite to form a potential person.

Every discussion of abortion must, in the final analysis, begin with what an individual thinks of the human fetus from the moment of conception. The legal profession has, in the past, recognized the fetus definitely as a potential person even though the Model Penal Code of the American Law Institute (ALI) suggests the fetus to be non-viable during almost two-thirds of the total fetal period. The ALI proposes that the life of a fetus not older than twenty-six weeks may be terminated if such action can be justified because of the physical or mental health of the mother.[40] This action by the ALI by no means is the unanimous opinion among all those in the legal profession. Thomas F. Lambert, Jr., the editor-in-chief of the American Trial Lawyers Association, writes: "The fetus or child in the womb should be treated as a person for purposes of tort law whenever that is necessary to prevent injustice."[41] For decades, Anglo-American courts denied recovery for prenatal injuries or death to the fetus due to the absence of a statute protecting the unborn child. Common law offered no precedents either, to protect the potential person.

Even though the opinion among many medical and legal minds tends to favor the fetus more as it develops toward full humanity, it still possesses rights from the moment of implantation in the mother's womb. In writing on the laws of wills and property, Lambert states: "It is emphasized that for the purposes of tort law, protection of the child in utero may well commence from the moment of conception."[42] In some recent court cases, decisions have been handed down in favor of an injured fetus. The argument of viability proved to be a false prerequisite to recovery for prenatal harm. Most states have favored the rights of the unborn child or fetus, whereby decisions have been rendered involving prenatal injuries. When actually faced with the issue for a decision, most states (a clear majority of those passing on the issue) have allowed compensation for the injured fetus, even though the injury occurred during the early weeks of the pregnancy when the fetus was neither viable nor quick. Most authorities consider a fetus to be viable or quick, that is, able to survive outside the mother's womb, beginning after the sixth month of pregnancy. The fact that a child can collect damages for an injury obtained during fetal growth is indicative of a ground swell of reforming jurisprudence. It is a further indication that a large number of legal minds recognize the fetus as a *potential human being* with inalienable rights.

This trend among many of the legal profession is in harmony with the majority of evangelical Christians who view the human fetus as a potential person demanding a deep concern, respect, and reverence for the fetus from the beginning of conception, or following the seven day blastocyst period when implantation takes place. This trend in jurisprudence is also in contradistinction to an opinion expressed by Rabbi Sanford E. Rosen, the president of the Northern California Board of Rabbis. In his 1964 testimony before the California State Assembly Interim Committee on Criminal Procedure at San Francisco, he said that the fetus was a part of the mother prior to birth, and as such can be sacrificed for the sake of the mother, just as an arm or leg could be amputated.[43] This view would eliminate the fetus even as a potential person. Yet, the fetus is considered by many attorneys and courts to possess rights as a human being coming into existence. Perhaps legal minds have come to their modern conclusions as to the fetus being a potential person by observing medical authorties who have recognized that a child was in existence from the moment of conception, and not merely a part of the mother's body.

Current medical and biological scientists in their research and knowledge lend support to the potential person concept or view. However, the biological scientist is hesitant in stating the precise moment that the fetus acquires the biological form and function of a human person. He views the mystery of human life in progressive stages as Thomas L. Hayes, a biophysicist at the University of California, Berkeley, has commented on when the fetus becomes a person. In fact, to him, such a point does not exist. The attributes and the form that designate the living system as a human individual are acquired at various times during development in a process that is continuous. "The transition occurs gradually, not at a single point in time."[44] The scientist knows that the fetus is not a nonentity. The accuracy of the genetic code reveals to him that the fetus is unmistakably a potential human being. The orderly arrangement of the genes and chromosomes, the directed multiplication of the dividing cells, is progressive proof of a potential person coming into being.

Professor Noonan interprets the findings of genetics to mean that this being in the uterus shares in the same essential characteristics that make us able to reason. It is only different from adult life in that it has not realized a number of its potentialities. We are all on our way to being human.[45] Paul Ramsey, and other ethicists, argue that medical research now supports the position of those who would impute full human dignity even to the non-viable fetus. Many theologians and ethicists oppose liberalization of abortion laws in the name of what they consider a helpless minority—unborn children. They consider the fetus a potential person, and they assign to fully human life a value which is very nearly absolute. These arrive at this view of the fetus as a potential person from the current knowledge of genetics, the mystery of procreation, and the image of God in man. Modern science supports the theological concept of the total person as an indivisible unit.

Whenever an induced abortion is proposed, regardless as to the stage of fetal development, a potential person is destroyed. There are exceptional cases whereby this appears as a necessary choice of lesser evil, as will be discussed later. This writer contends that potential human life begins at the moment of conception or at the implantation period. The argument of the viable or non-viable fetus appears to be irrelevant in view of new discoveries in medical and biological science. The theory of quickening was held to for centuries, that is, ninety days or three months following conception. No abortions were performed following this period except under extreme circumstances involving the life of the mother. New discoveries in science refute this traditional position. For instance, Gerald Waring reports in the *Canadian Medical Association Journal* at a recent commons meeting on health and welfare:

The committee heard evidence that there is electrocardiographic proof of independent heart beat at 11 weeks, saw a slide of an 18 week fetus sucking its thumb, and was told that even at six weeks, the fetus "is a living being" that should not be killed for any reason other than a condition gravely endangering the life of the woman.[46]

The fact that fetal heart function has been detected by means of the electrocardiogram (EKG) as early as the eleventh week of fetal growth and development shortens the traditional three month non-viable stage. Also, medical authorities inform us that the nervous system and the brain develop in the fetus or unborn child between the second and third months of pregnancy. In view of these facts, whereby the identity of the fetus leans heavily in the direction of personhood, it would appear that the viable and non-viable period of the fetus is too ambiguous to pinpoint for the identity of the potential person. Medical science appears to point out the weakness of viability in determining or establishing humanity. The shifting time of viability and quickening, as pointed out by medical authorities, tends to reinforce the "natural law" position shared by most Roman Catholic moralists and some Protestants. From the first week of a pregnancy, a *potential person* comes into existence, and from the Christian point of view, the image of God has been passed on to this new entity through the power of procreation.

*The Person*

The Scriptures are silent in defining when one becomes a person. Neither theology nor medical science can resolve unequivocally the question as to whether the fetus is a human being in a personal sense. It has been generally understood that a new person comes into being at birth. (The Chinese reckon their birthday from conception.) However, the biological development of a person does not end at birth. In fact, from the moment of conception until death, change occurs. The infant, especially, demands care and is as dependent after birth as during the prenatal period. In Exodus 20:12, the fifth commandment states: "Honor thy father and thy mother: that thy days may be long upon the land which the Lord thy God giveth thee." God has ordained that the human infant is more dependent and helpless for a longer period, and more utterly, than the young of any other animal. Its growth, which is to reach so much higher, is slower, and it is feebler during the process. The reason for this is very plain to the thoughtful observer. God has designed that the race of man should be bound together in the closest relationships. Every genuine mother bearing a child recognizes this relationship shortly after conception. She recognizes this new life in its distinctively human dimension, which is more than mere biology.

Scripture does not say per se that the fetus is a person. Yet, both the Old and New Testament support the "total person" and "unity of personality" concept of the nature of man. Also, the Bible does not say specifically that the fetus is the image of God. The creation narrative photographs man in a mature state. The mystery of life is imparted and infused in man as "the breath of life" (Gen. 2:7). This has led many to identify the modern person at birth, when individual breathing takes place. However, the mystery of life is also associated with the blood in Deut. 12:23: "Only be sure that thou eat not the blood: for the blood is the life; and thou mayest not eat the life with the flesh." The Hebrews were not to eat the blood of animals, which divine injunction was carried over into the Gentile Christian Church. In Acts 15:20 we read: "But, that we write unto them (Gentiles), that they abstain from pollutions of idols, and from fornication, and from things strangled, and from blood." In other words, the Gentile converts were to follow the instruction of Deut. 12:23. Still, the divine image of God in man would not be restricted to breath and blood, these are but parts—manifestations of the total person.

The image of God, though marred by the fall, is passed on by man to the fetus in his power to procreate. In Gen. 5:3, Adam fathered Seth after his image, and Adam's image was after the divine similitude. Thus, the idea of personhood is brought nearer the fetus in the Christian's view of man. Also the fetus receives more status when we view man as a composite whole and not a trichotomy or dichotomy. The apostle Paul's famous analogy of the gifts of the Spirit and the members of the body offer a kindred lesson to the total person concept, that is, what is the fetus apart from blastocyst, embryo, etc.? The individual from the union of two cells to the maturity of countless numbers of cells, are vital parts of the whole. He is near the definition of a person from the earliest stage of fetal development and growth.

The Psalmist identifies himself prior to birth in Ps. 139:13, 15: "For thou hast possessed (formed) my reins: thou hast covered (knit me together) me in my mother's womb. My substance (frame or bone) was not hid from thee when I was made in secret." Here, the Psalmist uses the personal pronoun to define himself in fetal development and growth. The passage implies that God and man are co-partners in initiating the life of a new person—God the Creator, and man the procreator. Even in pro-creation man is not alone. Indirectly, God gives man life, strength, and ability to accomplish every worthwhile endeavor (cf. Deut. 8:17, 18; Col. 1:18).

Theologians of the past and present have and can confuse the issue of the beginning of personhood with their anatomy of the soul. Rabbi David M. Feldman of Brooklyn said recently that God imparts a pure soul into the fetus untouched by original sin. When the fetus is killed, the soul goes to heaven.[47] The Roman Catholic view is that the soul is tainted by original sin, and if the fetus is killed, the soul, if unbaptized, goes either to limbo or hell. Both of these views appear to be incompatible with the Scriptural view of the total person. The total person concept is brought out in a second reference to his personhood in Ps. 51:5: "Behold, *I* was shapen in iniquity; and in sin did my mother conceive *me*" [italics mine]. The latter phrase of the passage by no means suggests an illicit act, but the writer is dealing with the hereditary aspect of sin. As in Ps. 139:14, 15, the Psalmist identifies "himself" by employing a personal pronoun to point out the beginning of his personhood. The passage is significant and relative to the current abortion crises. Whether the fetus is a person cannot be completely resolved. However, whether the fetus is a potential person cannot be denied in view of Scripture and medical science. The evidence of both tend to support the idea of the fetus with an independent personality. The total person concept, as offered in Scripture, certainly elevates the status of the fetus, and by no means subordinates it to a mere biological growth.

Jesus uses the significant term *brephos* (unborn child, embryo, infant) in Luke 18:15 to teach a lesson on God's grace. The same term is used in reference to the unborn John the Baptist. For the biblical writer, personhood in a most unique sense begins at conception; subsequent human behavior illustrates this personhood; it does not create it.[48]

The two Adams in Scripture afford us the best examples of personhood. The first man, Adam, as pointed out previously, was created as a mature person in the image of God. God gave him the power to procreate and to perpetuate God's image even though man had fallen. The second Adam, Christ, is portrayed in Scripture as beginning His personhood at conception, that is, His humanity began at the incarnation. Luke 1:35b refers to Jesus' nascent life as "that holy thing" (literally, the thing being born). His humanity began when He was conceived of Mary by the Holy Spirit. We read in Gal. 4:4 that "when the fulness of time was come, God sent forth his Son, made of a woman, made under the law." In Heb. 1:5, 6, the writer refers to the incarnation of Christ, using the phrase: "Thou art my Son, this day have I begotten thee," and again, "when he bringeth in the first begotten into the world." The word "begotten" could be better translated as "unique." The Father and Son terms are used in an ethical sense and not in a generic manner. The emphasis is on designation and not derivation. Therefore, the personhood of Christ, outlined in the New Testament, begins at the moment of His conception. He is viewed as a person, in fetal growth and development, as a child, and as a mature being. The writer is certainly cognizant of the sacredness and mystery of the ground he treads in dealing with the incarnation of Jesus Christ. However, His humanity does offer the Christian a better view of the total person in the abortion issue.

The exegetical aspect of Exodus 21:22-25 sheds light on the status of the fetus as a person. Exegetes have interpreted the passage in the following manner. Some have distinguished between the life of a pregnant mother and her fetus. They hold that an injury inflicted upon the mother would demand compensation; "an eye for an eye, and a tooth for a tooth." But compensation would not be demanded if the fetus were destroyed—at least full compensation would not be demanded whereby two men "were striving together" and the mother, or child, or both, were injured when the mother came between them for the purpose of making peace. Those who subordinate the quality of the life of the fetus follow the Septuagint translation of the Hebrew text. The Hellenizing Jew, Philo, spoke of the "fruit" (premature birth): if it had not yet developed into a human form, it was to be regarded in no sense as a human being. In such a case the giver was only required to pay a pecuniary compensation.[49] Exegetes who differ in their interpretation of the passage follow the 19th century Protestant Delitzsch, and the contemporary Jewish exegete, Cassuto. Delitzsch interprets the term "fruit" as a child, a fully developed human being. Cassuto renders the passage in the following manner:

When men strive together and they hurt unintentionally a woman with a child, and her child come forth but no mischief happens—that is, the woman and the children do not die—the one who hurt her shall surely be punished by a fine. But if any mischief happened, that is, if the woman dies or the children die, then you shall give life for life.[50]

Therefore, this passage along with the other Scriptural references lend support to the fetus as a person or potential person. By all means, the original text of Exodus 21:22-25 places a high value on fetal life equal to that accorded to a mature adult. Throughout Scripture, we find a deep respect and reverence for human life in any form. Therefore, the Christian view of man recognizes the fetus as a potential person or a person created in the image of God in some form, from the moment of conception and implantation.

Life is mysterious and sacred in all stages of human development. To terminate the life of a person, potential person, or possible person is truly a final recourse whereby man in this scientific age has more and more control over life and death. Man may take life, but he cannot give life; God alone gives life. Abortion, in any event, is laden with uncertainty and must be a last resort which is a lesser-of-evils ethical and moral decision. Our concluding section deals with reasons which justify abortions.

## Conditions Sanctioning Therapeutic Abortions

### The Life of the Mother in Jeopardy

For many years in this country, therapeutic or induced abortions have been permitted by law whereby the life of the mother was jeopardized if her pregnancy continued. Laws have been severe in dealing with those performing an abortion for causes other than the one mentioned. In the past few years, there have been concerted efforts put forth by many to liberalize abortion laws. Both the American Law Institute (ALI) and the American College of Obstetricians and Gynecologists have recently gone on record in recommending a more liberal position on therapeutic abortions. The official position of the American College of Obstetricians and Gynecologists at its May 9, 1968 meeting in Chicago is as follows:

Therapeutic abortion may be performed for the following established medical indications:
1. When continuation of the pregnancy may threaten the life of the woman or seriously impair her health. In determining whether or not there is such a risk to health,

account may be taken of the patient's total environment, actual or reasonably foreseeable.

2. When pregnancy has resulted from rape or incest. In this case the same medical criteria should be employed in the evaluation of the patient.
3. When continuation of the pregnancy would result in the birth of a child with grave physical deformities or mental retardation.[51]

This action follows basically the action taken by the American Law Institute in 1962 with the exception of point 1. The ALI was more specific in defining the mother's health. Apart from the physical or biological threat to the mother's health, they suggest a cause for abortion to include psychiatric reasons. The American College of Obstetricians and Gynecologists were more ambiguous in defining the mother's health.

The traditional Protestant view has been that an induced abortion is justifiable when the mother's life has been at stake. Yet, even in this extreme condition or cause, a genuine human life is terminated. God's revealed moral law in Scripture offers a high view on the sacredness of life. To cut off a human life is always a choice of lesser-evils. Yet the Christian's business is not to legislate moral standards. There is, and must always be, a distinction between the legal and the moral. The Christian must not be taken in, however, by the argument that a legalization of abortion would eliminate the lesser-of-evils practice of illegal abortions. The results of other countries legalizing abortion shows us that illegal abortions increased as well as legal abortions. The business of the Christian is to point out higher standards in sexual behavior and a deeper sense of responsibility in contraception and abortion. Such would help minimize the terrible choice that oftentimes must be made in terminating the life of the fetus which is a person or potential person. Among all the reasons given as justification for terminating fetal life, the life of the mother appears to be the one upon which most medical, legal, and moral experts agree. The issue is not as simply defined as Roman Catholic moralists teach, that is, a therapeutic abortion is a choice of one life over the other—the mother's life above the child's. The fact of the matter is, both lives in many instances would terminate if an abortion were not performed.

This writer takes the view that an abortion is understandable when the life of the mother is at stake. True, the total person is destroyed, yet it is purely a choice of lesser-evils, and the fetus should only be terminated as a final recourse when all the available facts are in in determining the case. I would further add that the husband and wife are the ones to make or agree with such a decision.

*Rape and Incest*

The justification of an induced abortion based on rape and incest appears to be acceptable to a large number of moral authorities. It seems intolerable to most medical and moral scientists that a woman who has been made a victim of such a brutal assault should be forced to bear the child under such circumstances. Those who advocate therapeutic abortions for rape and incest would also include statutory rape (a girl under 16 years of age) as justifiable grounds to terminate a pregnancy. In June, 1967, the American Medical Association (AMA) with its House of Delegates approved the first revision in 96 years of organized medicine's stand on abortion. The AMA endorsed the ALI proposal as outlined a few years previously in its recommendations on abortion. The American College of Obstetricians and Gynecologists (ACOG), as stated before, also followed the ALI recommendations.

Inasmuch as we have established the fact that the potential person begins with the union of two cells, and that human life in any form is sacred, the termination of a pregnancy even for the above reasons must be a lesser-of-evils' choice. A weightier value takes precedence over the newly conceived potential person. Scripture does not give a precise numbered value on the potential person from fertilized egg to birth. However, the total person, and the image of God as transmitted biologically through procreation, demands that the human fetus is of immeasurable value because of its potential. Such makes abortion a terrible choice under any circumstances. Nevertheless, abortion on the grounds of rape and incest appears to be justified, as will be discussed in the "interim solution to the abortion crises" section of this book.

The Roman Catholic Church sanctions a solution to the problem of rape and incest if medical attention can be administered within a 48 hour period. This would be the outer time limit whereby the sperm and the ovum unite. If rape or incest were established, then an injection or irrigation would be given to prevent conception. Yet, it would appear, as with the use of the morning-after pill, that even this approach could include abortion as well as contraception. This is not to say that either would be wrong; it merely points out an apparent inconsistency in Roman Catholic moral theology.

It would seem that Leroy Augenstein's suggestion on the establishment of regional committees would be helpful in dealing with the problem. These would coincide with circuit court districts and they could be authorized to decide on parental applications for abortions.[52] In the case of rape and incest, certainly the medical personnel and the committee would base their decision on the evidence supplied by the district attorney's office. The law should provide this abortion right, yet applications for abortion should be initiated by the parents.

Rape and incest, including statutory rape, have a profound emotional effect whether the pregnancy is terminated by a therapeutic abortion or whether a normal delivery is permitted. In addition to the severe psychological reactions to such a victim, there are always social traumas awaiting the child conceived in such a manner.

*Possible Fetal Deformity*

Four states have already adopted the recommendations of the above mentioned medical and legal bodies. None, however, have

111

adopted the extreme positions of the American Civil Liberties Union, which would remove all legal restraints of abortion. The state of California, among the five adopting the ALI and ACOG recommendations, did not include "possible fetal deformity" as a reason to terminate a pregnancy in their recent liberalization of the abortion law. The thalidomide tragedy a few years ago has no doubt influenced many in legal, medical, ethical, and theological circles to include possible fetal deformity as sufficient grounds for a therapeutic abortion. Considerations for an abortion on possible fetal deformity would include maternal rubella, known teratogenic drug exposure, and certain hereditary conditions.[53] There are a number of other genetic diseases which cause multiple malformations as well as mental retardation. The geneticists seem to suggest an average ratio of a one in four chance for fetal deformity by virtue of drugs, heredity, or contracting a disease which affects the fetus.

It is true that great strides have been made recently in biological science, especially in the field of genetics. The magnitude of the problem of fetal deformity is more sharply focused by current research and knowledge in this realm of science. The practical aspect of the problem or dilemma is portrayed by Augenstein in his recent book, *Come, Let Us Play God*:

> As far as I am concerned, anyone who votes for an abortion is taking a life. By the same token, anyone who says no to aborting the fetus in question is consigning those parents to endless worry, and almost certainly to a nervous breakdown if the child proves abnormal as suggested by the tests. Further, once the child develops amaurotic idiocy symptoms, that no vote has sentenced him to a long siege of dreadful suffering. Thus, either a yes or no represents a very godlike decision. Moreover, anyone who even becomes involved in counseling in such a situation assumes an awesome responsibility.[54]

Since genetic surgery must go through successful experimental stages, and absolute genetic proof of a fetal deformity is still lacking, a yes, or no, to an abortion in such an instance will be laden with uncertainty.

*Socioeconomic Reasons for Abortion*

Of all the reasons considered to justify abortion, the socioeconomic one appears to be the most serious ethical and moral violation. In this country, no such law has been enacted, although some have advocated this as the only sure means of population control. This would be employing abortion as a contraceptive measure, which most certainly disregards the biblical view of the sacredness and respect for human life.

Japan, Russia, Hungary, China, and Poland have permitted therapeutic abortions on socioeconomic grounds. Yet, our previous investigations as to the result of such practices should be ample warning to all who seek to go too far in liberalizing the current abortion laws. Such an approach borders too near "the end justifies the means" concept. It is also adjacent to Nietzsche's dehumanizing philosophy of the "survival of the fittest," which philosophy Hitler adopted, and thus darkened the pages of history.

The majority of evangelical Christians agree that it is time for a change relative to abortion laws—at least this is true among those who have spoken or written on the current issue. This trend or expression by many evangelicals by no means suggests that abortion should be available by the demand of any woman wishing to terminate her pregnancy. To take a human life, or the life of a potential person for socioeconomic reasons is, in the writer's opinion, a gross moral violation of the commandment: "Thou shalt not kill." This motive for terminating fetal life would be a clear-cut prerequisite for euthanasia, that is, a painless putting to death of persons suffering from incurable diseases. These persons, like the fetus, would not be wanted nor needed by such a society.

The economic benefits of abortion to society is a false premise. The Christian moral imperative is to help those who are impoverished in society. By far, the better solution to the population explosion and to improve the socioeconomic conditions of society is a concerted educational program in contraception, and making available contraceptive medications and devices.

It is the opinion of some, that those who advocate abortion for socioeconomic reasons do not fully realize the complexities of the abortion dilemma. It is the Christian's duty to point out the dignity of man who is created in the image of God. He must point out that human life from the moment of conception and implantation is mysterious, sacred, and as a potential person demands reverence and respect. In addition, the human fetus demands protection as an innocent person coming into being.

*Psychiatric Reasons for Abortion*

Among all reasons currently given for more liberal abortion laws, none are used more than psychiatric ones, to obtain a therapeutic abortion. Here, the subjective tends to bear influence over all other objective reasons for induced abortions. In most states that have liberalized abortion laws to include "psychiatric grounds" for the termination of fetal life, the number of abortions have risen sharply. The so-called psychiatric indications probably account for more abortions at present than any other cause. Some authors speak of the extra emotional burden the mother would have to bear if her pregnancy were not terminated. Such an approach is speculative and not realistic; in other words, a problem is prematurely erected.

The key psychiatric aspects as causes for terminating a pregnancy by an induced abortion are (1) the patient pressures the psychiatrist with suicidal threats, and (2) the patient will face dreadful social consequences if the pregnancy is allowed to continue until the delivery of a child. Yet, even among psychiatrists, an extreme range of opinion exists in relation to therapeutic abortions. A woman psychiatrist stated:

Pregnancy should be terminated when a woman is desperate enough to seek it, no matter what the reasons! Too many have died because moralistic clergymen and the mercenary underworld have driven them into the hands of unskilled individuals.[55]

114

A recent survey of members of the American Psychiatric Association showed that almost 90 percent of the U.S. members favored abortion when there is a significant risk that the mental or emotional health of the mother is jeopardized.

A well known English psychiatrist has stated that "there are no psychiatric grounds for the termination of pregnancy."[56] The diversity of opinion as to psychiatric reasons for abortion is not limited to the psychiatrist. Recently, the American Baptist Convention is reported to have come out in favor of abortion on request prior to the 13th week of pregnancy.[57]

Different conclusions as to the nature and value of the fetus have a profound bearing on attitudes toward induced abortions. The fetus is considered, by way of review: (1) as a new human life, thus the fetus must be treated as a person; (2) as a biological growth, or merely a part of the mother; and (3) as definitely a potential person. These views, or one of them, is held by many psychiatrists and clergymen and by Christians and non-Christians. Some estimate that 90 percent of all abortions are asked for on grounds of psychological distress.

### The Interim Solution to the Abortion Crises

If abortion is to be permitted, under what circumstances? Should the recommendations of the American Law Institute (ALI) and the American College of Obstetricians and Gynecologists (ACOG) serve as the criteria for terminating fetal life? The writer views the fetus as definitely human; therefore, the termination of this genesis of human life cannot be viewed as an insignificant decision. This conclusion has been arrived at from the Scriptural view of man, and the evidence afforded by biological and medical science. Abortion, under any circumstances, is an infringement upon the rights of the potential person. It is always a choice of lesser-of-evils.

The ALI and the ACOG have gone too far, in the writer's opinion, in their recommendations for therapeutic abortions. Their position on the life of the mother, as well as rape and incest, appears valid, but not on fetal deformity and psychiatric reasons. The mother's life has been valued above that of the fetus by most Protestants for many years. The American Medical Association agreed with this as the only cause for terminating fetal life for many years, the exception being in the case of rape and incest whereby injections and irrigations were performed within a 48 hour period. Also, a curettage could be performed during the blastocyst period, but like the morning-after pill, no one would ever know whether or not contraception or abortion were applied. Most all Protestant authorities in medicine and theology are united in approving an abortion whereby the life of the mother is jeopardized. Even this choice is a lesser-of-evils situation that appears to be unavoidable in exceptional and extreme cases. Such situations are minimized more and more in view of the progress in medical science and the skill of the obstetrician to see an expectant mother through a pregnancy even though she may be afflicted with difficult physical maladies.

The cases of rape and incest are social and moral violations with brutal physical, mental, and social overtones. In view of such, it appears proper to terminate fetal life, or possible fetal life. Yet, strong general guidelines should be followed or maintained. The ideal is to deal with such cases as recommended by the Roman Catholic Church, i.e., irrigations and injections administered within a 48 hour period. In addition, a curettage could be performed within the blastocyst period (approximately one week), and the morning-after pill could also be administered. In each of these solutions, no one would ever know whether or not the union of two cells took place. Such actions should be taken when approval has been granted by a representative regional committee that has considered the medical and legal evidence relative to a rape or incest case.

The victim of rape and incest and/or the parents of a minor should make their reports to both medical and legal authorities respectively. This should be done immediately following the crime in order that the case might be dealt with during the initial week of uncertainty as to whether or not conception had actually occurred. There are varied opinions as to when a potential person begins: at conception, or implantation? The writer is of the opinion that a potential person begins at the moment of conception and implantation. Scripture infers such (cf. Ps. 51 and 139), also, medical and biological science lend support to this view.

Therefore, in consideration of the above observations, it appears that both the ALI and the ACOG, as well as the AMA, have taken proper actions in their consideration of the total person in the case of rape and incest.

The writer views the "psychiatric" and "fetal deformity" reasons for abortion in an entirely different manner than the above two. Psychiatric reasons for terminating the life of a potential person is too subjective as a reason to terminate fetal life. The ambiguity of such decisions is revealed in the fact that most women requesting abortion on psychiatric grounds receive no therapy before and after an induced abortion. The present tendency to give the psychiatrist and the sociologist a greater voice in these matters does offer some problems. Traditional medicine has been much more objective in measuring and evaluating data than in the area of psychiatry. Therefore, psychiatric reasons for terminating the life of a potential person are freighted with speculation and ambiguity as a valid reason for terminating fetal life. More tangible evidence must be supplied before a flood-gate to abortions on psychiatric grounds is opened.

The possibility of fetal deformities, whether physical or mental, is also an infringement on the rights of the unborn child. The ability of genetic scientists to precisely predict a fetus as malformed due to genetic pollution or injury is not yet possible. As we previously stated, the average mathematical odds for possible fetal deformities are about one in four. This kind of genetic roulette is not only a leap of uncertainty, but the terminating of a life that is declared before birth to be unwelcome or unfit for society. The famous Helen Keller, although not afflicted by scarlet fever during pregnancy did contract the disease at the age of two. She lost her sight, hearing, and smell, yet her music has blessed millions. She could have been a victim of rubella prior to birth, and according to some spokesmen, her life could have been terminated in fetal growth. Milton was blind when he dictated one of the most sublime poems of the ages. Beethoven was so deaf that he could not hear the fortissimo of a full orchestra, and yet he composed one of the greatest oratorios. Has the world gained or lost from the services of the epileptic Michelangelo, of the deaf Edison, of the hunchbacked Steinmetz, or the Roosevelts—both the asthmatic Theodore and the polio paralyzed Franklin?

The argument for an abortion on the grounds of "possible fetal deformity" borders too close to euthanasia to be accepted as a valid cause for terminating fetal life.

### Notes to Chapter III

1. Gerald Kennedy, "The Nature of Heresy," in *Storm Over Ethics* (United Church Press, The Bethany Press, 1967), p. 131.

2. David T. Smith, ed., *Abortion and the Law* (Cleveland: The Press of Western Reserve University, 1967), p. 38.

3. Cf. Keil and Delitzsch, *Biblical Commentary*, II, 134-35.

4. Noonan, *Contraception: A History*, p. 85.

5. Ibid., p. 86.

6. Russell B. Shaw, *Abortion and Public Policy* (Washington, D.C.: Family Life Bureau, NCWC, February, 1966), p. 43.

7. Kalland, "Views and Position," p. 427.

8. Ibid.

9. Noonan, *Contraception: A History*, p. 87.

10. Shaw, *Abortion and Public Policy*, p. 44.

11. Russell Shaw, *Abortion on Trial* (Dayton: Pflaum Press, 1968), p. 157.

12. Kalland, "Views and Position," p. 429.

13. Noonan, *Contraception: A History*, p. 90.

14. Ibid., quoting Augustine.

15. Shaw, *Abortion on Trial*, p. 170.

16. Thielicke, *The Ethics of Sex*, p. 228.

17. Kalland, "Views and Position," p. 443.

18. *The New Catholic Encyclopedia*, quoted in Shaw, *Abortion on Trial*, p. 171.

19. James George, Jr., "Current Abortion Laws, Proposals and

Movements for Reform," in *Abortion and the Law,* ed. by Smith, p. 31.

20. Shaw, *Abortion and Public Policy,* p. 6.

21. "Contraception and Abortion," *Christianity Today,* Vol. XIII, No. 3 (November 8, 1968), p. 19.

22. Bernard J. Hanley, M.D., "The Right of the Unborn Child." Paper read before the 24th annual meeting of the Pacific Coast Obstetrical and Gynecological Society, Palm Springs, California, October 30 to November 2, 1957.

23. Fletcher, *Situation Ethics,* pp. 135-36.

24. Alton Blackeslee, "Abortion: Is It Woman's Right?" *Glendale News-Press,* November, 14, 1968.

25. A. C. and Norbert J. Mietus, "Criminal Abortion: A Failure of Law or a Challenge to Society" (Washington. D. C.: Family Life Bureau NCWC, 1966). This article originally appeared in *American Bar Journal,* October, 1965.

26. Shaw, *Abortion and Public Policy,* p. 35.

27. Ibid., pp. 36-37.

28. Ibid., p. 38.

29. Ibid.

30. Ibid.

31. Shaw, *Abortion on Trial,* p. 146.

32. Ibid., p. 147.

33. Ibid.

34. Thielicke, *The Ethics of Sex,* p. 230.

35. Shaw, *Abortion on Trial,* p. 153.

36. Mietus, *Criminal Abortion,* p. 1.

37. John Scanzoni, "A Sociological Perspective on Abortion and Sterilization," in *Birth Control and the Christian,* p. 317.

38. Shaw, *Abortion on Trial,* p. 1.

39. Augenstein, *Come, Let Us Play God,* p. 116.

40. Robert F. Drinan, S. J., "The Inviolability of the Right to Be Born," in *Abortion and the Law,* p. 109.

41. Thomas F. Lambert, Jr., "The Legal Rights of the Fetus," in *Birth Control and the Christian,* p. 378.

42. Ibid., p. 379.

43. Mietus, *Criminal Abortion.*

44. Shaw, *Abortion on Trial,* p. 86, quoting Thomas L. Hayes.

45. Robert E. Cook, et al., *The Terrible Choice: The Abortion Dilemma* (New York: Bantam Books Inc., 1968), p. 85.

46. Gerald Waring, "Report from Ottawa, Commons Committee on Health and Welfare," *Canadian Medical Association Journal,* XCVIII (February 24, 1968), 419.

47. "Rabbi Tells Why Jews Don't Believe Abortion Is Homicide,"

119

*Los Angeles Times*, December 18, 1968.

48. John Warwick Montgomery, "The Christian View of the Fetus," in *Birth Control and the Christian*, p. 83.

49. Montgomery, "The Christian View of the Fetus," p. 88.

50. Ibid., p. 89.

51. Lambert, "The Legal Rights of the Fetus," p. 409.

52. Augenstein, *Come, Let Us Play God*, p. 119.

53. Sara Crews Finley, "Genetics, Abortion and Sterilization," in *Birth Control and the Christian*, p. 543.

54. Augenstein, *Come, Let Us Play God*, p. 12.

55. Merville O. Vincent, "Psychiatric Indications for Therapeutic Abortion," in *Birth Control and the Christian*, p. 193.

56. Ibid., p. 192.

57. Ibid., p. 195.

# Chapter IV

# SUMMARY AND CONCLUSION

In our study of the total person in contraception and abortion, we discovered from Scripture and current scholarship in theology that man is a unity, a total, or holistic person. He is not a tripartite or a bipartite, a trichotomy or a dichotomy. He is not compartmentalized into body, soul, and spirit; these are but manifestations of his total person. These terms, and other ethical uses are often employed in Scripture, but they are but aspects of the whole man. The anthropology of the Bible is that man in all of his diversified representations is one grand psychophysical unit created in the image of God.

We also concluded that both the Old and New Testament are in agreement as to the nature of man. The Hebrew concept of the total person formed the background and basis for the New Testament anthropology, and not Greek thought, as was taught for so many years. Thus, the Testaments are not mutually exclusive, but compatible as to the unity of man.

The most profound statement in Scripture in regards to Biblical anthropology is: "Man was created in the image of God." This image of God concept involves the total person, not just a part of the individual. The fall of man marred, but did not obliterate the *Imago Dei* in man. The restoration of the image is made possible through the life, death, and resurrection of Jesus Christ. This full and complete restoration of the image of God is not complete until the body is glorified at the second coming of Christ. The image of God, though marred, was passed on to the human race by Adam to his posterity.

The total person created in the image of God has significance for the subjects of contraception and abortion. Contraception is viewed by the evangelical Christian as an option in the marriage

121

relationship. The total person, with his God-given power to procreate in His image, is to consider the sacredness of the sexual act within the bounds of the marriage experience. He is to recognize that in marriage one of the key purposes of coitus is that of procreation and the rearing of children to the glory of God. The sex act between the married couple involves more than a mere physical union when one considers the total person as a psychophysical unity. In view of this, contraception is a legitimate Christian option, inasmuch as husband and wife are "one flesh" both in *agape* and *eros*.

In the practice of contraception or in the use of contraceptive devices or medications, *possible* conception is prohibited. The argument against contraception as based on natural law by the Roman Catholic Church is invalid from the Scriptural view of the total person.

Contraception and the single person is simply laid to rest by the Christian due to the clear Biblical injunction against illicit sexual behavior. However, there may be exceptional cases in a subcultural environment whereby the physician feels compelled to prescribe a contraceptive measure, especially in the case of repeated illegitimacies.

The issue of contraception, although a burning one, is not as serious as is the problem of therapeutic abortions. The one involves the *possible* person, the other involves the fetus as a *potential* person. The decision not to have children is an unquestioned option afforded to couples in marriage. At least most Protestants subscribe to this view. The decision to terminate human life involves the total person, regardless as to the developmental stage.

Abortion involves the question of life or death. It is without a doubt one of the most challenging ethical and moral dilemmas confronting the medical, legal, social, and theological world today. The Biblical concept of the total person created in the image of God makes the choice of abortion a terrible one under any circumstances.

The Bible does not specifically point out the time when one

becomes a person. Yet, the inference from Scripture places a high value on human life regardless of the stage of development. Since man is an indivisible unit, his being from the moment of conception is to be respected and viewed with reverence. The creation narrator pictures man in a unique relationship to God (cf. Gen. 1:26, 27; 5:1-3). In Ex. 21:18-25, a number of notable exegetes equate the value of fetal life with that of the mother. Also, in Ps. 51 and Ps. 139, the Psalmist identifies himself in fetal development and growth. The second Adam, Jesus Christ, is identified in His humanity from the moment of conception. These observations along with the discoveries of medical and biological science, particularly the field of genetics, elevates the status of the fetus.

Paul's analogy on the parts of the body as they relate to the whole, offers a lesson in considering the fetus in relation to the mature person. Also, the Biblical teaching on the resurrection of the body lends support to the total person concept in the abortion dilemma.

Any abortion, whether justified or not, involves the total person. It is a choice of lesser evils. It is a terrible choice! The significance of fetal life cannot be fully appreciated apart from the view of man as pictured in Scripture, that is, he is a creature in the image of God. No one should counsel that a life be taken unless they know the value of a life; the total person as created in the image of God.

# BIBLIOGRAPHY

## Books

Arndt, William, F., and Gingrich, F. Wilbur. *A Greek English Lexicon of the New Testament and Other Early Christian Literature*. Chicago: The University of Chicago Press, 1957.

Augenstein, Leroy. *Come, Let Us Play God*. New York: Harper and Row, 1969.

Bagster, Samuel. *The Analytical Hebrew and Chaldee Lexicon*. New York: Harper and Bros.

Barth, Karl. *Dogmatics in Outline*. New York: Harper and Row, 1959.

Berkouwer, G. C. *Man: Image of God*. Grand Rapids: Wm. B. Eerdman's Publishing Company, 1962.

————. *The Person of Christ*. Grand Rapids: Wm. B. Eerdman's Publishing Company, 1966.

Bonhoeffer, Dietrich. *Creation and Fall: Temptation*. New York: The Macmillan Company, 1966.

Brown, Francis, Driver, S. R., and Briggs, Charles. *A Hebrew and English Lexicon of the Old Testament*. Boston, New York, and Chicago: Houghton, Mifflin and Company, 1906.

Brunner, Emil. *God and Man*. London: Student Christian Press, 1936.

————. *Man in Revolt: A Christian Anthropology*. Philadelphia: The Westminster Press, n.d.

Bultmann, Rudolf. *Theology of the New Testament*. New York: Charles Scribner's Sons, 1951.

Calderone, Mary. *Abortion in the United States*. New York: Hoeber and Harper, 1958.

Calvin, John. *Commentaries on the First Book of Moses, Called*

125

*Genesis.* Vol. I. Grand Rapids: Wm. B. Eerdman's Publishing Company, 1948.

Cook, Robert E., et. al. *The Terrible Choice: The Abortion Dilemma.* New York: Bantam Books Inc., 1968.

Cullman, Oscar. *Immortality of the Soul or Resurrection of the Dead?* New York: The Macmillan Company, 1958.

Daly, Mary. *The Church and the Second Sex.* New York: Harper and Row, 1968.

De Fraine, Jean S. J. *Adam and the Family of Man.* Translated by Daniel Raible, C.P.P.S. New York: Alba House, 1965.

─────. *The Bible and the Origin of Man.* New York: Desclee Company, 1962.

Deiltzsch, Franz. *A System of Biblical Psychology.* Edinburgh: T. & T. Clark, n.d.

Deissmann, Adolf. *Paul, A Study in Social and Religious History.* New York: Harper and Bros., 1957. A Harper Torchbook.

Dodd, C. H. *The Epistle of Paul to the Romans. The Moffat New Testament Commentary Series.* New York: Harper and Bros., n.d.

Drinkwater, F. H. *Birth Control and Natural Law.* Baltimore, Dublin: Billing & Sons Ltd., Guildford and London, for Helicon Press, Inc., 1965.

Duvall, Evelyn Millis. *Love and the Facts of Life.* New York: Association Press, 1967.

Fletcher, Joseph. *Situation Ethics, the New Morality.* Paperback. Philadelphia: The Westminster Press, n.d.

Flood, Dom Peter. *New Problems in Medical Ethics.* Book Two: *Sexual Problems of the Adolescent, Medical Responsibility.* Cork, Ireland: The Mercier Press, 1962.

Gelin, Albert S. S. *The Concept of Man in the Bible.* Translated by David M. Murphy. London: Geoffrey Chapman, 1968.

Harrison, Everett F., ed. *Baker's Dictionary of Theology.* Grand Rapids: Baker Book House, 1960.

Hill, Edmund D. P. *The Truth of Genesis 1-11.* The Quarterly of the Catholic Biblical Association. Vol. XVIII, No. 43. London: July, 1966.

126

Hodge, Charles. *Systematic Theology.* Vol. II. Grand Rapids: Wm. B. Eerdman's Publishing Co., n.d.

Horn, Siegfried H. *Seventh-day Adventist Bible Dictionary.* Washington, D. C.: Review & Herald Publishing Association, 1960.

*The Interpreter's Bible.* Vol. III. New York: Abingdon-Cokesbury Press, 1952.

Keil, C. F. and Delitzsch, F. *Biblical Commentary on the Old Testament.* Vol. I: *The Pentateuch.* Translated by James Martin. Grand Rapids: Wm. E. Eerdman's Publishing Company, n.d.

McQuarrie, John, ed. *Dictionary of Christian Ethics.* Philadelphia: The Westminster Press, 1967.

Mascall, E. L. *The Importance of Being Human.* New York: Columbia University Press, 1958.

Mietus, A. C. and Norbert. *Criminal Abortion: "A Failure of Law or a Challenge to Society."* Washington, D. C.: Family Life Bureau NCWC, 1966.

Neilson, John Robertson. *Everlasting Punishment.* London: Skeffington & Son, 1897.

*A New Catechism: Catholic Faith for Adults.* Commissioned by the Hierarchy of Netherlands. New York: Herder and Herder, 1967.

Nicoll, W. Robertson, ed. *The Expositor's Bible.* Grand Rapids; Wm. B. Eerdman's Publishing Co., 1940.

Noonan, John T., Jr. *The Church and Contraception.* New York: Paulist Press Deus Books, 1967.

————. *Contraception: A History of Its Treatment by the Catholic Theologians and Canonists.* Cambridge: Harvard University Press, 1966.

O'Connel, Hugh J. *Keeping Your Balance in the Modern Church.* Liquori, Missouri: Liquorian Pamphlets, Redemptorist Fathers, 1968.

Orr, James. *The Christian View of God and the World.* Edinburg: Andrew Elliot, 1893.

Ramm, Bernard. *The Christian View of Science and Scripture.*

Grand Rapids: Wm. B. Eerdman's Publishing Co., 1966.

Ramsey, Paul. *Deeds and Rules in Christian Ethics.* New York: Charles Scribner's Sons, 1967.

Reed, David H. C. *Christian Ethics.* Philadelphia: J. B. Lippincott Company, 1969.

Robinson, H. Wheeler. *The Christian Doctrine of Man.* Edinburgh: T & T. Clark, 1913.

Robinson, John A. T. *Honest to God.* Philadelphia: Westminster Press, 1963.

Schmithals, Walter. *An Introduction to the Theology of Rudolph Bultman.* London: SCM Press, Ltd., 1968.

Shaw, Russell B. *Abortion and Public Policy.* Washington, D. C.: Family Life Bureau, N.C.W.C., 1966.

————. *Abortion on Trial.* Dayton: Pflaum Press, 1968.

Smith, C. Ryder. *The Bible Doctrine of Man.* London: The EP Worth Press, 1951.

Smith, David T., ed. *Abortion and the Law.* Cleveland: The Press of Western Reserve University, 1967.

Snaith, Norman H. *The Distinctive Ideas of the Old Testament.* New York: Schocken Books, 1964.

Spitzer, Walter O. and Saylor, Carlyle L., eds. *Birth Control and the Christian.* Wheaton, Illinois: Tyndale House Publishers, 1969.

Stendahl, Krister, ed. *The Scrolls and the New Testament.* New York: Harper and Bros., 1957.

Teilhard de Chardin, Pierre. *The Phenomenon of Man.* New York: Harper and Bros., 1959.

Thielicke, Helmuth. *The Ethics of Sex.* Translated by John W. Doberstein. New York: Harper and Row, 1964.

————. *Man in God's World.* Translated by John W. Doberstein. New York: Evanston and London: Harper and Row, 1963.

Torrance, T. F. *Calvin's Doctrine of Man.* London: Lutterworth Press, 1949.

Tournier, Paul, et al., ed. *Are You Nobody.* Richmond: John Knox Press, 1967.

Vincent, Marvin R. *Word Studies in the New Testament.* Vol. II. Grand Rapids: Wm. B. Eerdman's Publishing Co., 1957.

Von Rad, Gerhard. *Old Testament Theology: The Theology of Israel's Historical Tradition.* Translated by D. M. G. Stalker. New York: Harper and Bros., 1962.

Vriezen, T. H. *An Outline of Old Testament Theology.* Oxford: Basil Blackwell, 1958.

Wace, Henry and Schaff, Philip. *The Seven Ecumenical Councils: Nicene and Post-Nicene Fathers,* Vol. XIV. New York: Charles Scribner's Sons, 1900.

Wendel, Francois. *Calvin: The Origins and Development of His Religious Thought.* New York: Harper and Row, 1963.

*What Then, Is Man?* A Symposium of Theology, Psychology and Psychiatry. St. Louis: Concordia Publishing House, 1958.


## Articles


Blackeslee, Alton. "Abortion: Is It Woman's Right?" *Glendale News-Press,* November 14, 1968.

"Contraception and Abortion." *Christianity Today,* Vol. XIII, No. 3 (November 8, 1968), p. 19.

Hanley, Bernard J., M.D. "The Right of the Unborn Child." Paper read before the twenty-fourth annual meeting of the Pacific Coast Obstetrical and Gynecological Society, Palm Springs, California, October 30 to November 2, 1957.

Hubbard, David Allan. "Old Testament Light on the Meaning of Marriage." Originally appeared as "Love and Marriage" in the *Covenant Companion,* January, 1969.

Jewett, Paul K. "The Divine Image." Lecture given in class at the Fuller Theological Seminary, Pasadena, California, November, 1968.

————. "The Relation of the Soul to the Fetus." *Christianity Today,* XII (November, 1968), 18-19.

Kennedy, Gerald. "The Nature of Heresy," in *Storm Over Ethics.* United Church Press. The Bethany Press, 1967.

Lederberg, Joshua. "A Geneticist Looks at Contraception and Abortion." *Annals of Internal Medicine*, Supplement 7, Vol. LXVII. Philadelphia, 1967.

Lo Bello, Nino. "Vatican Has Interest in the Pill." *Sacramento Bee*, March 23, 1969.

Meye, Robert P. "The New Testament and Birth Control." *Christianity Today*, XIII (November, 1968), 10-12.

Moskin, J. Robet. "Sweden: The Contraceptive Society." *The Reader's Digest*, April, 1969.

"A Protestant Affirmation of the Control of Human Reproduction." *Christianity Today*, XIII (November, 1968), 18-19.

Sternglass, Ernest J. "The Death of All Children." *Esquire*, Vol. LXXII, No. 3 (September, 1969).

*U.S. News & World Report*, Vol. LXII, No. 10 (March 17, 1969), p. 48.

*U.S. vs. One Package*. December 30, 1936. See Groves, Ernest R. *Marriage*, 2nd edition revised. New York: Host, 1947.

Vincent, M. O. "A Christian View of Contraception." *Christianity Today*, XIII (November, 1968), 14-15.

Waring, Gerald. "Report from Ottawa, Commons Committee on Health and Welfare." *Canadian Medical Association Journal*, Vol. XCVIII (February 24, 1968), p. 419.

10-4-65

the
pulpit
speaks
on
race

# the
# pulpit
# speaks
# on
# race

edited by
alfred t. davies

new york    abingdon press    nashville

Dedicated to the memory of those
whose lives have been taken
because of racial hatred

"Blessed are the peacemakers, for they shall
be called sons of God"

# preface

In recent months no one has been able to escape the barrage of words that have been both spoken and written on the civil rights struggle that grips our nation today. The Church, too, has made its contribution. The major denominations have frequently and prophetically spoken on the national board, conference, or assembly levels with official statements, pronouncements, and resolutions. But the words that are ultimately most effective must be uttered on the local level. Regrettably, however, the pulpit record on this level has been disappointing. In fact, most if not all of the civil rights leaders have written off the local congregations and many of their ministers as effective allies in this human rights movement.

But, disappointing as this has been, good things have been spoken in some pulpits of our churches, and it is my hope that this book will not only reflect the Christian concern that is present but will serve as a source book to stimulate a more articulate message in these critical days.

In bringing these sermons together I did not run an open "contest" from which I would choose the best. Instead, I invited men who have distinguished themselves both by their words and by their lives to submit their sermons to me. Some effort was made to maintain denominational and geographical balance, although quality, timeliness, and subject variety were the major factors in the final selection. With but a couple of exceptions each sermon was delivered to a congregation in the context of Christian worship.

I would be remiss if I did not express a brief "thank you" to at least a few of the many individuals who assisted me along the way. A special word of appreciation is due Dr. Kyle Haselden, Editor of the *Christian Century*, for his welcomed suggestions which have strengthened this book, and for his personal kindness which has strengthened me. To Mr. Clayton Hoskins for his helpful comments and encouragement, to Mrs. Margaret Dreifke for her efficiency in typing the manuscript and much of the correspondence, and finally to my wife, Wylene, who willingly gave me up to this task, cheerfully sacrificing time which rightfully belonged to her and our family, I owe a debt of gratitude.

Hilliard Presbyterian Church      ALFRED T. DAVIES, Editor
Hilliard, Ohio

# contents

## PART I
### THEOLOGICAL CONSIDERATIONS

9

*11*

# PART I
## THEOLOGICAL CONSIDERATIONS

# 1. long minutes

JAMES ARMSTRONG

*James Armstrong is pastor of the Broadway Methodist Church, Indianapolis, Indiana. He received his education from Florida Southern College (A.B.), which has also conferred a Doctor of Divinity degree upon him, and Emory University (B.D.), and did graduate study at Boston University and the University of Chicago. Dr. Armstrong has had wide experience in radio and television and has published articles in leading magazines. He also teaches Christian ethics at the Christian Theological Seminary (Disciples of Christ). In 1959 he was honored as the Outstanding Young Man of Indianapolis by the Junior Chamber of Commerce.*

The United States is on trial around the world. The Declaration of Independence, the Constitution, and Lincoln's Second Inaugural Address speak for themselves. But so do the public moods and deeds that deny the fundamental principles of our republic. It is interesting to note when traveling abroad that the first searching question generally asked by the critical inquirer is, "All right, but what about the American Negro?"

The so-called "race problem" is not just one item on our national agenda. In many respects it is *the* item. If we fail to produce at this point, our practice will deny our principle—and the whole world will be the victim.

Before moving toward possible solutions, we must explore the nature of the problem.

## I

*A part of the problem is prejudice,* which simply means prejudgment. All of us prejudge. That means we are all prejudiced, one way or another about one thing or another. Most of us, like it or not, would have to join Charles Lamb in his confession. "For myself," he said, "earthbound and fettered to the scene of my activities, I confess that I do feel the differences of mankind, national and individual. . . . I am, in plainer words, a bundle of prejudices." If you'll forgive me—all we, like Lamb, have gone astray.

In South Africa the English are against the Afrikaners, descendants of the Dutch settlers. Both are against the Jews. All three are opposed to the Indians. And all four conspire against the native blacks. Some Polish people call Ukrainians "reptiles." Germans call their neighbors to the east "Polish cattle," and the Poles return the compliment by calling them "Prussian swine." Malcolm X, of dubious fame, can say, "White people are born devils by nature," and add his fierce prejudices to the rest.

I grew up all over the country and thus saw firsthand a wide variety of prejudices. In northern Michigan prejudice was directed against the Scandinavian and central European miners. In Seattle it was turned against the Orientals. In southern California it lashed out at the Mexicans. In the South it vent its fury on the Negro. And in the heart of Anglo-Saxon Midwestern America there are about as many political, religious, and racial prejudices as you'll find anywhere.

Prejudice is universal. Therefore, we should not be surprised

16

to learn that white, middle-class Americans not only direct their hostilities toward others; they are on the receiving end of prejudice as well.

A generation or so ago a Chinese student, when asked what he thought of Americans, reluctantly confessed that he considered them "the best of the foreign devils." And in England during the war it was said, "The only trouble with the Yanks is that they are overpaid, oversexed, and over here." Now all this may seem innocent enough, but when they start talking like that about the "Yanks" we arch our backs. "Didn't we save their island? Didn't we win their war? And anyway, I know some of the Americans who were in England, and they were as fine as any people on the face of the earth." "Overpaid and oversexed" to be sure!

This is the fallacy of prejudice. Prejudice talks about the Yank or the Catholic or the Mexican or the Negro or the Jew only as a member of a group. He has no identity apart from his group. Prejudice does not see the *individual* as a growing, dreaming, yearning, laughing, crying, aching child of God. And that's exactly what he is, no matter who he is or where he's from.

But the problem is deeper than prejudice. It becomes most hurtful when linked with patterns of cruel discrimination, when we begin to react *against* a person because of the accident of his birth and the blindness of our souls.

Jackie Robinson comes to town to campaign for the Republicans. He is denied the right to stay in a downtown hotel. It's not because he's a Republican. It's because of the color of his skin. Think of those whose names don't happen to be Jackie Robinson to whom this happens every day. You say, "Yes, but the hotel owner has his rights." But think what it would be like to stand in the other fellow's shoes.

A doctor moves into a newly developed residential section of the city. His wife is of another race. Immediately, his life is threatened, his property is threatened, insults are hurled, and a cross is burned. A man works around the clock bringing health to life, but every time he comes home a threat of violence hangs over his own. You say you have serious misgivings about mixed marriages. Many people do. But there are other values involved here. Put yourself in the other fellow's shoes.

A North Carolina college student is critically injured in an automobile accident. He is turned away from two hospitals because of the color of his skin. He is bounced back and forth over country roads between one town and another as his friends seek some sort of helping hand. He finally dies.

Riots break out in Chicago. Men are beaten. Cars are overturned. A Negro preacher tells his people—and his sermon is broadcast—"I've said you should have faith. I've said you should pray. But the time for prayer and faith have passed. It is time we carried more than Bibles to protect ourselves." Hard words! But I wonder what you would say if you stood in his shoes.

Police dogs bite and maul Negro demonstrators. An old man is beaten to the ground and kicked in Jackson. A bomb is thrown and children die in Birmingham. Medgar Evers is shot in the back of the head. How would we react if we were Negro? We need not agree with all that James Baldwin writes or Malcolm X says in order to understand the blind, cruel fates that have molded them and theirs.

Patterns of segregation and discrimination have splintered the countryside. They have pitted man against brother man. And this has happened in a land that proudly says to all the world, "All men are created equal, . . . they are endowed by their Creator with certain inalienable Rights." Do you see why a smirk plays about the lips of nations that have turned toward us looking for a leader, for a symbol, for an example to follow? They hear our noble words and then they see us trample them in the dust.

Oh, I know—it isn't your fault; it isn't my fault. I never owned a slave in my life. I never burned a cross. I never wrote an anonymous letter. I've never thrown rocks or used clubs or jeered at anyone. Broadway Church has its Negro members. Negro children are in our church school. Our community service program is 95 per cent Negro. We have developed no self-conscious jargon about being an "integrated" church or an "inclusive" church. We are simply a church doing the work of the church. This isn't "our" problem. *But, is there any human problem that is not, in part, our own?*

One of the things that led Albert Schweitzer to Africa was the burning memory of a statue that stood in the village where he lived as a boy. The statue was that of a Negro in chains. He had not placed the chains there, but he felt that his fathers before him had created the tragedy and it was up to him to make atonement for their sins. Dr. Schweitzer, with all his limitations, is one of the towering figures of Christendom. He felt a personal responsibility for the redemption of a history he had not forged. But Schweitzer is only one man. What about you and me? In what directions can we move toward solutions?

## II

Certainly there is *education.* Just as our prejudices are learned, so can they be unlearned.

There is *dialogue.* We cannot function in isolated pockets and understand the wider world of which we are a part. We should get acquainted with our neighbors of other races. We can work with them in the P.T.A. and on the community council. As we learn to talk across the back fence and in the conference room we are tearing down long-standing barriers.

There is *political action.* For the past twenty-five years both national political parties have said the "right" things, giving lip service to a concept of complete equality.

There is *law.* Every major stride taken by a minority group in our country has been made possible by the passage and enforcement of law. We are a "constitutional" people. We believe in the validity of the law.

We need to bear in mind, however, that the race problem is basically a problem in human relations; *it is a religious problem.*

Thus it becomes our responsibility as members of the Church of Jesus Christ to create an atmosphere in which the right kind of education, conversation, political action, and lawmaking can take place.

I have said that this is fundamentally a religious problem. Let me be more specific: Where human relationships break down, where blind prejudice infects the climate of society, where cruel patterns of discrimination lash out at particular persons because of their religion or their nationality or their color—*there sin exists.*

The Lord of the church summed up his entire teaching in one law. It had two parts, indivisible. It consisted of a wholehearted response to God and a wholehearted love for brother man. Where that law is broken man's covenant with God is fractured. There man lives in sin. This is a religious problem, and its solution, finally, must be determined in the realm of the Spirit.

The words of the psalmist are the words of any oppressed segment of mankind:

> "How long, O Lord? Wilt thou forget me for ever?
> How long wilt thou hide thy face from me?
> How long must I bear pain in my soul?
>
> . . . . . . . .
>
> How long shall my enemy be exalted over me?

The anguished soul cries out, "How long, O Lord, how long?" And we hear the cry and make our response—one way or another.

Jesus heard the cry and went to a cross. He refused to turn away from "the winebibbers and the gluttonous," from the publican and the sinner, from the despised Samaritan—and he went to a cross. He stooped to the lowliest of men and lifted them into the presence of God—and he went to a cross. He offended the self-righteous and the pharasiac with his pleas for brotherhood—and he went to a cross. Even on the cross he was love incarnate. He extended mercy to the miserable soul of a dying thief and forgave his screaming, jeering murderers. The problem is religious, but so is the answer. The ground is level at the foot of the cross.

20

Lillian E. Smith in her novel *Strange Fruit*, tells of the lynching of Henry McIntosh, an innocent Negro. After McIntosh is seized by a frenzied mob old Dr. Sam rushes to the office of Mr. Harris, one of the foremost citizens of the white community. The colored doctor pleads for the life of his friend, begging the white man to intervene. Finally Harris wheels on the old man and says, "Sam, I'm the black man's friend. . . . But I've got to work in the set up we got down here. I'm no radical, no addlebrained red trying . . . to turn a hundred years upside down in a minute." Just then the telephone rings. Harris lifts the receiver. As he does so Dr. Sam replies quietly, *"It's been a long minute for the Negro."*

The first Negro slave was brought to our shores in 1619, and in one form or another his slavery has continued to the present hour. The American Negro has been the victim of our long minutes of hesitation, shortsightedness, and sadistic inhumanity. But, the clock on the wall ticks on. The fool says, "Time will take care of these matters." Time takes care of nothing! Only persons *in time* can function redemptively. We are such persons. In the name of Jesus Christ let us, then, turn long minutes of humiliation, and suffering into "the time of the Lord," when justice and righteousness will prevail as the ethic of the cross is related to the most grievous scandal of the here and now.

# 2. love in action

## MARTIN LUTHER KING, JR.

*The name Martin Luther King is synonymous with the non-violent demonstrations which have largely characterized the civil rights movement in this country. Dr. King came into national prominence as the leader of the successful Montgomery "walk for freedom" in 1956 and has since led long-term demonstrations in Albany, Georgia; Birmingham, Alabama; and St. Augustine, Florida. He is founder and president of the Southern Christian Leadership Conference and the co-pastor of the Ebenezer Baptist Church in Atlanta. He was formerly the pastor of the Dexter Avenue Baptist Church in Montgomery.*

*Dr. King was educated at Morehouse College (A.B.), Crozer Theological Seminary (B.D.), and Boston University (Ph.D.). He has received several honorary degrees, and numerous honors and awards have been bestowed upon him, including "Man of the Year" by Time, Inc., for 1963, and the 1964 Nobel Peace Prize. He has written three books and many articles. His sermon "Love in Action" was written while in a Georgia jail.*

Then said Jesus, Father, forgive them; for they know not what they do.     (Luke 23:34 KJV.)

Few words in the New Testament more clearly and solemnly express the magnanimity of Jesus' spirit than that sublime utterance from the cross, "Father, forgive them; for they know not what they do." This is love at its best.

We shall not fully understand the great meaning of Jesus' prayer unless we first notice that the text opens with the word "then." The verse immediately preceding reads thus: "And when they were come to the place, which is called Calvary, there they crucified him, and the malefactors, one on the right hand, and the other on the left." Then said Jesus, Father, forgive them. *Then*—when he was being plunged into the abyss of nagging agony. *Then*—when man had stooped to his worst. *Then*—when he was dying, a most ignominious death. *Then*—when the wicked hands of the creature had dared to crucify the only begotten Son of the Creator. Then said Jesus, "Father, forgive them." That "then" might well have been otherwise. He could have said, "Father, get even with them," or "Father, let loose the mighty thunderbolts of righteous wrath and destroy them," or "Father, open the flood gates of justice and permit the staggering avalanche of retribution to pour upon them." But none of these was his response. Though subjected to inexpressible agony, suffering excruciating pain, and despised and rejected, nevertheless, he cried, "Father, forgive them."

Let us take note of two basic lessons to be gleaned from this text.

## I

First, it is a marvelous expression of Jesus' ability to match words with actions. One of the great tragedies of life is that men seldom bridge the gulf between practice and profession, between doing and saying. A persistent schizophrenia leaves so many of us tragically divided against ourselves. On the one hand, we proudly profess certain sublime and noble principles, but on the other hand, we sadly practice the very antithesis of those principles. How often are our lives characterized by a high blood pressure of creeds and an anemia of deeds! We talk eloquently about our commitment to the principles of Christianity, and yet our lives are saturated with the practices of paganism. We proclaim our devotion to democracy, but we sadly practice the very opposite of the democratic creed. We talk passionately about peace, and at the same time we assiduously prepare for war. We make our fervent pleas for the high road of justice, and then we tread unflinchingly the low road of injustice. This strange dichotomy, this agonizing gulf between the *ought* and the *is*, represents the tragic theme of man's earthly pilgrimage.

But in the life of Jesus we find that the gulf is bridged. Never in history was there a more sublime example of the consistency of word and deed. During his ministry in the sunny villages of Galilee, Jesus talked passionately about forgiveness. This strange doctrine awakened the questioning mind of Peter. "How oft," he asked, "shall my brother sin against me, and I forgive him? till seven times?" Peter wanted to be legal and statistical. But Jesus responded by affirming that there is no limit to forgiveness. "I say not unto thee, Until seven times: but, Until seventy times seven." In other words, forgiveness is not a matter of quantity, but of quality. A man cannot forgive up to four hundred and ninety times without forgiveness becoming a part of the habit structure of his being. Forgiveness is not an occasional act; it is a permanent attitude.

Jesus also admonished his followers to love their enemies and to pray for them that despitefully used them. This teaching fell upon the ears of many of his hearers like a strange music from a foreign land. Their ears were not attuned to the tonal qualities of such amazing love. They had been taught to love their friends and hate their enemies. Their lives had been conditioned to seek redress in the time-honored tradition of retaliation. Yet Jesus taught them that only through a creative love for their enemies could they be children of their Father in heaven and also that love and forgiveness were absolute necessities for spiritual maturity.

The moment of testing emerges. Christ, the innocent Son of God, is stretched in painful agony on an uplifted cross. What place

24

is there for love and forgiveness now? How will Jesus react? What will he say? The answer to these questions bursts forth in majestic splendor. Jesus lifts his thorn-crowned head and cries in words of cosmic proportions: "Father, forgive them; for they know not what they do." This was Jesus' finest hour; this was his heavenly response to his earthly rendezvous with destiny.

We sense the greatness of this prayer by contrasting it with nature, which caught in the finality of her own impersonal structure, does not forgive. In spite of the agonizing pleas of men trapped in the path of an onrushing hurricane or the anguishing cry of the builder falling from the scaffold, nature expresses only a cold, serene, and passionless indifference. She must honor everlastingly her fixed, immutable laws. When these laws are violated, she has no alternative except to follow inexorably her path of uniformity. Nature does not and cannot forgive.

Or contrast Jesus' prayer with the slowness of man to forgive. We live according to the philosophy that life is a matter of getting even and of saving face. We bow before the altar of revenge. Samson, eyeless at Gaza, prays fervently for his enemies—but only for their utter destruction. The potential beauty of human life is constantly made ugly by man's ever-recurring song of retaliation.

Or contrast the prayer with a society that is even less prone to forgive. Society must have its standards, norms, and mores. It must have its legal checks and judicial restraints. Those who fall below the standards and those who disobey the laws are often left in a dark abyss of condemnation and have no hope for a second chance. Ask an innocent young lady, who, after a moment of overriding passion, becomes the mother of an illegitimate child. She will tell you that society is slow to forgive. Ask a public official, who, in a moment's carelessness, betrays the public trust. He will tell you that society is slow to forgive. Go to any prison and ask the inhabitants, who have written shameful lines across the pages of their lives. From behind the bars they will tell you that society is slow to forgive. Make your way to death row and speak with the tragic victims of criminality. As they prepare to make their pathetic walk to the electric chair, their hopeless cry is that society will not forgive. Capital punishment is society's final assertion that it will not forgive.

Such is the persistent story of mortal life. The oceans of history are made turbulent by the ever-rising tides of revenge. Man has never risen above the injunction of the *lex talionis:* "Life for life, eye for eye, tooth for tooth, hand for hand, foot for foot." In spite of the fact that the law of revenge solves no social problems, men continue to follow its disastrous leading. History is cluttered with the wreckage of nations and individuals that pursued this self-defeating path.

Jesus eloquently affirmed from the cross a higher law. He knew that the old eye-for-an-eye philosophy would leave everyone blind. He did not seek to overcome evil with evil. He overcame evil with good. Although crucified by hate, he responded with aggressive love.

What a magnificent lesson! Generations will rise and fall; men will continue to worship the god of revenge and bow before the altar of retaliation; but ever and again this noble lesson of Calvary will be a nagging reminder that only goodness can drive out evil and only love can conquer hate.

II

A second lesson comes to us from Jesus' prayer on the cross. It is an expression of Jesus' awareness of man's intellectual and spiritual blindness. "They know not what they do," said Jesus. Blindness was their trouble; enlightenment was their need. We must recognize that Jesus was nailed to the cross not simply by sin but also by blindness. The men who cried, "Crucify him," were not bad men but rather blind men. The jeering mob that lined the roadside which led to Calvary was composed not of evil people but of blind people. They knew not what they did. What a tragedy!

History reverberates with testimonies of this shameful tragedy. Centuries ago a sage named Socrates was forced to drink hemlock. The men who called for his death were not bad men with demonic blood running through their veins. On the contrary, they were sincere and respectable citizens of Greece. They genuinely thought that Socrates was an atheist because his idea of God had a philosophical depth that probed beyond traditional concepts. Not badness but blindness killed Socrates. Saul was not an evil-intentioned man when he persecuted Christians. He was a sincere, conscientious devotee of Israel's faith. He thought he was right. He persecuted Christians, not because he was devoid of integrity, but because he was devoid of enlightenment. The Christians who engaged in infamous persecutions and shameful inquisitions were not evil men but misguided men. The churchmen who felt that they had an edict from God to withstand the progress of science, whether in the form of a Copernician revolution or a Darwinian theory of natural selection, were not mischievous men but misinformed men. And so Christ's words from the cross are written in sharp-etched terms across some of the most inexpressible tragedies of history: "They know not what they do."

This tragic blindness expresses itself in many ominous ways in our own day. Some men still feel that war is the answer to the problems of the world. They are not evil people. On the contrary, they are good, respectable citizens whose ideas are robed in the garments of patriotism. They talk of brinkmanship and a balance of terror. They sincerely feel that a continuation of the arms race will be conducive to more beneficent than maleficent consequences. So they passionately call for bigger bombs, larger nuclear stockpiles, and faster ballistic missiles.

Wisdom born of experience should tell us that war is obsolete. There may have been a time when war served as a negative good by preventing the spread and growth of an evil force, but the destructive power of modern weapons eliminates even the possibility that war may serve as a negative good. If we assume that life is worth living and that man has a right to survival, then we must find an alternative to war. In a day when vehicles hurtle through outer space and guided ballistic missiles carve highways of death through the stratosphere, no nation can claim victory in war. A so-called limited war will leave little more than a calamitous legacy of human suffering, political turmoil, and spiritual disillusionment. A world war—God forbid!—will leave only smouldering ashes as a mute testimony of a human race whose folly led inexorably to untimely death. Yet there are those who sincerely feel that disarmament is an evil and international negotiation is an abominable waste of time. Our world is threatened by the grim prospect of atomic annihilation because there are still too many men who know not what they do.

Notice, too, how the truth of this text is revealed in race relations. Slavery in America was perpetuated not merely by human badness but also by human blindness. True, the causal basis for the system of slavery must to a large extent be traced back to the economic factor. Men convinced themselves that a system which was so economically profitable must be morally justifiable. They formulated elaborate theories of racial superiority. Their rationalizations clothed obvious wrongs in the beautiful garments of righteousness. This tragic attempt to give moral sanction to an economically profitable system gave birth to the doctrine of white supremacy. Religion and the Bible were cited to crystallize the status quo. Science was commandeered to prove the biological inferiority of the Negro. Even philosophical logic was manipulated to give intellectual credence to the system of slavery. Someone formulated the argument of the inferiority of the Negro according to the framework of an Aristotelian syllogism:

> All men are made in the image of God;
> God, as everyone knows, is not a Negro;
> Therefore, the Negro is not a man.

So men conveniently twisted the insights of religion, science, and philosophy to give sanction to the doctrine of white supremacy. Soon this idea was imbedded in every textbook and preached in practically every pulpit. It became a structured part of the culture. And men then embraced this philosophy, not as the rationalization of a lie, but as the expression of a final truth. They sincerely came to believe that the Negro was inferior by nature and that slavery

28

was ordained by God. In 1857, the system of slavery was given its greatest legal support by the deliberations of the Supreme Court of the United States in the Dred Scott decision. The Court affirmed that the Negro had no rights which the white man was bound to respect. The justices who rendered this decision were not wicked men. On the contrary, they were decent and dedicated men. But they were victims of spiritual and intellectual blindness. They knew not what they did. The whole system of slavery was largely perpetuated by sincere though spiritually ignorant persons.

This tragic blindness is also found in racial segregation, the not-too-distant cousin of slavery. Some of the most vigorous defenders of segregation are sincere in their beliefs and earnest in their motives. Although some men are segregationists merely for reasons of political expediency and economic gain, not all of the resistance to integration is the rear-guard action of professional bigots. Some people feel that their attempt to preserve segregation is best for themselves, their children, and their nation. Many are good church people, anchored in the religious faith of their mothers and fathers. Pressed for a religious vindication for their conviction, they will even argue that God was the first segregationist. "Red birds and blue birds don't fly together," they contend. Their views about segregation, they insist, can be rationally explained and morally justified. Pressed for a justification of their belief in the inferiority of the Negro, they turn to some pseudoscientific writing and argue that the Negro's brain is smaller than the white man's brain. They do not know, or they refuse to know, that the idea of an inferior or superior race has been refuted by the best evidence of the science of anthropology. Great anthropologists, like Ruth Benedict, Margaret Mead, and Melville J. Herskovits, agree that, although there may be inferior and superior individuals within all races, there is no superior or inferior race. And segregationists refuse to acknowledge that science has demonstrated that there are four types of blood and that these four types are found within every racial group. They blindly believe in the eternal validity of an evil called segregation and the timeless truth of a myth called white supremacy. What

29

a tragedy! Millions of Negroes have been crucified by conscientious blindness. With Jesus on the cross, we must look lovingly at our oppressors and say, "Father, forgive them; for they know not what they do."

## III

From all that I have attempted to say it should now be apparent that sincerity and conscientiousness in themselves are not enough. History has proven that these noble virtues may degenerate into tragic vices. Nothing in all the world is more dangerous than sincere ignorance and conscientious stupidity. Shakespeare wrote:

> For sweetest things turn sourest by their deeds;
> Lilies that fester smell far worse than weeds.

As the chief moral guardian of the community, the church must implore men to be good and well-intentioned and must extol the virtues of kindheartedness and conscientiousness. But somewhere along the way the church must remind men that devoid of intelligence, goodness and conscientiousness will become brutal forces leading to shameful crucifixions. Never must the church tire of reminding men that they have a moral responsibility to be intelligent.

Must we not admit that the church has often overlooked this moral demand for enlightenment? At times it has talked as though ignorance were a virtue and intelligence a crime. Through its obscurantism, closemindedness, and obstinancy to new truth the church has often unconsciously encouraged its worshipers to look askance upon intelligence.

But if we are to call ourselves Christians, we had better avoid intellectual and moral blindness. Throughout the New Testament we are reminded of the need for enlightenment. We are commanded to love God, not only with our hearts and souls, but also with our minds. When the Apostle Paul noticed the blindness of many of his opponents, he said, "I bear them record that they have

30

a zeal of God, but not according to knowledge." Over and again the Bible reminds us of the danger of zeal without knowledge and sincerity without intelligence.

So we have a mandate both to conquer sin and also to conquer ignorance. Modern man is presently having a rendezvous with chaos, not merely because of human badness, but also because of human stupidity. If Western civilization continues to degenerate until it, like twenty-four of its predecessors, falls hopelessly into a bottomless void, the cause will be not only its undeniable sinfulness, but also its appalling blindness. And if American democracy gradually disintegrates, it will be due as much to a lack of insight as to a lack of commitment to right. If modern man continues to flirt unhesitatingly with war and eventually transforms his earthly habitat into an inferno such as even the mind of Dante could not imagine, it will have resulted from downright badness and also from downright stupidity.

"They know not what they do," said Jesus. Blindness was their besetting trouble. And the crux of the matter lies here: we do need to be blind. Unlike physical blindness that is usually inflicted upon individuals as a result of natural forces beyond their control, intellectual and moral blindness is a dilemma which man inflicts upon himself by his tragic misuse of freedom and his failure to use his mind to its fullest capacity. One day we will learn that the heart can never be totally right if the head is totally wrong. This is not to say that the head can be right if the heart is wrong. Only through the bringing together of head and heart—intelligence and goodness —shall man rise to a fulfillment of his true nature. Neither is this to say that one must be a philosopher or a possessor of extensive academic training before he can achieve the good life. I know many people of limited formal training who have amazing intelligence and foresight. The call for intelligence is a call for open-mindedness, sound judgment, and love for truth. It is a call for men to rise above the stagnation of closedmindedness and the paralysis of gullibility. One does not need to be a profound scholar to be open-

31

minded, nor a keen academician to engage in an assiduous pursuit for truth.

Light has come into the world. A voice crying through the vista of time calls men to walk in the light. Man's earthly life will become a tragic cosmic elegy if he fails to heed this call. "This is the condemnation," says John, "that light is come into the world, and men loved darkness rather than light."

Jesus was right about those men who crucified him. They knew not what they did. They were inflicted with a terrible blindness.

Every time I look at the cross I am reminded of the greatness of God and the redemptive power of Jesus Christ. I am reminded of the beauty of sacrificial love and the majesty of unswerving devotion to truth. It causes me to say with John Bowring:

> In the cross of Christ I glory,
> Towering o'er the wrecks of time;
> All the light of sacred story
> Gathers round its head sublime.

It would be wonderful were I to look at the cross and sense only such a sublime reaction. But somehow I can never turn my eyes from that cross without also realizing that it symbolizes a strange mixture of greatness and smallness, of good and evil. As I behold that uplifted cross I am reminded not only of the unlimited power of God, but also of the sordid weakness of man. I think not only of the radiance of the divine, but also of the tang of the human. I am reminded not only of Christ at his best, but of man at his worst.

We must see the cross as the magnificent symbol of love conquering hate and of light overcoming darkness. But in the midst of this glowing affirmation, let us never forget that our Lord and Master was nailed to that cross because of human blindness. Those who crucified him knew not what they did.

# 3. a question of belonging

WILLIAM SLOANE COFFIN, JR.

*William Sloane Coffin has been university chaplain and pastor of the Church of Christ at Yale University since 1958. He is a graduate of Yale University (B.A.) and Yale Divinity School (B.D.) and was chaplain at Phillips Academy and Williams College before coming to Yale. Mr. Coffin's fluency in several languages led him into liaison work with the French and the Russians during World War II and the Korean War. When the Peace Corps was started in early 1961 Coffin was named an adviser, and later he became the first director of the Peace Corps' Field Training Center in Puerto Rico. In 1962 he was one of the one hundred men in America under forty years old selected by Life Magazine as outstanding in "the take-over generation." Articles from his pen have appeared in leading journals.*

*In May, 1961, Coffin was one of seven "Freedom Riders" arrested in Montgomery, Alabama, while protesting local Southern segregation laws and arguing that such laws were in conflict with the integration ruling of the U. S. Supreme Court. The group was found guilty of unlawful assembly and disturbance of the peace in the local courts, but it is appealing the decision. Because of his belief that the church in this country has been remiss in assuming its prophetic role, Coffin has been active in many social and political issues.*

33

*This sermon, "A Question of Belonging," was preached in Battell Chapel, Yale University.*

> For by one spirit we were all baptized into one body—Jews or Greeks, slaves or free—and all were made to drink of one Spirit.     (I Cor. 12:13.)

On the occasion of T. S. Eliot's seventy-fifth birthday W. H. Auden wrote him to this effect: "Because you found the right words to interpret our situation to us, you prevented our fear from becoming panic."

What a wonderful tribute, and what a wonderful role, not only for an artist, but also for the churches to play—for finally what other answer is there to the question, "Why should a man go to church?" than simply, "To hear the truth," to hear the word of God interpreted to the life of the age?

"You prevented our fear from becoming panic." According to C. Vann Woodward 1945 marked the end of free security, the security long afforded Americans by the Atlantic, the Pacific, and the Ice Cap. The end of this security, he suggested, is going to have an effect on the American character comparable to that caused by the end of free land in the 1890's. Add to the loss of free security the loss of confidence the world over in traditional political, economic, moral, and even esthetic structures; and add to these losses the realization that the test-ban treaty has only slightly thickened the single hair holding up the sword of Damocles—add up all these features of our contemporary situation and is it surprising that America the beautiful has become America the insecure? With real nostalgia one can recall the good old days of F.D.R. when we had nothing to fear but fear itself.

But who is finding the right words to interpret our situation to us—who apart from artists like Eliot and Auden; and certain wonderful theologians like Tillich, with his understanding of sin as estrangement from self, neighbor, and God, and like Bonhoeffer

34

who has written, and in his own blood, of the Christian style of life in a world, as he puts it, "come of age"?

Certainly the politicians are of little help, with their familiar and now inept jargon, calling one and the same thing now "government interference," now "guided capitalism," depending on whose ox is being gored at the moment. And while some theologians are helpful, most churches are not. Church bells, far from calling men to hear the truth, generally produce a sort of Pavlovian piety, the sworn enemy of intellectual integrity. Or when churches try to be honest they are generally honest in too limited a context of responsibility. Our stronger churches are now in the suburbs, and the trouble with the suburbs is not that they are sub-urban, but that they are anti-urban. They are residential communities deliberately segregating themselves not only geographically, but socially and culturally as well from the economic and political structures of our society. As Gibson Winter has dramatically pointed out in his book *The Suburban Captivity of the Churches* the churches are so preoccupied by the concerns of middle-class domesticity that they are irresponsible towards the total context of American life.

As a corrective, then, let us try to think of American life as a whole and to see if there are not biblical insights that can interpret our situation to us in such a way as to prevent our current fear from becoming panic. 1323748

It seems to me that society the world over is operating today on two sensationally new bases. Since the time of Paul we have progressed from slavery through serfdom, feudalism, and aristocracy to legal equality. From the presupposition of slavery society has moved to the presupposition of freedom, for today everyone has to pay lip service at least to the notion of national and individual equality. In the second place we have moved from a time of personal and national independence—functionally speaking—to a day of striking interdependence, with the result that more and more society is looking like an organism—diversity through unity.

At first glance this fact should hardly strike panic in the breasts of Christians. Does not Paul himself write of the church as an

35

organism, as a body with many members, all of which are "inspired by one and the same Spirit"? But just how committed to this Christian insight are American Christians? It seems to me that while our personal—i.e., suburban—lives have been informed by Christian insights our public life has reflected far more a form of social Darwinism, the philosophical rationale for the free enterprise system, a philosophy stressing the survival of the fittest and hence one more interested in dividing than in uniting the various members of society.

To be sure, as a coherent theory social Darwinism has been discredited by the great depression and subsequent regressions. But while discredited, it has not been rejected, certainly not by many Yale alumni, whose pulses still quicken to these succinct words of that great Yale professor of yore, William Graham Sumner: "If we do not like the survival of the fittest, we have only one possible alternative, and that is the survival of the unfittest. The former is the law of civilization, the latter is the law of anti-civilization."

To be sure, also, Christian influence and a certain balance of power have tempered this view so that the "have nots" now have at least a little. But the churches have not consistently and openly challenged social Darwinism on the crucial question, which is not a question of men's having or not having but of their belonging to one another. "For by one Spirit we were all baptized into one body."

From a Christian point of view all members of society *belong* to one another. God made them that way and Christ died to keep them that way, and our sin is that through our suburban lives, through our treatment of the aged, the sick, the criminal, the poor, through our exclusion of those who cannot fulfill a utilitarian purpose, which alone gives men value according to the tenets of social Darwinism, we are trying to put asunder what God has joined together. And our fear is turning into panic because we know at some level of our being that God will not be mocked. For we are, to use Tillich's term, estranging ourselves from that from which we cannot finally be estranged. We are attempting to split at the circumference of life that which cannot be split at the center. Am I my brother's keeper? No, I am my brother's brother. "For by one Spirit we were all baptized into one body."

Christianity never supplies blueprints, something we have to keep telling ourselves—those of us who feel the Lord's annointed will one day appear in the ranks of the Democratic party and those of us who feel he already has appeared in the right wing of the GOP, clearly God's faithful remnant! But while Christianity does not give specific answers to specific social problems, it does shed light on these problems, and each of us must try as best he can to carry his Christian insights out into the streets and byways of life. So let us spend a few minutes trying to apply this truth of our oneness to two concrete questions: The question of property rights and the question of the poor, both questions vital to the present civil rights struggle.

At the end of the mythological story of the Fall—the truth of a myth being an eternally contemporary truth—as Adam and Eve are being rather brutally ejected from the Garden, we read this touching line, "And the Lord God made for Adam and for his wife garments of skins, and clothed them." Now this statement illumines not only marital but social relations as well. (And here I am indebted to Paul Ramsey of Princeton.) Were all of us as innocent as were Adam and Eve before the Fall, we could, like them, live in direct uninhibited relationship one with another. But in a fallen world for our own protection we need to be distanced from one another. In a fallen world absolute oneness leads either to an excess of submission—I identify myself with you—or to an excess of imperialism—I identify you with me. So these garments of skin that the Lord gives Adam and Eve can indicate the rightness of private ownership in social relations. But the question of ownership must not obscure the more important question of *use*. "To each is given the manifestation of the Spirit for the common good." We must remember that Adam and Eve are clothed in order to facilitate their relationship. Men are distanced not in order to be separated, but in order the better to be related. Private property is good not because of the precariousness of our separate existences, but because of the

37

precariousness of our life together. We have, only in order to belong, in order to belong to the one body into which we were baptized by one Spirit. Thus the question of ownership is always subordinate to the question of use, and property rights at a minimum should always reflect and not reject human rights.

As an ancient story sheds light on the problem of property, so a modern one illumines our treatment of the poor. In a deeply disturbing book, *Dark Eye in Africa*, Laurens Van der Post describes a conversation with the Governor General of Java in 1948, at a time when the Indonesians were pressing hard for the Dutch to leave. The Governor General could not understand. "Look what we have done for them. Look at the schools and hospitals. . . . A hundred years ago the population was only a few millions, today it is nearly sixty millions. We have done away with malaria, plague and dysentery. . . . We have given them an honest and efficient administration and abolished civil war and piracy. Look at the roads, the railways, the industries—and yet they want us to go. Can you tell me why they want us to go?"

"I'm afraid," replied Van der Post, "it is because you've never had the right look in the eye when you spoke to them."

Again the question of having is confused with the question of belonging. Think of the millions we have spent in slum clearance, moving people out of wood and into brick and mortar, and with what result? Instead of "slum dwellers" we now have "project people"—and we still have the wrong look in the eye. We think the problem is to get people out of the slums, but instead, the basic problem is to get the slums out of the people—the apathy and resentment that a sense of exclusion breeds. How is this to be done? Not by a charity which gives from within the circle to those without; not by relief programs which manage to keep men alive while depriving them of the possibility of human dignity; but by far more —by concretely asserting our solidarity with the lives of men whose dignity we preach. Why shouldn't we too, for instance, live in the slums, being lawyers, doctors, teachers, ministers, for the poor, or at least pledge a large portion of our extracurricular or extra-vocational time to the valiant efforts of urban renewal? This we can do without condescension if we remember what we have read: "God has so adjusted the body, giving the greater honor to the inferior part, that there may be no discord in the body." This I read to mean that the poor are not so much a problem to us as we are a problem to them.

"For by one Spirit we were all baptized into one body." Diversity through unity—a question not of having, but of belonging, a question really of receiving and giving for

> All things come of Thee, O Lord,
> And of Thine own have we given Thee.

Only those holding this view are fit. Only they survive in any meaningful sense. "For what does it profit a man, to gain the whole world and forfeit his life?"

In the Holy Land are two ancient bodies of water. Both are fed by the Jordan River. In one fish play and roots find sustenance. In the other there is no splash of fish, no sound of bird, no leaf around. The difference is not in the river Jordan for it empties into both, but in the Sea of Galilee, because for every drop taken in one goes out. It gives and lives. The other gives nothing and is, therefore, called the Dead Sea.

"For by one Spirit we were all baptized into one body—Jews or Greeks, slaves or free—and all were made to drink of one Spirit."

# 4. god's plan:
## to unite all things in christ

JOSEPH W. ELLWANGER

*Joseph Ellwanger is pastor of St. Paul Lutheran Church in Bir-
mingham, Alabama, his first charge after receiving his education from
Concordia College (B.A.) and Concordia Seminary (B.D. and M.S.T.).
St. Paul is located in a Negro community, and thus Mr. Ellwanger has
had an opportunity to serve in the midst of the struggle for racial
equality. He has been chairman of Birmingham's Council on Human
Relations and was the only white member of the committee which
initiated and carried out the demonstrations begun in Birmingham in
the spring of 1963. He is the pastor of the parents of one of the four
girls killed in the tragic church bombing on September 15, 1963.*

> He has made known . . . his purpose which he set
> forth in Christ . . . to unite all things in him.
> (Eph. 1:9-10.)

A young, seminary-trained, dedicated pastor startled me with
this carefully-thought-out position on the racial issue—and he was
taking this position in the midst of a fierce racial storm in his own
city:

40

## god's plan: to unite all things in christ

I don't see why the church is suddenly so interested in integration. There was a time when the church said nothing at all about this matter. Or if it did speak, it often preached segregation—because that was the thing to do. I think the only reason why church officials and church periodicals are speaking out in favor of integration today is because it is the melody that happens to be in the air. They're just jumping on the political and sociological bandwagon of the day.

As far as I am concerned, you can be a good Christian—and be a segregationist or an integrationist. Segregation and integration are two types of culture, and you can be a Christian in either of them. I don't think the church has any business supporting the one or the other.

There are two things about this young pastor's statement that ought to disturb us. First, his judgment that some Christians are favoring integration simply because it is the thing to do undoubtedly is correct in some instances. It ought to disturb us that the motivation of Christians working toward an integrated church in an integrated society is often little different from the motivation of the non-Christian who is working toward an integrated society.

But even more disturbing is the young pastor's conviction that God is neutral toward segregation and integration. If this is correct, then segregation is not morally wrong, and the Christian has no responsibility to uphold or to oppose segregation. He can honestly forget about the whole issue—and go on about his business.

It is important for us as followers of the Christ to see clearly that God is not neutral toward segregation—nor can we be neutral— because, as Paul wrote several times in his letter to the Ephesians, it is God's plan to unite all things in Christ.

To fully grasp God's great plan for unity in Christ we must first see what made this plan necessary—the fragmentation and the disunity that man has insisted on down through the years.

Ever since the first man and woman broke their relationship with God and with each other man has been working overtime to shatter the unity designed by God from the time of creation.

We foolishly think that by withdrawing ourselves from God and living for ourselves and our family we will achieve the security and

41

the happiness that we are looking for. We call this withdrawal from God by many names—materialism, self-centeredness, faithlessness, secularism. But always it means that we are breaking our oneness with God.

Like a chain reaction, when we pull ourselves away from God we begin pulling ourselves loose from the people who were made by him and who are loved by him. Jealousy, envy, pride, hatred, prejudice, coldness, fickleness, suspicion—all run like a cancerous infection in man's bloodstream. And all of them separate—husband from wife, neighbor from neighbor, family from family, clan from clan, nation from nation, race from race.

And so plans to divide and shatter the family of man have been devised through the years—all expressions of men who have broken away from God and therefore have no more concern for God's plan of unity.

Many Jews at the time of Paul were contributing their part to the brokenness of man. They had taken God's prohibitions against intermarriage with Gentiles as a command hinging on racial and ethnic considerations rather than on religious considerations. God gave these commands because he did not want the unbelieving Gentiles to "turn away your sons from following me." (See Deut. 7:3, 4) He wanted to keep Israel strong in the faith, ready for the coming of Christ.

But it was an easy twist of the mind for the Jews to begin to think themselves better than everyone else, to remain separate from unbelieving Gentiles on all levels of life, and to make a distinction between Jew and Gentile even when the Gentile became a believer. The natural pride of the flesh had an easy time of developing the attitude that "we are to be separate from Gentiles because we are superior people who do not want to contaminate ourselves by contact with the Gentiles."

The Book of Jonah in the Old Testament is the prophetic voice calling Israel to a different kind of relationship with the Gentiles— a relationship in which Israel would energetically carry God's word to the Gentiles—even to such a place as the wicked Gentile city of

42

Nineveh. Israel's general attitude toward Gentiles, symbolized by Jonah's refusal to take the word of God to Nineveh, was one of disdain, or at best indifference.

It was this kind of aloof attitude that Paul faced in almost every Mediterranean city where he attempted to establish a Christian congregation—and where there were both Jews and Gentiles. It was this feeling of superiority, buttressed by real differences in the observance of Old Testament ceremonial laws, that separated Jewish and Gentile Christians in most of Paul's fledgling congregations.

And so Paul did not write these transcendent first three chapters of Ephesians on God's unifying purpose in Jesus Christ because he just happened to pull the topic out of his theological bag. He wrote it because Jewish and Gentile Christian were not getting along together. Jewish Christians were demanding that the Gentile Christians do certain things before they would consider accepting them on their level, and Gentile Christians were becoming skeptical about "this Jewish religion" where the Jews were holding themselves on a privileged level.

It does not take much imagination to reconstruct the suspicion and rumor and rationalization and emotionalism that permeated such a situation. It is clear that the varying degrees of discrimination that existed between Jew and Gentile in the early church were a part of the sinful thread of man's separation from God and from his fellow man that ruins God's design of unity for human history. This is not just a matter of yesteryear. Were Paul writing today he would have the same need to write the same letter on God's plan of unity. In our country the class lines that creep into the church are horrible breaches of God's great plan of oneness. The flight of the churches to the suburbs, the subtle coldness toward people from across the tracks, the failure to evangelize certain communities because "they aren't our kind and wouldn't take to the gospel anyway," the complete indifference to the physical needs of the economically deprived—all register the class consciousness which shatters the unity of the body of Christ.

Even more devastating than the class barrier in the church is the

43

racial barrier. It is still possible for a Negro woman in Pittsburgh to say, "I would like to go to a particular church in my community, but I go across town to church because I know I would meet with the rebuffs and coldness of the world at the church in my neighborhood." Congregations in the South are still seceding from their respective church bodies rather than participate with them in the burial of segregation. Pastors are still losing their pulpits because they are becoming too articulate in the scriptural application of the gospel to the racial situation. There are still all-white churches in a sea of darker peoples.

There are still Christians who sense no responsibility in working earnestly to eliminate racial barriers in society—in employment, housing, education, voting, and the like. Surely there is no need to document the shameful existence of obvious and subtle racial walls right in Christ's church.

The more difficult and the more important point to see, however, is that all this racial difference and prejudice separates and is contrary to God's plan of unity. It is not a matter of social preference. It is not a matter of the right to choose one's closest friends as one pleases. It is not a matter of how to reach the most people with the gospel without hurting too many persons' feelings and without jeopardizing the financial support of the highest contributing member. It is not a matter of public relations—keeping a "good image" in the community. It is not a matter to be decided by the majority or by the prevailing winds of opinion in the community. It is not a neutral issue that may be decided either way.

Racial prejudice, discrimination, and segregation are going against the plan of the almighty and loving God who created man in unity and sent his Son to restore that unity. Racial bias shatters the unity of believers, hurts both oppressor and oppressed, and blasphemes the crucified and risen Christ who died to make men one.

No man can recognize another man as his brother in Christ, truly love him, and then add, "But why don't you go to your own church?

44

"And don't you dare send your children to school with my children.

"And if you have trouble getting a decent job because of the color of your skin that's too bad. We all have our obstacles.

"If you have trouble registering to vote, keep trying. Times will change.

"And don't embarrass my wife and me by coming over to our house with your family.

"If I see you out in public you understand why I will not be able to shake hands with you.

"True enough, you will not be able to go into restaurants and hotels with me, but you will understand that too, of course.

"I'm all for your having your constitutional rights like me, but don't push so hard. Some people don't like that.

"And I know you've got a raw deal in our country, but don't ever let me catch you bitter, or angry, or sullen.

"I know, too, that the injustices of racial discrimination are part of the reason for the higher incidence of crime in your community, but you know that we cannot remove the injustices until all of you shape up.

"And whatever you do, don't ever let me catch your teenage son talking with my teenage daughter. You ought to know better than that."

It is completely laughable to talk about such thinking as love—or to talk about such thinking as though it were in keeping with God's plan of unity. To the contrary, it is hatred. It pulverizes the spirit of the person who is the object of the prejudice, and it saps the spiritual vitality of the prejudiced. It shatters God's plan for unity.

But for all of man's fracturing of God's intentions, it is still God's plan to pull together all things in Christ.

That God in his mercy should plan to do this indicates the depth of his displeasure with the fragmentation of the human family. Surely God had to see all this brokenness of man as a contradiction

45

of all that he had planned for man—or else the sending of Christ to pick up the broken pieces would not have been necessary.

God's plan of heading up all things in Christ also indicates the nature of the problem. The problem of man's broken relations with his fellow man is more than a matter of bad manners that can eventually be rectified by education. It is more than simply a lack of cultural progress. It is a matter of a broken relationship with God. A matter so deep that only God, entering the arena of human history in the person of his Son and mending that relationship with himself, can really get to the bottom of man's ancient problem.

God's amazing plan also shows the depth of his conviction that man—for all his hatred and separation and prejudice—can be brought back together into the unified whole that he had intended in creation.

God's plan, said Paul, is to "head up all things," "to unite all things," "to consummate all things," in Jesus Christ. God was in Christ not only reaching down his hand to the individual person to rescue him from his own self-centeredness and to lift him into a living relationship with himself. But he was also reaching his arms around all humanity and all history and gathering it together into one throbbing, meaningful whole. Of course there are those who may wiggle out of God's sweeping, unifying armreach. But those who remain discover life as it was intended to be—in intimate fellowship with God and with the other sons of God.

This is God's plan of unifying all things—and we cannot stress too hard the little phrase interjected so often by Paul, "in Christ." The whole plan was to unite all things "in him." "In him we have redemption through his blood" (1:7). "He has made known to us in all wisdom and insight the mystery of his will, according to his purpose which he set forth in Christ" (1:9). Surely Paul has in mind here the whole life, death, resurrection, ascension, and current lordship of Christ over heaven and earth.

It is in Christ that we get a glimpse of what God's great plan of unity really means. It is not just a resolution about unity broadcast from heaven. It is a unity lived out here on earth by Jesus Christ.

We see it to be a unity that always flows from the unity that already exists with the Father in heaven. A unity that seeks to identify with people in the depths of their needs—like the deep-seated needs of harlots and tax collectors. A unity that shares the total life of joys and sorrows, of wedding parties and funeral processions. A unity that constantly is willing to accept and forgive and use an impetuous Peter and a doubting Thomas. A unity that seeks to change the vicious patterns of landlords who overcharge the widows and the poverty stricken. A unity that is capable of hoping for a change—even in a Zaccheus.

But more than just seeing God's plan come into focus in the person and life of Jesus Christ, we can say that in him the plan begins actually to unfold in this cold world of broken human relationships. It is because of the unique act of forgiveness and reconciliation accomplished by the life and sacrificial death of Jesus Christ that man was reunited with his God and with his fellow man. This gracious act of forgiveness for the rebellion and of actual reunion is God's plan of unity—initiated and launched. It is all brought about through the person and work of Jesus Christ.

Now this magnificent plan of God's, which has been demonstrated and catapulted in Christ is continued and carried out through Christ's body, the church—"the fulness of him who fills all in all." It is not enough for us to say today that God's unifying plan is under way, so let it move on. In one sense God's great plan does move forward in spite of us, and even in spite of the church. We may do all we wish to block God's great plan. The church may foolishly try to weave the thread of racial prejudice and aloofness into the fabric of God's kingdom. But God will carry out his plan in spite of those who would crucify Christ anew.

Yet in the long run God carries out his plan set forth in Christ through the church—through people who have been reconciled to God and to one another. Just as people could look at Jesus' life and sense something of God's great plan of unity, so people ought to be able to look at the church and see the same amazing plan. The world ought to look at the church and see a group of people utterly

47

unconcerned about society's labels and living a visible unity. The world ought to see a group of people identifying themselves with the oppressed and the needy.

The church is Christ's body fulfilling God's plan of unity. It has the message of God's great reconciliation in Jesus Christ whereby men can be brought into this great plan, and it has the power of Christ himself, who is Lord of the church, to bring about lasting unity.

Now that God has made it clear what he wants—unity—the big question for each of us to face up to is, "Where are we in this great plan?"

Have we first of all unreservedly permitted God to sweep us up into his great reunion with himself and with our brothers? And do we clearly see that this gracious reconciliation is through Christ alone? Are we wholeheartedly fulfilling our role in the body of Christ to unify all things in him? Or are we frustrating God's great plans? Are we naïvely saying that "time will take care of things"? Or are we utilizing the time to fulfill God's transcendent plan of unity?

Does our congregation clearly portray to the world that in Jesus Christ class and race are of no consequence? Am I identifying myself with the oppressor and the oppressed and actively working to bring about justice in society as an extension of the body of him who identified himself with all men? Or am I just an onlooker as I see men, women, and youth struggling—even giving their lives for the cause of oneness in the church and justice in society? Am I working for the elimination of racial discrimination for the right reason—because it is God's great plan to unify all things in Jesus Christ?

At times God's plan of pulling together all the broken pieces in Jesus Christ seems like little more than a pipe dream. Surely Paul and the readers of Paul's letters must have felt despondent and frustrated as they were caught up in the realities of the brokenness of mankind. We are no different.

We would do well to say to one another what Paul said at the

48

end of the third chapter of Ephesians, after taking his readers on a breathtaking journey into the almost unbelievable possibilities for the unity of man through Jesus Christ: "Now to him who . . . is able to do far more abundantly than all that we ask or think, to him be glory in the church and in Christ Jesus to all generations for ever and ever. Amen."

# 5. on loving one's neighbor as oneself

### FRANCIS GERALD ENSLEY

*Bishop Ensley, one of America's most distinguished preachers, since 1952 has been Bishop of The Methodist Church, first in the Iowa Area and, beginning in mid-1964, in the Ohio Western Area. From 1938 to 1944 he was professor of homiletics at Boston University and for eight years was minister of the North Broadway Methodist Church in Columbus, Ohio. After graduation from Ohio Wesleyan University (A.B.) he pursued his theological studies at Boston University where he was awarded both the S.T.B. and the Ph.D. degrees. Four honorary degrees have been awarded to Dr. Ensley.*

*This sermon was delivered at the Second Methodist Conference on Human Relations in Chicago on August 26, 1963.*

"You shall love your neighbor as yourself."
(Matt. 19:19.)

Broadly speaking there are two ways of interpreting our text. The first is what we may call the *quantitative:* "You shall love your neighbor *as much as yourself.*" I will give as much concern for the other man's welfare as I do for my own. I shall seek his happiness with the same earnestness as my own. I shall endeavor to screen him from what may hurt him as truly as I seek to escape hurt myself. I shall treat the other man's good as intrinsically as valuable as my own good. The guiding principle is equality—50-50 all the way around.

This conception means—laudably—that my neighbor's rights are quite as worthy of regard as my own. But it could mean also "separate but equal" facilities! If the community spends as much on Negro schools as on white, then my conscience need not be troubled about segregation. If the Jim Crow car is as modern and well-furnished as my own I do not need to ride with my Negro brother, for I can tell myself that I am doing as well by him as I am by myself. Certainly "love" in this quantitative sense—really justice—still far exceeds our attainment. But is this what Christ died to make real?

There is a second possible interpretation of our text which I should call the *qualitative*. "You shall love your neighbor as yourself"—not as much as yourself, but *as though he were yourself*. It means tying my sensibilities to my neighbor's nerve endings so that I feel things as he does. It means crawling under my neighbor's skin and experiencing the world as he does. It means endeavoring to look at the world through his eyes. It means trying to comprehend *his reasons* for doing what he does. We tap people's telephones. Christian love presupposes the imaginative power necessary to tap what the other fellow is saying to himself. It means tuning in on the other man's aspirations. Christian love presupposes an imaginative sympathy with the joys, the pains, and the hopes of every man who crosses our path.

Christian love does not signify that we feel the same toward the casual acquaintance that we do toward our own flesh and blood. I do not imagine that Christ on the cross felt the same tenderness toward his enemies as he did toward his mother. Christian love does not mean that we approve of the other man or that sentiment makes law and discipline unnecessary. Christian love doesn't mean that we are candidates for marriage with anyone we meet—that putrid old herring that is always being dragged out when race is up for discussion. Christian love means, as Paul put it, being members one of another. By the power of imagination we are to share in the inner life of every human being with whom we deal. "You shall love your neighbor as yourself"—as though he were yourself.

Every true parent understands the meaning of what I am saying. A parent, physically speaking, is a distinct entity from his child. But nothing hurts the child that does not hurt the parent, because spiritually they are one organism. Did you ever sit through a piano recital when one of your youngsters was performing—and a bit shakily? Every bad note hits you as though someone were striking your spinal column with a mallet! Two bodies but one unit of sympathy! A great teacher has this imaginative power. As a recent biographer has put it with regard to "Copey" Copeland of Harvard, "He never needed to be told; he always sensed his pupils' difficulty." A great artist has this power. Isn't it interesting that we know so little about Shakespeare's life and personality despite his voluminous writing? He entered so skillfully into the mind of his every character, from Falstaff to Macbeth, that we do not know what his own philosophy was. How wonderfully Lincoln possessed this power to feel with the other man! When the Battle of Shiloh was at its height he hastened to the War Department, where he found the brother and sister-in-law of General Lew Wallace, who was in the thick of the fight. "Oh!" the sister-in-law exclaimed, with a sense of relief in her voice. "We had heard that a General Wallace was among the killed, and we were afraid it was *our* Wallace. But it wasn't."

"Ah," Lincoln replied, looking down into her face with sad eyes, "but it was *somebody's* Wallace." Everybody's Wallace belonged to him! "You shall love your neighbor as yourself"—love every person as though he were your very own.

I advance this interpretation of Christian love because it is so conspicuously absent when it comes to the question of race. We "feel for" the other person in our family or among our friends, or perhaps among our social class, but somehow the power of fellow feeling dies for so many of us at the color line. I don't think that we of the white race understand the burden of spirit which our Negro brethren carry. Have we ever projected ourselves into the Negro's place and asked how some of the experiences which are almost daily for him would feel to us? Have you ever thought how it would feel to be driven from a restaurant or a market when you had the money to pay just because your color was not right? What would it be like to be a world-famous scientist like George Washington Carver and to be required to ride on a freight elevator to address a learned society? How would you feel if you were required to live in a sixty-year-old house in need of repair and decoration, cold in winter and hot in summer, in a deteriorating neighborhood conveniently located to a smoking factory or the animal smells of a stockyard, because custom will not permit you to live elsewhere? I wonder how many of us appreciate in the most remote way the aspiration of the colored people of the world for the advantages that we take for granted. Did you notice the article in *Time* Magazine a while ago which told of an international ink manufacturer who found that his African sales were skyrocketing and native retailers were asking for gallon bottles? The company finally discovered that its popularity was due to a thirst for education. Pregnant mothers were drinking ink in the hope their children would be born with the capacity to write! Can anyone of us really comprehend such a fact?

"You want to know what it's like being colored?" asks Waring Cuney.

> Well,
> It's like going to bat
> With two strikes
> Already called on you—
> It's like playing pool
> With your name
> Written on the eight ball.
> Did you ever say

"Thank you, sir,"
For an umbrella full of holes?
Did you ever dream
You had a million bucks,
And wake up with nothing to pawn?
You want to know what it's like
Being colored?—
Well,
The only way to know
Is to be born that way.

The Master wasn't "born that way," yet he had the power to feel with the other man. He lived in a segregated society. "Jews have no dealings with Samaritans." Yet, he could make a Samaritan the hero of a parable. He lived at a time when Rome and all her lackeys were hated as were the Nazis by the Europe they subdued a quarter century ago. Yet, he healed a centurion's servant and called a publican—a Roman henchman—down out of a tree to eat with him. He lived in a day when every orthodox priest offered a Temple prayer, thanking God that he was not a woman. Yet, the Master responded to the touch of a woman's pain upon the hem of his garment and forgave a guilty woman in Simon's house before the icy self-righteousness of the Pharisees. "You shall love your neighbor as yourself"—as though he were yourself, whatever your race.

Let's consider what this qualitative view of Christian love means.

Let's begin by noting that *this kind of love bypasses altogether the question of equality*. If my heart is tinged by Christian love I don't ask if my neighbor is my equal. I only put myself in his place and ask how he feels. I don't ask whether the foot is equal to the hand, to use Paul's figure—both are essential to the body's well-being. I simply make sure that nothing the hand does hurts the foot. Equality is in essence a mathematical category. It does not truly apply to human qualities. Human beings are different; they are not equal or unequal. To ask whether white is intrinsically superior to brown is like asking whether the name Smith is intrinsically better than Jones. Is straight hair superior to curly hair?

### on loving one's neighbor as oneself

I am told that some Negroes believe it is, while a whole host of white ladies spend their husbands' and fathers' money trying to make theirs permanently curly! Is one sex superior to another? (Some time ago a pompous male made the public statement that men had proved themselves superior to women in all the professions. To which the president of one of our women's colleges replied, "No wonder, the poor women don't have wives to look after them!" It was a sufficient answer, because equality in the strict sense does not have a place in the human equation.)

I sometimes wish we could superannuate the notion of "equality." It is the silent partner of so much of our prejudice. Gordon W. Allport in his notable study of prejudice says there are two ingredients of prejudice. First is the notion that other groups are not the equal of our group. The white man is superior to the Negro; the Gentile is superior to the Jew; the Protestant is superior to the Catholic. (I do not know how you would ever prove such judgments to an impartial jury.) The first ingredient of prejudice is the belief that other groups are unequal to mine. The second ingredient of prejudice, Allport said, is the belief that within the inferior group all members are equal. That is, all Negroes are equally Negroid; all Jews are sly and materialistic; all Indians are lazy, et cetera. Again, such judgments have no standing in fact. As most anthropologists acknowledge, the average Negro has as much white ancestry behind him as Negro. Most whites, too, are mixtures, and no race has a monopoly of good or evil. As Will Rogers once observed with a sly wink, "I'm ⅛ cigar-store Indian; I have just enough white blood in me to make my honesty questionable!" Away with equality! When the good Samaritan came upon the bruised and bleeding man beside the Jericho Road he didn't stop to inquire whether the unfortunate fellow was his equal. He merely sensed that he was in need. He intuited by the power of imaginative sympathy how it must feel to be in that condition. Then he picked him up and took him to an inn and cared for him. He bypassed altogether the notion of equality. "You shall love your neighbor as yourself"—the antidote to the spurious notion of equality.

In the second place, when this qualitative conception of love is accepted *we'll bring race relations in America in line with the twentieth century.* Human relationships resemble everything else in an evolutionary world. Things that were good in one age cease to be in the next. I hear some of my friends proclaiming the virtues of segregation. Well, confessedly there was a day when segregation was good, when it represented a step forward. Certainly segregation is good compared with slavery, as slavery is good compared with the killing of one's captives, as primitive men did. Now the time has come, however, when segregation is out-of-date.

A study of Henry Ford and the Ford Motor Company was published by distinguished Pulitzer-Prize-winning historian Allan Nevins. The book makes this judgment about Henry Ford. It says that for sixty years he was ahead of his time and for the last twenty years he was behind his time. For six decades he was an industrial pioneer. He introduced the assembly line, the five-dollar wage, and a cheap, useful product that set America on wheels. But he refused to keep up with the developing world, and at last his time passed him. He refused to style his cars. He fought the rising labor movement. He insisted on the same autocratic one-man rule when he had 100,000 employees that he had enjoyed when he had 100 employees. The consequence was that by 1933 General Motors had overtaken him, and by 1943 he was on the threshold of destruction, spared only by the rising up of the Ford family itself to take away his power. That is a parable of what happens at every level of experience when we fail to keep up with the calendar.

Our present racial situation is out-of-date. There is a new Negro. There is a rising professional class—the Negro doctor, for instance —who nets 500 dollars a week, drives a Cadillac, and lives in a ranch-style house. He is not going to take the treatment that a sharecropper would. The Negro of today is not the field hand of Civil War days; he is capable of producing from his ranks a Ralph Bunche, with his Ph.D., his Harvard professorship, and his Nobel Prize. The Negro is not an indigent class as it was in the days of Reconstruction. According to the *New York Times* Negro purchasing power in this country is now equal to our total foreign exports.

There is a new world. Time has marched along. The colored peoples of the world are in the majority, and in nation after nation they are sitting in the driver's seat. In land after land they are evicting their erstwhile masters. Can we put our heads in the sand and pretend it isn't so? So often we hear it said by defenders of the old order, "Now don't push us. This thing must be done gradually." No one likes to be pushed, but have we forgotten that the Emancipation Proclamation was enunciated a hundred years ago? And nullification was smashed, not by the Supreme Court in 1954, but by a Tennessean, Andrew Jackson, in 1833. How slow is slow? How near to the absolutely motionless may one be and still be gradual?

There is a new conscience in the world. Many a white person is chagrined that we have come so little way in a hundred years. No, it isn't pleasant to be pushed, but it isn't pleasant to be hobbled either when the Christian conscience speaks. Christian love means not only that we shall sympathetically feel with the Negro, but also that we shall sympathetically feel with the white conscience that feels with the Negro.

"You shall love your neighbor as yourself." When we begin to think in terms of the brotherhood of unity we shall forget altogether about time; yet strange to say, we'll find ourselves up-to-date.

Well, how do we acquire this ability to feel with other people? Let me make three brief suggestions. The first is that we "take thought," as the Bible puts it. Let us project ourselves imaginatively into the place of others. Let us ask *why* they do as they do. The papers not long ago reported a unique school in Britain which endeavors to teach sensitivity to others. For a day the children are blindfolded and must get around without eyes, which teaches them to appreciate the blind. For a day their ears are stopped; this multiplies their understanding of the deaf. Perhaps there ought to be a day when we could take on the complexion of the other race and see how it feels. At least this is possible in imagination. Instead of looking out we might look within. This was Jesus' suggestion in the Golden Rule. Let us ask how this feels to me, and I have a clue to the way others feel it. A woman said the other day that she felt very much like everybody else at the center but different around the edge. This was her way of saying she was a human being at heart and an individual on the circumference. Take thought then; consult your heart and you will understand the pulsing heart of your neighbor.

Secondly, if we would learn to love the neighbor *we will associate with him.* Association does not *guarantee* love; indeed, some of the hardest persons to love are one's neighbors! Practically all the studies of prejudice show that acquaintance lessens prejudice. In the Army the white and Negro soldiers who fought in the same platoons had the least objection to one another, according to the tests. Instead of familiarity's breeding contempt, experience shows that it begets a sense of value. This is why segregation is such an iniquitous thing. It not only poisons the relations of the present, it builds a wall of hindrance that prevents a better relationship that ought to be. We white people have discovered these last few months that we did not know our Negro brethren as we thought we did. Their resistance has surprised us. Their willingness to risk danger for their cause has been a marvel. But it would not have happened, I surmise, if we had been in brotherly fellowship with one another. Segregation has destroyed the very access to each other which might have saved the tragedy we have been going through.

Finally, we achieve love for others by *realizing the love of God.* Love begets love. Love, believed in, produces love. The law of human nature is that we love in reply to love. "We love, because he first loved us." "Beloved, if God so loved us, we also ought to love one another." If a person believes that God really loves him he will find it impossible to hate those whom God loves. When we lose sight of God's love, on the other hand, the heart sours and men no longer seem worth the loving. Let a person ponder the great love God has for him, unworthy though he may be, and he can never treat others with disrespect.

In the long run, human rights rest upon community of feeling.

American history is instructive on this point. The American Constitution is the basic body of law and right. What is behind it? The War for Independence, climaxing in a Declaration of Independence. What is behind that? A sense of unity residing in the thirteen colonies, transcending their differences. Historians tell us now that months, years, before Paul Revere rode that night to Concord and Lexington to warn of the British advance, he and other bold riders had been moving up and down the Atlantic seaboard carrying messages to and from the patriots. Like shuttles they sped back and forth, weaving a fabric of unity. They did their work so well that when the crucial hour came and the British attacked Massachusetts distant Virginia felt it was an attack on her, and George Washington went at once to her aid. Out of that community of feeling came independence, and finally a new and greater unity.

Well, the first task of the church is to weave a fabric of sympathy by which our minority brethren may lose their bonds and be united in a stronger and closer fellowship. When love becomes *qualitative,* a feeling for the other person's feelings, racial exclusiveness in the church will cease.

# 6. civil rights
# from a christian point of view

THEODORE PARKER FERRIS

*Dr. Ferris, one of America's outstanding preachers, has been rector of Trinity Church (Episcopal) in Boston since 1952. He was educated at Harvard University (A.B.) and the General Theological Seminary (B.D.) and four times has been honored with the Doctor of Divinity degree. He lectures in homiletics at the Episcopal Theological School in Cambridge and is the author of nine books, including the exposition of "The Acts of the Apostles" in the* Interpreter's Bible.

On Wednesday, August 28, 1963, 200,000 people marched into the city of Washington, D.C. Most of them were Negroes; many of them were not. It was a demonstration for equal rights. The amazing thing about it was that there was no disorder, no violence. On the following Friday James Reston wrote about the March in his column. He is one of the interpreters of events whom I admire most and to whose mind I turn most confidently. Some of you may not, but I do.

The first sentence of his article struck me like a blow. This was it: "The first significant test of the Negro march on Washington will come in the churches and synagogues of the country this weekend." It was quite clear that the implication was that if nothing happened in the churches nothing would happen in Congress. He went on to say, "As moral principles preceded and inspired political principles, as the Church preceded the Congress, so there will have to be a moral revulsion to the humiliation of the Negro before there can be significant political relief."

Then I stopped to think about this church. What happened in this church on that weekend? Nothing. At least nothing was said that had anything to do with the March or its purpose. I did not intend to say anything about it at that particular time, for reasons that I need not go into now. I am not sure that something had not already happened in this church and in many other churches, and I wonder whether James Reston fully appreciated how much has been happening in the churches. Granted, the churches have not done all that they should, but they have done infinitely more than that particular article of his would lead an outsider to guess.

I am not sure that preaching in and by itself will change anybody's mind, but Reston's article has lain heavily on my conscience, and for better or worse I am going to say now what I think about civil rights from a Christian point of view.

## I

First, there are no specific directions about this particular matter in the Bible, none whatever. Slavery is taken for granted in both the Old Testament and the New Testament. Words like integration, segregation, desegregation, interracial do not appear anywhere in the Bible, for the situation to which they refer did not exist then as it does now. The first thing that I would like to make as plain as I possibly can is this: You can neither defend nor oppose the idea that the colored and white are separate on the basis of some particular passage in the Bible. Many people have tried to do it. Some have tried to defend the idea that the colored and white are separate, and some have tried to oppose it, on the basis of a fragment, a scrap, taken out of its biblical context. You cannot do it.

You cannot defend or oppose the idea that the earth goes around the sun on the basis of any particular passage in the Bible. The Bible is too early for that idea, and it is likewise too early for the particular social revolution which is now raging full tilt.

There is something much more powerful in the Bible than specific directions. There is in the Bible a movement toward the emancipation of men and women. That is the important thing about the Bible. From the first page to the last page the Bible is the story of a movement toward the freedom of a man to be himself and to live his own life within the limits of his human condition.

The movement began at the Red Sea when one small tribe broke loose from bondage to another people. It was the beginning of the movement. It ends supremely on Calvary where Jesus, one single human being in whom the fullness of God revealed itself, was free to be himself and as a consequence frees other people to be themselves. It is liberty born out of sacrifice. It's the only real liberty there is.

During his brief ministry Jesus never spoke about Negroes or said anything that has anything to do with the problem that we are now dealing with. For one thing there weren't many Negroes in his neighborhood. There were, however, a great many Samaritans, and the Samaritans were as thoroughly segregated from the Jews as Negroes are from the whites. Segregation was a habit peculiarly congenial to the Jewish people. Yet as far as we know Jesus never talked about integration or segregation in principle or in theory. One time he told an unforgettable story about "a certain Samaritan" who helped a Jew who was in a bad way—the last person in the world you would expect to stop to help a Jew. And when ten lepers ran to him for help he healed them all, but only one went back to thank him, "and he was a Samaritan."

In his own behavior Jesus treated people like human beings no matter who they were, whether they came from the aristocracy or from the gutter, and no matter what they had done, whether they had a magnificent record or whether they had only the record of failure. Regardless of their present status, he treated them like human beings. The essential thing is that in his dealings with people he brought them into the presence of God, the same God from whom they all originally came, from whom they all derived their lives, in the sight of whom they all failed, and by whose tender, understanding love they could all be made new. He brought them all into the presence of that God, and the equality they had was the equality that he gave them as he drew them into the presence of his Father.

There on Calvary stands Jesus. I wonder if you can see it clearly as you look back across the centuries. I know that some think that the images of Christianity will have to be changed in a radical way. The years go by, the generations pass, and the fashions of thought change, but Jesus remains on Calvary. There he stands, the center of human dignity and integrity, where the cross-purposes of life are accepted and saved from desperate remedies.

Gradually people begin to see what it means to be associated with him. They don't see it all at once. Even Paul didn't see it completely; he saw the great thing, but he didn't have time to work out the details. But gradually people see that to be associated with Jesus means to treat other human beings the way he treats you. It's quite a thing to see! If you once see it, you won't always be able to do it, but you will never be the same again.

Copernicus declared that the earth went around the sun, and to his satisfaction he proved it. It took a hundred years for the plain people of the Western world to take in that idea, and they are still working out the implications of it. Jesus declared that every human being revolves around God. It took a long time for people to take in that idea; they were so used to thinking that God revolved around them. He began a movement toward freedom, and it took some people a long time to see that that movement toward freedom includes, and this is very important, not only freedom from hell, but also freedom from humiliation. It is much easier to reach for one than the other.

Let me tell you something that happened as I was working on

these notes in the rectory. A great many people go to Mass in the Roman Catholic Church just up Newbury Street, and they park their cars all around the rectory. Across the street from the rectory was parked a small foreign car in which was a little French poodle. While the owner of the car was in church praying for salvation from hell the poodle spent the entire time yelping to be saved from the humiliation of being locked up in a car for three quarters of an hour. If the door had not been locked I would have opened it; at least I would have been tempted to. Jesus began a movement to do something for the people who are crying for help.

## II

This movement has now reached a new front. In this country Negroes have never been treated like human beings, by and large. I know that that is a general statement, and I know that some of you will take exception to it. I stand by the statement, however, that Negroes in this country have never been treated before the law as human beings. Many of them have been dearly loved and treated with great kindness—the way you would treat a child— but when they wanted to vote they were treated another way.

In the last few years two things have happened. The first is that the Negroes in this country now demand to be treated as human beings. Some of you would prefer that they didn't, but they have the numbers and the intelligence to demand it, and they will continue to demand it until they get it. They have waited for one hundred years, and they might well say to us, "We've waited long enough." The longer they wait, the more insistent their demands will become.

The other thing that has happened is that some white people, many white people, sincerely want this. They are people who have caught up with the movement of Jesus. Nominally they may not be Christian, but they are a part of this movement toward freedom, and I am proud to claim my association with them. The Christians who want this see the difficulties involved if they have any eyesight at all. They are enormous. Imagine what is involved in changing a whole social pattern; for many people it's like an earthquake. They see the difficulties, but they cannot deny the principle, and they begin to move bravely toward it.

Take, for example, one of the many difficulties. If you give Negroes equal social rights, they may intermarry with whites. A great many people believe that this is highly undesirable and that the intermarriage of white and colored people causes all sorts of difficulties. Their solution is not to give them equal social rights. If equal social rights encourage intermarriage, and if intermarriage is not good, then withhold the rights. Keep them in their place.

The Christian, I believe, takes a different position. The Christian says, "Give them equal social rights because it is right." If there are undesirable consequences as a result you deal with those as well as you can when they arise. This is essentially what we said in another situation fifty years ago. You give labor the right to organize because it is right; if there are undesirable consequences, and there certainly have been, you handle those as they arise as well as you can.

We are now standing on the new front, and as we stand there we can see real gains in every direction. As we look toward the South we can see real gains in many Southern cities and towns, gains that have been made quietly, white and colored people working together, both realizing how difficult it is, with patience, intelligence, and lovingkindness. Right here in our own state the gains are easy to see. We see a Negro in the office of Attorney General of the Commonwealth of Massachusetts. We see a Negro on the staff of the Cathedral.

Looking more closely at our own parish, we see that there are Negroes—not many, but there are some—who belong to this church, with all its rights and privileges. They have been accepted as members of this parish for years. We see that there are white people in this church who are working for this movement, quietly, not necessarily talking about it, but working for it, to give to people who crave to be treated as human beings the right to live as human

65

beings in a community which includes both white and colored people.

There are some in this church, I am sure, who think that this whole movement is in the wrong direction. There are some who think that it is contrary to the Bible, and a few who think that it is inspired by Communism. And there are some, I am sure, who are in sympathy with the article that David Lawrence wrote about the March, which he called "The Day of Disgrace." I welcome those people to this congregation. We will never all be of one mind. I do not agree with them. I think they are wrong, but I love them, and I want them to be here.

I am speaking only for myself and for those whose consciences are stirring, for those who know that Christians belong to a movement begun originally by God, brought to a head by Christ, and worked out imperfectly by individuals like you and me.

I am speaking for all those who see, even though dimly, what Paul was aiming at. He didn't see it himself, but he was aiming at something great, the fullness of which he never attained. I am speaking for those who see what he was aiming at when he wrote, "There is neither Jew nor Greek, there is neither bond nor free, there is neither male nor female; for you are all one in Christ Jesus."

# 7. dedicated to a proposition

### GERALD KENNEDY

*Gerald Kennedy, since 1952 Bishop of The Methodist Church, Los Angeles area, has had a most distinguished career. For eighteen years before his election to bishop he was a pastor. He has taught in various theological schools, lectured frequently, written twenty books, traveled the world over, and has been awarded ten honorary degrees. After study at the University of the Pacific (B.A.) and the Pacific School of Religion (M.A. and B.D.) he received the M.S.T. and Ph.D. degrees from Hartford Theological Seminary. In 1955 Newsweek listed him as one of the ten greatest American preachers.*

*The sermon "Dedicated to a Proposition" was preached in Chicago on August 30, 1963, at the Second Methodist Conference on Human Relations.*

He created every race of men of one stock.

(Acts 11:26 NEB.)

Our ambassador to the United Nations, Adlai Stevenson, wrote an article, "The Hard Kind of Patriotism," for *Harper's Magazine,*

67

July, 1963. Stevenson pointed out that this nation differs from others in its principle of unity. We are not bound together by a common heritage, since we came from many different countries. We are not people of a single culture, and we have not been united through conquest. We are, he says, a land "dedicated to a proposition," and our unity centers around a principle. He was referring, of course, to the phrase used by Abraham Lincoln in the Gettysburg Address. In that crucial, tragic moment in our history the President said that we were testing whether or not the proposition that had given us birth could withstand the strains of civil war.

Today our society has been forced to pay new attention to our faith. On the hundredth anniversary of the issuing of the Emancipation Proclamation Negro Americans by their demonstrations are forcing our society to consider seriously the original proposition which gave us birth. It is a painful time for white as well as for black citizens. We are confronted by our dilatoriness and our willingness to preach one thing while we practice another. We are face to face with the judgment of the denial of our heritage. This is a time of suffering and shock. It is a time when we must reexamine who we are, where we came from, and what we believe.

I

The first thing I want to say is that we always live by faith. Or to put it in another way, we live on the basis of propositions which we cannot prove but which we commit ourselves to live by.

It is amazing how much we assume. The so-called scientific laws oftentimes grow outdated. Not long ago it was discovered that inert gases will combine with chemical elements. Through all the previous years it was thought that this was not possible, so that now the scientific textbooks have to be changed and a scientific law has to be amended. When we deal with the material things of life we must live by faith even as we do in the spiritual realm. We are always moving out beyond the evidence, and indeed, we could not live for ten minutes on what we can prove.

## dedicated to a proposition

It would seem that economics could be resolved to a few solid rules so that we would know how to be prosperous and how to prevent depression. There comes to my desk a little paper put out by a New York bank which proposes to give the economic trends for the future. I stopped reading it long ago because it does not really say anything. Its articles announce that if such and such a thing happens, and if such and such a thing does not happen, then perhaps this result may be expected. There is so much hedging in economic forecasting that it becomes obvious that nobody really knows. The only sure thing is J. P. Morgan's prediction concerning the stock market, "It will fluctuate." An outstanding CPA told me one time that his work was as much art as science and that ultimately we must depend upon the character of the accountant himself.

Sociology is far from scientific. We cannot say for sure why juveniles become delinquent, and we do not know why one boy goes wrong and another boy goes right. Just when we think we have the principles announced there appears so many exceptions that we have to admit our inability to forecast human behavior. People are the most unpredictable creatures in the world, and the heart has secrets which no science can explain.

If a man considers a day in his own life he knows how uncertain things are. He begins with plans, which oftentimes are frustrated, and the end of the day seldom reveals what he had expected. We plan for the future the best way we can, but the wise man knows that the future is beyond his control. My father always used the phrase "the good Lord willing." The older I grow, the more I understand the wisdom of that spirit. Remember the wise word of the epistle of James: "What is your life? For you are a mist that appears for a little time and then vanishes. Instead you ought to say, 'If the Lord wills, we shall live and we shall do this or that'" (4:14-15.) God has made our life so that we are driven to commit ourselves to propositions we must live by, but which are always in a realm beyond proof.

I marvel at the ability of men to forecast happenings in the universe. A physical scientist may be able to tell us to a split second the time of the next eclipse of the sun. He may be able to forecast the exact position of Saturn in the year 2,000. But that same scientist cannot be sure what his teen-age boy is going to do tomorrow. We live by faith.

## II

Now the second thing that needs to be said is that life is a dedication. The strength of the nation lies primarily in a willingness to commit itself to its faith. What we believe was announced by the founding Fathers in their Declaration of Independence. They had a high regard for the public opinion of the world, and when they severed their relationship with Great Britain they wanted to make sure that the rest of the world knew why they were doing it and what they had in mind. So we have in that great document not only a Declaration of Independence, but really a declaration of faith. They wrote, "We hold these truths to be self-evident, that all men are created equal, that they are endowed by their Creator with certain inalienable Rights." America was to be something different, for it was to be a land where every man could expect equal justice and equal opportunity regardless of race or class. Some of us have forgotten how through the years New York Harbor has been the gateway to equal opportunity for every man. When, in the darkness of the Civil War slaughter, people stood in the presence of their dead President Lincoln reminded them again of the ideas for which these men had died. Faith becomes powerful only when it becomes something more than intellectual assent. It calls for complete commitment from those who have announced what they believe.

The future of any society depends on the greatness of its faith and the strength which men dedicate to its fulfillment. In all our talk these days about defense and foreign aid we need to keep this truth very clear in our minds. It is an unseen spirit of devotion which produces the power to live by. A nation will find its chief temptation is to compromise in the name of expediency. As our awareness of our chief purposes grows dim we become more like the enemy, and our allies and friends become confused and uncertain. We cannot conquer without a continuing renewal of our dedication to the purposes of the nation. This means that our chief enemy is always within our borders, and indeed, it is usually within our own hearts. The hesitancy which Americans have felt in taking seriously the commitments of the Declaration of Independence has spelled weakness and not strength. It is time to recover knowledge of the propositions and find a great new voice to proclaim this faith abroad.

The Christian church comes into our world with an idea about man and his ultimate nature. It proclaims the worth of every human creature and the universal brotherhood of all of us. There is no biblical support for prejudice or for the artificial distinctions of color and class. When the church ceases to be dedicated to that philosophy, or when it ceases to practice it within its own fellowship, it destroys one of the main foundationstones and surrenders its claim to universality.

We are committed to a society in which every child has his opportunity. We must be forevermore opposed to saddling any youngster with man-made handicaps. When we put these millstones around the necks of children because they happen to be born in a certain place and of a certain race we are guilty of denying our Lord. Our compromise in this field has led to nothing but failure. If the church is to have any authoritative word in our time it must come from commitment to our belief in all men.

In my own poor life and yours this principle of the necessity of dedication finally brings us to judgment. All that we are worth are the propositions we have given ourselves to serve. Our test finally is the extent to which we have been faithful to our principles. The measure of any man's life is ultimately the measure of his dedication to the propositions he accepted.

Logan Pearsall Smith once wrote in his diary: "What a bore it is to wake up every morning the same person!" But it would be very confusing and frustrating to wake up every morning a different person. Actually the thing that saves us from boredom is to wake up every morning with a sense of privilege and adventure which comes from our commitment to great issues. And if we have a dream of wider brotherhood and more justice each day becomes a more exciting adventure.

## III

A third thing we need to observe is that our commitments have become vague. It is too easy to believe that yesterday was better than today and that our modern problems are unique. It does seem true to me, however, that there is a kind of uncertainty in our contemporary situation which makes it very difficult for us to determine the propositions which are important.

A few years ago the Council of Bishops of The Methodist Church met in Washington, D. C. We called on President Dwight Eisenhower at the White House. The secretary of our council read to the President the greetings which had been delivered to President Washington by the first Methodist bishop of America, Francis Asbury, more than 150 years before. In his reply to this greeting the President remarked how simple life seemed to be in those days compared with life today. There were so few government employees and so few international involvements, unlike the present situation. Then he went on to say that the more involved and complicated life becomes the more important it is that men should have a clear vision of the underlying principles. It is this clear vision that is lacking with us. The complications of our present life blur the sharp lines of our principles.

We see it in the movies. Now and again, there is a picture which is downright suggestive, and people with some sense of moral decency are shocked. In some ways a more serious defect, however, is the motion picture which stays within the laws of decency but offers only a meaningless hodgepodge of activity as our way of life. The thing that troubles me more than anything else in modern pictures is this lack of moral awareness and a loss of the ability to distinguish between what is good and what is evil. It is a

72

tendency which we see in city, state, and national government and is observed in all our society.

This is a disease which attacks the church. The modern church in some ways looks very imposing. We rejoice in the billions of dollars worth of property represented by the churches in America. We can be proud of the number of people who claim membership in American churches, for it is at the highest point in all our history. We have been prosperous and we have had less trouble with budgets than ever before. But the sharp outline of our commitment is no longer observable. The unique witness of Christians seems to have faded into a twilight atmosphere of blurred images. A sickness which could be unto death is the loss of our sense of ultimate loyalties.

John Steinbeck drove leisurely across the nation from east to west and then back again. He wrote about his experience in a book, *Travels with Charlie.* He tells of a conversation with a New Hampshire farmer by the roadside. He asked what people around there were saying and thinking about the November elections and about the world in general. The farmer said the people didn't say much about any of these things. Steinbeck asked him if it was because they were scared. The farmer said some of them are scared, but not all of them, and even those who were not scared did not have much to say. Then as the two men wondered why this was, the farmer said, "Well, you take my grandfather and his father. . . . They knew some things they were sure about. . . . But now. . . . Nobody knows. . . . We've got nothing to go on—got no way to think about things."

Surely it is an amazing thing that the more success we have achieved the less sure we are of the meaning of life. The more wealth we pile up the more doubt we seem to gather at the same time. Bitterness between races does not disappear with prosperity. Military might has failed to provide us with confidence, with love, or with power.

I despair over young people who are outside the church and have no religious upbringing. To what shall they dedicate themselves if they believe only in atheism and in existential despair. They have seen very few good examples, and they have heard very little clear proclamation of faith. How desperately we need someone to stand before us and define anew the propositions to which we are dedicated as American Christians.

A student in a ninth-grade English class concluded his book report with this appraisal, "I think the author was a pretty good writer not to make the book no duller than it was." Those are often my sentiments when I realize how little opportunity many of our young people have had to be confronted by faith. It is a wonder they are not worse than they are. How little they have been taught about what has brought us on our way and makes us different from other nations! It is a time of darkness and danger because the vision has faded and the darkness of our doubts obscures the path.

## IV

The last thing to say is that here is where Christ helps us. When we are confronted by God in Christ we see the issues which demand our decisions. Christianity is not a mere coloring of morality with a little emotion but light on our path.

When on Sunday morning in our churches we stand and say, "We believe in God Almighty," we are saying something of such serious importance that I do not know how we say it so easily. The truth is that the reality of God brings a man's life under a searching judgment. If we believe in God, then we believe that our lives have meaning and we have responsibilities one to another. If God is, then life has a plot and a purpose.

We believe in brotherhood, which is to say that no man lives unto himself. It is to say that every man is responsible for every other man and that the artificial barriers we place between men are the signs of our sin. No Christian can withdraw unto himself or retreat into his own little circle. He is committed to the belief that since God is the Father of all of us the withholding of fellowship from any human being is a severing of our relationship with God.

The thing that Christ does for us above all else is to make clear that justice is not a gift we have a right to ration. It is apparent in our Christian faith that justice is something God has decreed for all men. When we talk about civil rights we are not talking about privileges to be bestowed or withheld at anyone's whim. God demands justice for all of us, and we must demand it for one another. The Christian church has no other choice but to dedicate itself to these propositions.

This is painful, and it hurts, and we will not play down this part of the process. But it seems perfectly clear that every conference, every council, every leader of any Christian church, must promise the support of the whole Christian fellowship to any man, black or white, who seeks equal rights for himself and his family. It is too bad that we could not see this for ourselves but must be reminded of it by the sacrifices of our Negro brethren.

Men need God's help to see that evil is evil, nonsense is nonsense, and good is good. The world is in need of men who can make plain the propositions by which we live. This is the task and the responsibility of churchmen. More than that, it is the tremendous privilege that Christians enjoy. In Christ we know that there is neither male nor female, neither Gentile nor Jew. Indeed, we find in him the fulfillment of our search for peace and brotherhood.

Many years ago I saw Marc Connelly's *The Green Pastures.* I went to the play unexpectantly, for I thought it would have nothing to say to an American seminary student. But if I went to scoff, I remained to pray. I remember yet the scene where Moses appeared before Pharaoh demanding freedom for his people. The miracles impressed Pharaoh. "I don' say you ain't a good tricker, Moses," the king admitted. "You is one of de best I ever seen."

Moses replied, "It ain't only me dat's goin' to wukk dis trick. It's me an' de Lawd."

It will be neither our cleverness nor our virtue which will bring us through this struggle for human rights, but the power of God.

It is for us to remind ourselves of the propositions of our faith. There is a little of the black Muslim in every Negro and a little of the Ku Klux Klan in every white man, but there is also the cleansing power of God. This struggle belongs to all of us, and we can engage in it with the confidence that our victory is the will of God.

# 8.  a death and life matter

### BRUCE WILLIAM KLUNDER

*Bruce Klunder became known around the world as a result of a protest demonstration accident which tragically took his life, April 7, 1964. While participating in a civil rights effort to halt the construction of a new elementary school in Cleveland he was crushed beneath a moving bulldozer. At his memorial service it was said of him, "He died in the front lines of those who, having pledged themselves to nonviolence, are pledged also to stay in the struggle until the victory is won."*

*Mr. Klunder, a United Presbyterian, grew up in Oregon and graduated from Oregon State University. He received his theological training from Yale Divinity School, from which he graduated in 1961. For two and a half years, until his death, he was Associate Executive Secretary of the Student Christian Union in Cleveland, ministering to students at Western Reserve University and Case Institute of Technology.*

*This remarkably prophetic sermon was preached in his hometown in Oregon nine months prior to his death.*

The glory which thou hast given me I have given
to them, that they may be one even as we are one . . .

77

> so that the world may know that thou hast sent me
> and hast loved them. (John 17:22, 23.)

Strange as it may seem, I have chosen today to preach an Easter sermon. Thus I have read as the Scripture lesson for the day portions of the Passion narrative as recorded by John. We have read from the prayer that Jesus offered with his disciples before his betrayal. We have read of the crucifixion itself, and finally, we have read of the presence of Jesus with his disciples in the post-Easter community. This is the stuff of which Easter sermons are made, and to make it complete we shall sing a very familiar Easter hymn at the conclusion of our worship.

I hope that it will become clear as we progress why the sermon of the day must be an Easter sermon.

Now, while the title I have put to the sermon—"A Death and Life Matter"—is no mistake, I would like first of all to turn it around and address our attention to what must necessarily be termed a *life* and *death* matter. At this point I want to attempt to interpret certain of my own experiences and feelings about an issue which can no longer be ignored by any of us.

It is no secret to anyone that the past few years and especially the last few months have been for our nation a period of turmoil and finally a test of courage and purpose, the result of which cannot be seen with any great certainty at this point. Since the Emancipation Proclamation of one hundred years ago now, we have been faced with the problem of conscience which is posed by the disparity between an official policy of universal human freedom and the daily observation that *in fact* for many of our fellows this proclamation of freedom is a hollow thing indeed. We are faced with the discrepancy between the American dream of unlimited upward mobility for each person and the fact that the American Negro lives surrounded by walls and covered with a nearly immovable ceiling.

These last two years, since I have settled with my family in Cleveland, Ohio, has been a period of real confrontation for us with the many ways that the Negro in America finds the American

78

dream to be a hollow one for him. It has also been a period of increasing personal involvement and identification with the movement that is protesting radically against the closed door which our Negro brethren confront as they seek to enter the mainstream of our society and economy.

It seems that the thing we most readily think of as we ponder the scandal of American race relations is the fact that some white persons are prejudiced and, therefore, discriminate against colored persons; or conversely, the fact that some whites are not prejudiced, have Negro friends, and thus treat these friends and other Negroes justly and equitably. We then try to think of ways that might work to change those who are prejudiced to be more like those who are not. But to view the major problem in race relations in this fashion—that is, to try to change the attitudes of individual prejudiced people—could have no result, I should think, other than to leave one baffled by the current tactics of the Negro freedom movement with its demonstrations, marches, sit-ins, and freedom rides. It is obvious that such measures do little to make the prejudiced person less prejudiced. In fact, the opposite is most often the case. Prejudiced people in the face of such tactics have something real to retaliate against, and most often that is precisely what they do.

If, however, the experience of living two years in a city with a Negro population of over 300,000 has taught us one thing, it is that the issue of race relations must be approached much differently than this. It can no longer be a question of strictly interpersonal relations, as if my responsibility ended with my attitudes toward those five, ten, twenty, or fifty Negro individuals with whom I come in contact in the course of a week. I must, of course, be concerned with personal attitudes, but finally the problem is one which involves institutions. It involves questions about the structures of society; it involves my behavior in the voting booth, the apportionment of my tax dollar, my buying and selling habits; it involves these things in a profoundly important way whether or not I can claim to have any Negro friends or even any Negro acquaintances to my name.

Now the question of whether the bulk of white America can see this difference becomes the life and death matter. It is the question of whether we can cease hiding behind the all-too-familiar expression, "Some of my best friends are Negroes," and begin seeing the issue in terms of the structures which serve as the imprisoning walls for all too many Negro citizens. This is the question which the rapidly moving freedom movement forces us to answer.

It is my intention then to lay bare as far as my limited experience makes possible some of these institutionalized structures which continually add up to the keeping of the white man's foot on the neck of his Negro brother. After this I would like to return to the original title, which I think captures the essence of the Christian faith's direction for this issue.

The United States Civil Rights Commission has issued a report documenting the full range of racial discrimination in this country. It is because they look at discrimination in terms of the structures of our society that they can preface the entire report with a section entitled "the iron ring"—the iron ring of law and custom that forces an *inferior status* upon its victims. What are some of the elements of that iron ring? The interesting and important thing is that you can't pick out any one element without already implying all the other elements. This is what makes it a ring, or in more common language, a vicious circle.

Since we must start somewhere, let's start with the question of where Negroes live in a city like Cleveland. Cleveland, like almost every large urban community, is a cluster of cities. Cleveland is made up of some sixty separate municipalities. The largest of these, of course, is Cleveland, but the other fifty-nine together have as many people as does the city of Cleveland. Some of these communities are among the nicest, most prosperous residential areas in the country. Many new schools have been built to serve developments made possible by FHA and VA insured loans. But are these areas for the Negro? The answer is an overwhelming No! A recent census count found that all these suburban communities were by actual count 99.44 per cent white. Why is it that 300,000 of Cleveland proper's 800,000 residents are Negro, living in a rapidly deteriorating community? Why is it that they crowd themselves into overcrowded, run-down flats and apartments in areas where trees and grass are all but unknown? Is it because they like so well to live so closely together? Hardly! Is it because the 800,000 whites in suburbia have discriminated against them? Most of these would deny it vigorously. It is primarily because of certain structures which have grown up for which few people take any personal responsibility. It is because the FHA and VA housing developments that mushroomed in the late forties did so as consciously segregated communities with the blessing and guidance of these agencies. Now, while policy has changed, the legacy remains. It is because integrated neighborhoods have appeared to be poor financial risks, and therefore, the policy of all the major banks in Cleveland prohibits the making of loans to Negroes, regardless of collateral, if they wish to buy or build in a predominantly white neighborhood. It is because real estate agents and brokers refuse in a unanimous way to make such sales even if the money is available. It is because until recently renters and sellers advertised blatantly in the major newspapers "white only" or "colored only." It is structures like this, not individual acts of discrimination, that lead to the fact that of Cleveland's 300,000 Negroes probably less than fifteen or twenty families are the first occupants of the homes in which they live. New homes are built by the dozens, but they are *not* for Negroes.

What is the result? Quite obviously the result is a Negro ghetto made up of inadequate and anything but low-cost housing. In one of the really deteriorated slum sections of Cleveland the average monthly rent is seventy-eight dollars. This is for three or four rooms to house large families.

And so around the ring we go. The fact that we have Negro ghettos in our inner-city neighborhoods has meant necessarily that we have had segregated schools—schools where close to 100 per cent of the pupils were Negro. What kind of schools are they?

They are in areas cut off from the tax revenue of the prosperous suburbs. Thus the schools are crowded—often they are on half-day sessions. They are understaffed, and facilities are inadequate. It is just here where special remedial and individualized programs are needed most that they are usually not present at all. In one area the only accelerated program is for children from several different schools who have to walk through two classrooms in order to meet in an attic. And for what? For instruction with the standard curriculum of most suburban schools.

High rents and low incomes lead to frequent moves to find better housing or to avoid rents that cannot be paid. Consequently many of the schools experience close to 100 per cent turnover in their student body in the space of a year. And another thing, even where all students are Negro nothing is read in the textbooks about Negroes in America because these books are written on the assumption that all people in America are white. Inferior education, therefore, with a lack of any personal interest leads many to drop out of school prior to graduation.

What about the employability of these school dropouts? Of course it is low, but the depressing thing is that it is not very different from the employability of all Negroes; thus the incentive to finish school is not high. Here we have come to a third element of the ring of discrimination, the element of employment. If there were ever a crucial issue it is this one, for without steady employment one can hardly hope to be a member of mainstream American society. What are the facts here? The American economy has been compared to a "train in which the Negro is the caboose and the number of cars between the engine and the caboose is constantly being increased."

The fact that the Negro is in the caboose can be illustrated in a few striking ways. In our economy we have learned to live with a certain amount of unemployment. Still we must remember that America's Negroes have had to learn to live with an unemployment rate between two and a half and three times as large as the whites. One summer in a section of Cleveland with a population of over 60,000 Negroes a group of college students voluntarily tutored junior-high students. They had to learn that as a fact of life in this community, unemployment for men sixteen to twenty-one years old is about 85 per cent. For the rest unemployment runs around 50 per cent and of those who are full-time employees few are making more than fifty dollars a week. Partly it is because education and skills are lacking. But, on the other hand, it has been ten years since a large technical high school there has placed anyone in a job. This is not because of the lack of skills, but because the unions do not accept Negro apprentices and because semiskilled jobs are rapidly disappearing due to automation.

Then try to sense the mounting frustration of many highly educated Negroes who have taken what was available to them and year after year either carry the mail or drive buses, while displaying M.A. or Ph.D. degrees at home.

We are beginning to have large communities of those who could be termed permanently unemployed. These are those who live in a culture of poverty which guarantees that the ring of oppression will continue—in housing, in education, and in the world of work.

We also see the breaking up of home life which further guarantees a continuation of the vicious circle. In Ohio mothers can receive aid for dependent children only if no father is present at home. This means that for many unemployed, unproductive fathers the only altruistic act is to desert, thus making the family eligible for this aid. We find in many areas that only about a third of the families have any father figure present.

This may all sound like a horror story from somewhere far away. It is not at all intended as such. These are the facts with which millions of people live daily. And my point is that they are the responsibility of every American regardless of where he lives, for they are consequences of structures which we through our disbelief, or apathy, or smugness have allowed to develop and to continue for far too many years.

It is a life and death matter for all who exist as oppressed people. It is a life and death matter for all of us, for our times are explosive. None can claim the luxury of not having to decide. The structures are being radically attacked, and each of us must respond even if it is only a personal response to the reading of a newspaper account of some action somewhere. It is an American dilemma.

How did you respond to the freedom rides or lunch counter sit-ins as they challenged the structure of separate facilities? How would you respond to the sit-ins in which I participated in a governor's office and in a state legislature protesting inaction on a pending fair housing bill? How do you respond to the idea of thousands of students boycotting their schools in protest against schools which are all Negro because neighborhoods are all Negro? How do you respond to massive boycotts of certain brands and certain products in an attempt to force employers to be nondiscriminating in their hiring practices? These are the questions which every newspaper is forcing us to answer.

Now where does the Christian faith, especially the faith based on the Easter event come in? Let us ponder for a moment the nature of this central event in our faith. At its core, to participate in the Easter faith is to affirm that, in spite of—*in spite of*—our rebellion against God who is our Father and to whom we owe our total existence, we have been accepted. We have been reconciled to this God not because we turned to him, but because he continued to turn to us. He loves us not because we are lovable, but because he chooses to suffer with us in our very unloveliness. His love for us as expressed for us in its supreme form in the agony of Jesus in the garden and on the cross is not a sentimental, comforting, warming thing. It is a love which pursues us relentlessly and finally causes us to become radically new creatures. It is a love which challenges much more than it comforts and which finally wins its victory in its willingness to suffer even the death on the cross. This kind of love is at the center of our faith, and because it is we cannot avoid involvement in the crisis which I have attempted to describe. Our central affirmation is that through Jesus Christ we are all one—one with God and one with each other. But this

84

is not the oneness of jolly good fellowship. This instead is the oneness of suffering *with* and *for* one another. If it seeks to be anything less it ceases to be the oneness of Christian faith. Thus, we see what I mean by the title—a death and life matter. Life for the Christian is life which does not deny or ignore pain, suffering, and death. It is life which emerges victorious from the pain of our dying to what we once were.

What this suggests as a guideline for me is that we *must*—each in his own way—suffer with and for those who are oppressed by those structures of injustice which we have described. This will mean that we must learn to feel their pain as *our own* and that we must be willing to bear personally some of the cost of that pain's removal. The policy of many of us has been that justice is fine if it doesn't cost us anything—economically, socially, or politically. That time is past. Changes are taking place which will inevitably cost us all something. Are we willing to bear this cost, with a realization that it is only a small part of what many have been forced to pay for many years? We must learn to feel the injustices of the structures of our society as do those who are oppressed by them. We must know what it is like to be a man for whom our economy has no use and who thus can be of no use to his family. We must try to know the feelings of one who has spent a lifetime hearing, "No, not here; not for you; you're not wanted," and we must learn to repent to those who come to believe our charges of inferiority.

Finally, I think we must identify with those in the freedom movement who are acting on the faith that suffering love can overcome hate. We must understand the depth of feeling expressed in a statement by a veteran of the freedom rides with whom we talked in Nashville. Still bearing the marks of numerous stitches on his face, he replied when questioned why he could say he did not hate his attackers, "Would you hate a blind man if he stepped on your foot?" This person and this movement are willing to endure pain without hating in return; yet how long is this possible, and what can we do to support it?

To understand suffering and to make it your own will not dictate a particular strategy of action, but it will throw you into the battle to make your own decisions as a follower of him who suffered all that we might be one. Our Lord is risen! In him we have peace and life. Amen.

# 9. from these stones

CARLYLE MARNEY

*Carlyle Marney has gained a national reputation as a lecturer and preacher. He has lectured on more than fifty university and college campuses and has preached in many well-known university chapels, churches, and military bases in this country and abroad. For ten years he was pastor of the First Baptist Church, Austin, Texas, and while there served on the faculty of Austin Presbyterian Seminary. Currently he is Senior Minister at Myers Park Baptist Church in Charlotte, North Carolina.*

*Dr. Marney has written five books and has contributed numerous articles to theological journals. He received his education from Carson-Newman College (A.B.) and the Southern Baptist Theological Seminary (Th.M. and Th.D.). Wake Forest has conferred the Doctor of Literature upon him.*

Bear fruit that befits repentance, and do not presume to say to yourselves, "We have Abraham as our father"; for I tell you, God is able from these stones to raise up children to Abraham. Even now the axe is laid to the root of the trees; every tree

therefore that does not bear good fruit is cut down
and thrown into the fire.     (Matt. 3:8-10.)

Out of the Palestinian wilderness, perhaps from a little community of hardly known Essenes, there came a wild sort of fellow, and he got a hearing. Eternal voices frequently have come from wilderness places, and sometimes such voices are heard by people who are not wild at all.

To the contrary, John's hearers were a *religious* people. They comprised the largest population group within their nation. They enrolled the most respected elements of their culture. They were a participating group in the respected institutional religion of their day. Their salvation was being constantly reassured to them by annual blood atonement. They were favored in their own eyes and in God's—especially blessed, picked, chosen. How often they had heard preached the doctrine of their own chosen-ness! Like our own "eternal security of the believer," it had become common property of the layman on the street: We are God's own!

The extent of their personal religion, however, like ours, was another matter. In the main it consisted of attendance upon the public functions, reasonable observance of custom and law, enjoyment of traditional assurances, with a grand seasonal series of revival as diversion. It was upon a people much like us that this wilderness bomber burst with his strange doctrine that when people have repented they ought to give evidence of it. No wonder they listened. So John preached in the wilderness towns, and his words fell like hot shrapnel at the first. "Repent! Who? Me?"

The thing that jarred even Jerusalem in John's preaching was his flat denial of their indispensableness. Their pet doctrine said, *"Chosen!"* John said, *"God does not have to use you!"* There is no most favored nation with God. He is able of these stones to raise up his needs. And he did. In less than twenty years God was raising up men to do his will from stones—Gentile rubble off the hills of southeast Europe.

He raised us up from rubble; our ancestors were but stones to these chosen, satisfied Jews. Now we have replaced the Jews as God's chosen ones—strange it sounds to our ears that God does not have to have us. Repent! Who, me? And for what?

There are moments in history, moments in the life of races, of nations, of cultures, and of churches, which if seized lead to immortality and which if lost issue in decadence. This is ours! And the weight of historical evidence is against our waking up. Whole civilizations will die, have died, rather than wake up! Must God raise up his seed of Abraham from another race? Must he whet his sword?

It would seem so, for now we are numerous enough to be a majority; *established* long enough to be comparatively unchallenged; settled enough that not even an earthquake disturbs our worship; old enough to have dignity, poise, and some beauty; rich enough to be social leaders; powerful enough to rewrite laws if we are hemmed too tightly; content enough to be beyond the reach of new social pressures; *pious* enough to know no real conviction for sin; strong enough to need no brothers; and complacent enough to be highly discriminating about the responsibilities we admit beyond ourselves. Hence, John's "bear fruit that befits repentance" has its hard way to make among us. We do not look for new seed of Abraham—God has got us! Let him be content.

We were not always rich, or numerous, or powerful, or so sure of our chosen-ness.

Once there was less than thirty of us at Williamsburg, and our women wept at the blood dripping from our pastor's hands as he preached through the bars of the town gaol. Before that, once there were but four of us screaming to our executioners that we were not a part of that Muenster madness, but our bones bleached in a cage on the town-hall roof for decades just the same. And once there was but one of us to whom our precious immersion-baptism was not only "a threat of death," but became death itself, as Dame Hubmaier, strapped to her ducking stool, was buried "with him" till she died. Not even in death could she have her companion, for Dr. Hubmaier got his from sulfur and fire. We have not all been so gently and genteelly baptized! Once when there were more of us we loaded our pathetic possessions on our ox wagons and came to the high wilds of West Virginia and East Kentucky to escape the taxes and the sacraments of the state-supported Anglicans. Often we have bought our privacy and freedom at the price of isolation and ignorance.

But one of us took his ideas to James Madison, and they got in the "Bill of Rights" for Virginia—and later they became the bedrock of our system of personal freedom. Some of us got to school, even started schools, while others rode the backroads in early days. And in the forests where a bear killed the first pastor of the first full church I served there is now a city of adherents to his faith and ours. We won our way. God raised us up from stones—the stones of Maine, from which Kittery's little congregation moved to Charleston, and the stones of Wales and England and Holland's sand flats. We won our way to this that we have. On the backs of grand men preaching five grand ideas we came to this.

The individual soul is both competent and responsible for that encounter with God in Christ in so far as any human agency is concerned. The church is composed of men who have so encountered God and bear witness to such a meeting of grace by immersion in "believer's baptism." Such a company of believers is responsible to no earthly or churchly authority except Jesus Christ and its understanding of his will, while within that church all members are equal—no expertness bringing obeisance. Such a fellowship remains completely separate from the state, its cogs never enmeshing with the cogs of state, while its members live as citizens of two kingdoms. Finally, only the Scriptures provide for such a fellowship its authority in all matters of faith and practice.

Fundamental to each principle, underlying every one, was the great broad concept of the worth of any individual man, every individual man. Since every major tenet we held put us fairly in the center of the almost irresistible rise of the common man in this hemisphere, the "Century of the Common Man" saw us lifted to an unbelievable level of size, power, wealth, and influence. But we left someone behind, and here appears the fundamental cleavage in our personality. Here appears the cleft that threatens to make us schizophrenic and calls for God to raise up from *saner* stones a people he can trust. We left someone behind, and in order to reconcile us we added five principles to these other.

Accursed day that ever we theologized and falsely biologized our great discrepancy!

About 120 years ago when first we began to assume some place of numerical strength in the South a fundamental contradiction between our mighty tenet—all men equal—and our common practice—some white men equal—began to appear to our conscience. The thing just didn't look right! And even though we brought hundreds of slaves into our communions and called them "our people" it still did not look right. Yet slavery for the "new South" was so vital an economic institution, and prosperity was so obviously God's desire for us, that it had to be right. There had to be an explanation, and there was.

In the mid-1800's we could not call biology to our rescue, for she was barely a science. In the South theology was queen of the sciences, for astronomy and geology could not replace her without biology's help and Darwin had not yet written. So, without Darwin to call on, we went a notch higher and used God. Theology would explain this contradiction—and it did, until biology came to bolster the spots where theology sagged at the seams.

God did this thing! He made races; he intended races; and we violate his will if we try to unmake anything he has made. He makes some superior and some inferior. Some are sons of Ham, "drawers of water," "hewers of wood." Let us not tamper with God's decree. And though such reasoning seeped through the seams of our conscious here and there, the theology did it, and it survives a hundred years later to form the bulwark of the Dutch Reformed grasp at preserving economic superiority by means of "apartheid" in South Africa. They are preaching our 1840 theology!

Meanwhile Darwin came through, and modern biology was no longer the work of naturalists and bird watchers. It became a *science.* And under the twisting of Huxley and Spencer, Darwin, poor Darwin, was made to claim claims he never dreamed. Malthus and Mendel and Darwin, what crimes committed in thy names! A word that once referred to families of flowers now began to be used in a new sense. *Race* came to mean the difference in color pigmentation of human hide, and there were other differences. Gobineau expanded them; Chamberlain copied Gobineau; Nietzsche used them to build Superman; Hitler lived them into *Mein Kampf.* But worst of all, here in the South we used a butchered biology to bolster a biased theology, and it threatens to destroy not only our major principle of equality, but our very personality as a people of God.

Since about 1875 a blend of poor theology and poorer biology has crystallized in our minds to form the five great principles of pseudo-racism by which we preserve our vaunted superiority. They are every one as false as deadly. They all appear in the first volume of Gobineau's *Essay on the Differences in Races* (which explains why volumes two and three are still in French, since we needed only volume one). Every single one has been offered by some "educator" during the past year as being the fruit of vast research and earnest inquiry. And worse, it is done and accepted with a straight face. What are these vaunted principles by which racism thrives?

1. All cultural advance, and at bottom, all human progress is the work of and a result of the gifts of the great Aryan, primarily Germanic, predominantly Anglo-Saxon race.

2. All other races, especially colored of any kind, derive their advantage from the Aryan race and by nature are imitators, except where they are despoilers.

3. Race itself means the existence of certain psychic differences as pronounced as physical differences and by these native traits, some races are "hewers of wood and drawers of water," incapable of better things.

4. Human prosperity requires the presence within a culture of a race of conquerors and a race of vanquished, so that all types of functions may be filled. Aryan superiority being obvious, the racial disposition

of the problem is the most obvious and the most profitable to the "superior" group.

5. Any race mixture is a mongrelization which breeds out the better race qualities of each group and leaves always an inferior product.

And so it goes. Recently a woman telephoned to ask if it were not true that any child of Negro-white parentage would have skin like a garfish, and a man asked in earnest if King David were really Anglo-Saxon, while in Poland an old lady was quite upset to discover that Jesus was a Jew—she had thought he was a Pole!

Meanwhile, modern anthropology knows nothing of any racial, psychic characteristics. Modern sociology knows nothing of any racial, psychic characteristics. Modern sociology knows no intra-cultural tie-up of prejudice, for prejudice is everywhere a product of provincialism times institutionalism. There is no organic connection between race prejudice in South Africa and South Alabama. Modern biology knows no valid racism; there is only invalid stereotyping which refuses to see men as individuals and prefers to keep them in nice, safe categories. And most important, an honest biblical theology knows that *race* is strictly a modern concept, biologically and theologically false, for "God has made from one every nation."

Meanwhile, the cleavage is sharp in our consciences. We cannot ignore the economic, selfish, fear that provokes our poor theology of racism. We cannot close off the emotional set of automatic switches that guarantee our automatic racial reactions. Nor can we forget that haunting, throbbing undertone caused by the deep violation of that great hope that led us to freedom—all men are born equal. We begin to suspect that the Creator wills it so, that the four-fifths of the earth's millions who are "colored" in our eyes will not continue long to cooperate with our superiority. The tensions of Asia and Africa spill over into our county-seat towns, our school boards, our deacons' meetings, our coffee houses. And it doesn't help at all that John the Baptist keeps telling us to "bear fruit that befits repentance."

93

Nor does it help for us to remind ourselves that we are strong enough, in God's grace, to fix it—and it frightens us that he may expect us to achieve this thing as the seed of Abraham. Sometimes we wake up in the night remembering that Ephesus too was a strong and mighty church when the angel of the Lord called her to "Repent . . . . If not, I will come to you." And for nearly 1,700 years, since the Goths came, Ephesus has been a heap, thirty miles from any house.

Meanwhile, twenty-seven rifle balls blazed through an old Negro woman's house as she prayed in Gregg county. A while ago a Negro lad, with his new school clothes laid out to wear and thirty dollars worth of cotton-picking money in his pockets, died from a rifle bullet fired at random from a car at the roadside stand where he stopped for his "soda-water." A pastor is "frozen-out" east of here for refusing to vote against his conscience; a thousand towns, in a thousand ways, continue the thousands of hurts to the spirit of man. And the hackles rise on trustees' necks if we ever get too "Christian."

We were not always rich. Once we were poor, but how strange the ways of minority people where they have grown to majority! Sometimes we forget the principles whose throbbing gave us birth, and when we do we lose our history. Does the axe now lie at the root of the tree? This thing that lies before us is no "illustration" of the gospel's claim. It is its prime expression in our time, and a new kind of Pentecost lies beyond it.

Meanwhile, is there hope? Thin and well-greyed at fifty-five, with two children in the university, all his money gone, a modest salary, a small-town church, his eyes puffed with worry and fatigue, and in tears, he said, "I'll vote my conscience if it kills me." In him and his kind, who keep speaking their piece, there is hope, high hope, all we have. We get our peace when we achieve it, not before.

Once we were weak and had a great high love: The belief that in our Lord Christ's name men are really men, ends in themselves, never means to an end. Once the great church at Ephesus heard "but I have this against you, that you have abandoned the love you had at first. Remember then from what you have fallen, repent and do the works you did at first. If not, I will come to you."

Maranatha!
Even so, come, Lord Jesus, and show us how to do this great thing.

# 10. segregation
## and the ten commandments

EVERETT TILSON

*Everett Tilson, a Methodist and graduate of King College (B.A.),
was for eight years on the faculty of Vanderbilt University Divinity
School, where he had earlier received his B.D. and Ph.D. degrees. He
is now professor of Old Testament at the Methodist Theological School
in Ohio and frequently contributes articles to leading journals. In 1958
he published the book* Segregation and the Bible.

*In 1959 Dr. Tilson participated vigorously in the series of demonstra-
tions against segregation in Nashville, Tennessee. On behalf of the
faculty of the Divinity School at Vanderbilt University he helped
negotiate the release from jail of student James Lawson and was a critic
of Lawson's expulsion from Vanderbilt. More recently Dr. Tilson, with
six other Methodist ministers, was arrested on Easter Sunday, 1964,
in Jackson, Mississippi, while trying to attend worship. The sermon
"Segregation and the Ten Commandments" was preached at a Nashville
mass rally shortly before that city's downtown lunch counters were de-
segregated.*

96

## segregation and the ten commandments

Almost universally the churches officially condemn segregation. They do so, not on constitutional grounds, but because of the demands of their Lord. Our Christian churches do not oppose segregation because it is illegal; they oppose segregation because it is immoral. They do not oppose it because it is unconstitutional; they oppose it because it is unchristian. They do not oppose it because it breaches the ten amendments; they oppose it because it breaches the ten commandments.

Segregation breaches the first commandment: "You shall have no other gods before me." It substitutes race for God as the organizing center of life. It measures the worth and growth of human existence by an altogether human yardstick. And this, as we all know, is worse than immoral; it is idolatrous. Christian segregationists think they have an answer to this charge. In unqualified commitment to their race, they assure us, they have escaped that bondage to self which Christian faith sees as the root evil of human existence. But this assurance can hardly survive close scrutiny. Quite the contrary, segregation furnishes us with a center for the organization of our pride and ambition. No matter how physically weak, mentally dull, or morally obtuse they may be, so long as men of distinction wear a white skin, they can take pride in their common heritage with Al Capone and John Dillinger, not to mention John Kasper and Senator James Eastland.

Segregationists do not betray their self-centeredness in their hymn of praise to the white man; they do it by their private refrain: "Just think of it! I am a member of the Master Race!" They do not take pride in their race because it is white; they take pride in the white race because it is theirs. They do not idolize white skin because it is a mark of distinction; they make white skin a mark of distinction because possession is nine-tenths of idolatry. They idolize the white race because they belong to the white race. Because of their possession of the skin of the superior man's color, they can idolize themselves. Worse yet, thanks to the presence among them of other men of this same color, vocal altruism becomes a shield for covert egocentrism. Segregation does worse than put the god of race before the God of the universe. It puts the maker of me and mine before the Maker of heaven and earth.

I

Segregation breaches the second commandment: "You shall not make yourself a graven image, or any likeness of anything . . . in heaven above, . . . in the earth beneath, or . . . in the water under the earth." It turns a pale face into a graven image, then bows down and worships "the likeness" of what is "in the earth beneath." If here I were to substitute the platform of the Marxists or the ritual of the Canaanites for the platform or the ritual of the Eastlands, the breach of the second commandment would become quite clear. We Americans have remarkable skill in uncovering and shattering the graven images of the Russians and the Canaanites. Unfortunately, we do not fare so well in the struggle against the graven image of Jefferson Davis. But the graven image is there, and it is exceedingly dangerous. What must be set down as one of the most ironic facts of our time is the readiness of the most blatant anti-Marxists among us to let segregation take the same place in our life that Communism occupies in the Kremlin.

Segregation breaches the third commandment: "You shall not take the name of the Lord your God in vain." It asks God to bless us in our refusal to identify our neighbor by the love of God. Bishop Nygren reminds us, "When it is said that God loves man, this is not a judgment on what man is like, but what God is like." By the same token, when the New Testament confronts us with the demand to love neighbor as self it tells us nothing at all about our neighbor. Nothing about the size of his fortune, nothing about the state of his soul, nothing about the color of his skin. It tells us only that our neighbor, whoever, wherever, and whatever he is, is beloved of God. And God loves our neighbor not because he is lovable, but because God is loving. If God's love for neighbor be blind love—value blind, creed blind, color-blind—and our love be conscious love—value conscious, creed conscious, and color conscious, we should hardly be surprised at Jesus' stinging rebuke of our unctious piety: "Not every one who says to me, 'Lord, Lord,' shall enter the kingdom of heaven, but he who does the will of my Father who is in heaven."

Segregation breaches the fourth commandment: "Remember the sabbath day, to keep it holy." It sunders those whom God would join together. Instead of bringing Christians together because of a common faith, it keeps them apart despite a common faith. A local minister in a recent sermon on "The Almighty Race Question" illustrates the deep tragedy of the relation between segregation and the fourth commandment. The church bulletin which carried this sermon contained the following word of welcome: "Ours is a friendly church—visitors are always welcome." But the sermon made it quite clear that this applied only to certain visitors. There the minister said: "It is . . . the opinion of the official board that . . . in this time of tension any member of our church desiring to bring . . . Negroes must previously have cleared the matter with the pastor-in-charge, securing a written note from him to the effect that it is permissible." And some people are shocked by the requirement of a pass book in South Africa.

Segregation breaches the fifth commandment: "Honor your father and your mother." It defines kinship in terms of blood rather than faith. That is not the way Jesus defined it. One day as Jesus was speaking to a crowd someone said to him, " 'Your mother and your brothers are outside, asking for you.' And he replied, 'Who are my mother and my brothers?' And looking around on those who sat about him, he said, 'Here are my mother and my brothers! Whoever does the will of God is my brother, and sister, and mother.' "

## II

Segregation breaches the sixth commandment: "You shall not kill." It kills the noblest impulses in man. As Jesus so clearly saw, you can kill men without taking up the sword against them. The vitriolic tongues or pens of angry little men can be just as murderous as the sword or bomb in the hands of a maniac. Our Lord said:

"You have heard . . . it . . . said . . . 'You shall not kill; and whoever kills shall be liable to judgment.' But I say to you that every one who is angry with his brother shall be liable to judgment; whoever insults his brother shall be liable to the council, and whoever says 'You fool!' shall be liable to the hell of fire."

If Mr. and Mrs. Alexander Looby had been killed in the explosion that rocked Nashville who would have been responsible for their murder? A lot of people would have been responsible for their murder. The jails of Nashville could not begin to accommodate all the people who helped to set the stage for that crime. A whole host of Nashvillians aided and abetted the men who threw that bomb. All of us who have in any way insulted Negroes—we, as well as the droppers of the bomb, would have been guilty of this crime.

Here I do not refer alone to the merchants who turned "thumbs down" on the request of the Negroes for service at downtown lunch counters, thus forcing people to have to wage demonstrations for rights you and I take for granted. I do not refer alone to the people who in one breath hail as patriots the American revolutionaries who took up arms in protest against "taxation without representation" and then in the next condemn Negroes as anarchists for sitting down in protest against "equal prices without equal privileges." I do not refer alone to the people who, though many of them know better, trace this whole movement to a few outside "agitators." I do not refer alone to the operators of local television stations who in the midst of a controversial issue fail to ask any Negro leader to interpret for Nashville the other side of this controversy. I do not refer alone to the churchman who after two months of eloquent silence in Nashville calls the church in Denver to speak with "a clear voice" on race relations, but even at that safe distance fails to say what it is the church ought to say with "a clear voice." I do not refer alone to the tea-and-cocktail experts on human relations who, between their semiannual teas with Negro friends, drink cocktails once a week with Christian segregationists. I do not refer alone to the whites who believe cultured Negroes ought to play the role of guinea pigs that we might be convinced one by one of their readiness for admission into high civilization, as if the burden of proof rested on the shoulders of the Negro to show to you and me that he is our equal. I do not refer alone to the moderates who until the Negroes laid siege to the wall of segregation said it must fall, then after reading a few objective editorials on the subject decided that Nashville is not the place, now is not the time, and these are not the Negroes. I do not refer alone to the people who when Northern industrialists show up at downtown restaurants treat them as distinguished guests, yet insult Americans from Mississippi or South Carolina because of a difference in the pigmentation of their skin.

I refer to those of us who insult the Negro by failing to translate his quest into human terms. I refer to all of us who when we see a Negro man directing his thirsty child away from a water fountain, his hungry wife away from a lunch counter, or his frail mother away from a comfortable seat, insult him by failing to exclaim, "But for the accident of birth there I go." I refer to all of us who when we see a Negro mother leave her children alone while she goes to another part of the city to keep those of a white socialite insult her by failing to say, "But for the accident of birth there goes my sister."

There are endless ways of smothering the life of the oppressed. One of the oldest and most common is simply to close our minds and hearts to the fact of their existence.

The relation of segregation to the seventh commandment, "You shall not commit adultery," cannot be stated quite so simply. But one fact lies beyond dispute: Segregation has not prevented the violation of the commandment against adultery on an interracial basis. Here we do not even have to redefine adultery, as Jesus did, in terms of the lustful look. Under segregation, as under integration, men and women of both races have broken the seventh command-

*101*

ment. To paraphrase Lincoln: The fact that some white men will not have the black woman as a wife does not keep them from using her as a mistress.

Segregation breaches the ninth commandment: "You shall not steal." It robs the white man, and it robs the Negro. It robs the white man of a chance to discover that it is not the race but the segregation of the Negro that keeps him, in all too many of his places, in slums and poverty. It robs him of a chance to discover that beneath the skin Negroes and whites share a common humanity: They rejoice alike at birth; they weep alike at death; they suffer alike in pain; they hope alike in marriage; and they dream alike as parents. But what segregation steals from the Negro, as pointed out in the report of the President's Committee on Civil Rights, is much more basic and elementary. It robs him of equal access to public facilities. It robs him of equal access to educational opportunities. It robs him of equal access to decent housing in good neighborhoods. It robs him of equal access to a typical workweek and favorable working conditions. It robs him of equal access to hospital facilities. It robs him of the respect and dignity due him as a human being.

Segregation breaches the ninth commandment: "You shall not bear false witness against your neighbor." Segregation bears false witness against the white man, and it bears false witness against the Negro. Segregation bears false witness against the white man by ascribing his advantages to extraneous considerations. If he has a stratospheric intelligence quotient it is traced not to his genius but to his race. If he enjoys superior economic advantages it is traced not to his industry but to his race. If he is especially good it is traced not to the purity of his heart but to the whiteness of his skin. If such logic held a Negro of virtue, wealth, or intelligence would be an impossibility.

Segregation prompts men to bear false witness against the Negro. If he lives in a slum the Negro is charged not with poverty, but laziness. If he works in a kitchen the reason is not discrimination, but limitation. If he fails as an engineer the reason is not a lack of education, but a shortage of intelligence. If he goes to jail the reason is not environment, but heredity. If this logic held there would be no Negroes in engineering, kitchens, or slums. All Negroes would be behind bars.

Segregation has betrayed us into bearing false witness about both races. It has betrayed us into granting the white man undeserved advantages. It has betrayed us into denying the Negro basic rights. In short, thanks in part at least to segregation we have broken the ninth commandment against members of both races.

Segregation breaches the tenth commandment: "You shall not covet . . . anything that is your neighbor's." It prompts the white man to covet what belongs to the Negro. The Universal Declaration of Human Rights asserts that all men have a right to protection against any "inhuman or degrading treatment," against "any discrimination," against any denial of "equal access to public service," against any refusal of "equal pay for equal work," against "any restriction of full participation in the cultural and scientific advancements and benefits of society." If true we cannot deny the Negro, or any other person, his enjoyment of these rights without coveting what belongs to our neighbor. Therefore, insofar as segregation does involve men in the denial of these rights, by the same token it involves them in the breach of the tenth commandment.

The future of desegregation depends on our point of departure in times of crisis. How we answer the questions, "When do we start?" and, "How fast do we travel?" will hinge largely on the authority from whom we take our orders. If we take our cues from our neighbors' prejudices we shall move slowly and in all probability in the wrong direction at the wrong time for the wrong reason. On the other hand, if we take our cues from God's commandments who among us would dare answer, "Be patient, Lord, and I'll do what you say, but not here and not yet." It may be later than we think. This may be the hour for the tribe of Elijah to rise up and say to this generation: "How long will you go limping with two different opinions? If Jesus Christ is Lord follow him; but if Jim Crow, then follow him."

# PART II

CHRISTIAN AND SOCIAL IMPLICATIONS

# 11. law and order and christian duty

### EUGENE CARSON BLAKE

*One of the leading Protestant voices today, Eugene Carson Blake
has been since 1951 the Stated Clerk of the United Presbyterian Church
in the U.S.A. (until 1958 the Presbyterian Church in the U.S.A.).
Prior to his election to this highest position in his denomination he was
a pastor of congregations in New York state and of the Pasadena
(California) Presbyterian Church. Outside Presbyterian circles he is
known as a former president of the National Council of Churches
(1954-57), as the author of the now famous Blake-Pike proposal for
church union, for his frequent attendance at ecumenical conferences
and assemblies, and as one of the speakers at the March on Washington.
In recent months he has received several significant awards for his
strong leadership in the civil rights movement. Dr. Blake received his
education from Princeton University (A.B.), New College, Edinburgh,
and Princeton Theological Seminary (Th.B.). He has received honorary
degrees from sixteen colleges and universities.*

*In his sermon, which was preached at Riverside Presbyterian Church,
New York, he speaks about his arrest in Baltimore County, July 4, 1963.*

But Peter and the Apostles answered, "We must
obey God rather than men."     (Acts 5:29.)

the pulpit speaks on race

Almost everyone in our nation knows by now that the Negro community is no longer satisfied with the measure of freedom they now have received and earned in the hundred years since the Proclamation of Emancipation by Abraham Lincoln.

What appears to be still in question is whether white America will be converted in its pattern of thinking and living with regard to race and will voluntarily change the laws and customs of the nation soon enough so that freedom, justice, and equality will be established for Negroes in an orderly and nonviolent way.

Change is coming and soon. It is not a question "whether" or even of "when." The only question is "how." How will justice, freedom, and equality be established—voluntarily and by law, or violently and by revolt, rebellion, and revolution?

As James Reston clearly pointed out after the August 28, 1963, March on Washington, the most critical place for decision on this is in the churches of the nation. Unless people like you, largely white, professing Christians, make the Negro cause your cause; unless we transform the just demands of Negroes for their own rights into our demands as Americans for the rights of all Americans, we will be responsible for the violence that will come.

As I judge it there are three reasons for our hesitation.

1. Some are fearful of any change and will resist any reduction of the special privileges white people enjoy. These are the Negro haters, the Negro baiters. Fortunately, these are a small minority in the United States and an even smaller minority in New York.

2. Some say, "Yes—Negroes ought to have their rights, but they are pushing too hard. They want too much too quickly." Negroes rightly reply, "A hundred years marks the end of our patience."

3. Others say, "I would be for them, but they break the law with their demonstrations—civilization is based on law and order. We won't ally ourselves with law breakers."

From this you can see why I feel it important to preach to you about "Law and Order and Christian Duty," since this is my first sermon in New York since July 4, when, as I believe all of you must know, I was arrested just outside Baltimore, Maryland, for having, with others, ministers and laymen, Negro and white, broken deliberately the trespass law of that state. The occasion was a demonstration organized by the Congress on Racial Equality (CORE) designed to protest the standing indignity offered the large Negro community by a private amusement park which regularly advertised that it was open to the public (it even appears in Rand McNally Maps) and just as regularly has refused admittance to all dark-skinned Negroes.

One of the most distinguished Presbyterians of Baltimore, Furman Templeton, an elder, the Director of Baltimore's Urban League, was with me. He is a Negro. We approached the gate of the amusement park together. The guard stopped us, saying that we could not enter. I protested. The guard said that I could go in but Mr. Templeton could not. I protested again. The trespass law, in digest form, was read to us. We were asked to leave the private property. We refused, continuing our protest, and were arrested. Scores of others were arrested too, including six Roman Catholic priests, a Jewish Rabbi, a dozen Protestant ministers, and many young people of both races. I was there as acting Chairman of the Commission on Religion and Race of the National Council of Churches. Three others representing the National Council of Churches went with me from New York, including Bishop Corrigan of the Protestant Episcopal Church. The question is, Is this kind of action right or is it wrong? The fact that the demonstration was successful, that the owners stopped their discrimination last month, and that it is reported that business has been excellent since is not really relevant to my question.

When, if ever, is it right to break the law? That is the question that I want you to think about with me. The lawyers among you will quickly note that deep legal questions with which I cannot deal even were I qualified are raised in this sermon. I remind those of you who may be lawyers that in the eighteenth century lawyers were leaders in the legal, theological, and political discussions having to do with civil disobedience and revolution. It was an easier thing for a lawyer to do then than it appears to be now, since in eighteenth-century jurisprudence almost all lawyers thought of statute law as based upon or arising out of common law which in turn was thought to rest on "natural law"—something objective and given by nature, or more often by nature's God. In the twentieth century most lawyers have been taught to think of law in positive terms only. What does the law on the statute books say, and how, in fact, has it been interpreted by actual courts? The twentieth-century lawyer has made his day-by-day task easier by eliminating from consideration such concepts as "abstract justice" or "natural law." The effect of this means that most Protestant lawyers today, as lawyers, have not thought very much about the deep question of this sermon. My correspondence since July 4 reveals a rather naïve shock in the minds of many lawyers that anyone like me could deliberately break a law. All I can say here is that I wish more lawyers today would buckle down to the ultimate task of harmonizing their theology and their law, for I am conscious of the fact that lawyers will pay little heed to theologians or ministers in their own field.

I return then to my question, "When, if ever, is it right to break the law?" First, let me make it perfectly clear that breaking law is not something to be done lightly. Anarchy is a terrible thing. Disorder makes civilization impossible. Anyone who has lived through a riot or a revolution knows how much all of us ought to appreciate civil order and the police who enforce it for us. And some fear especially the breaking of a trespass law. These say that in our free society all freedom is based on the protection of property rights. This is partly true—but no Christian dare ultimately or finally put property rights above human rights. Did you never read Les Miserables? The most conservative of us knows better. No one has an absolute right that allows him to use his property against the general dignity of human beings. That is why equality in public accommodations is crucial.

So let us be entirely clear that law is not God. It has always from the first been a basic Christian conviction that there are times when a Christian ought to break law, any law. Let us look at a New Testament precedent.

Peter and some of his fellow apostles had been officially and legally ordered not to preach publicly that Jesus the Christ had been raised from the dead. They were in and out of jail several times for refusing to obey the injunction established by the church and state officials—high priest, council, and senate.

As Christians Peter and the apostles believed that they must not obey any order, however legal, which would stop them from making their witness to the Lord Jesus Christ. They said, "We must obey God rather than men."

I do not believe that any of you would argue in general that it is never right to break a law. What about Christians or Jews under Hitler? What about the Boston Tea Party? What about the whole series of arrests in the New Testament when Christians regularly refused to obey some laws even when they were taught through the Apostle Paul that the powers that be were ordained of God?

Has the present day effort by American Negroes to win equality now in voting, in education, in job opportunity and advancement, in housing, and in public facilities (even amusement parks) anything to do with witnessing to Jesus Christ, as did law violation in the first century?

It is quite clear that all the highest authorities in the Church of Jesus Christ do so believe. The general assembly of my own church has repeatedly made it clear that the white man's treatment of the Negro in our free nation is morally and spiritually wrong and that our normal treatment of the Negro even in the church itself is morally wrong. The World Council of Churches said it is "a betrayal of Christ." The Pope has made it clear that this is also the Roman Catholic understanding. The presiding bishop of the Protestant Episcopal Church, in an address based on the Scriptures and on the actions of their convention, has spoken officially and most eloquently in the same vein. So have all the major churches in the whole world!

The World Council of Churches has been willing to lose from

its membership several South African churches rather than to weaken its witness to the Christian importance of racial equality and justice.

The general board of the National Council of Churches has asked us all to begin now to act in harmony with our Christian profession. But why just now? Why do we act now, apparently encouraging an increasing lawlessness on the part of the Negro community? It is because we wouldn't listen that now we run risks of lawlessness and violence.

It is clear enough that we should have begun to witness to our convictions in this matter much sooner, but there are at least two reasons why I plead with each of you today to consider what may be your Christian duty in this battle for justice and equality in the United States.

First, the nation faces a crisis. It is not a sectional crisis; it is a national crisis. For a hundred years, since their fathers were freed from chattel slavery, the Negro community has on the whole followed Christian nonviolent leadership in trying to win a place of dignity and equality according to our American Constitution.

In some states they do not yet have the right to vote, because of either intimidation or unjust local laws. Due to interrelated discrimination in getting jobs, in finding housing, and in opportunities for education most Negroes find it almost impossible to move out of the lowest social and economic strata of our society. It was not long ago that we had in my town in California Negro college graduates dumping garbage trucks because they were discriminated against in jobs for which they had prepared at great effort and sacrifice. Is it then surprising that many other Negroes drop out of high school when they see how hard it is to get ahead, even if you are good? Is it surprising that there are not enough Negroes ready for good jobs when some do open up? Why are we surprised that Negroes generally are forced into crowded housing (high priced), because they do not qualify for other communities as "our kind of people?"

I say these inequalities are all interrelated—a push towards

112

solving them all together, along with the right to vote everywhere and the right to public accommodation everywhere, is the only racial solution. And the people who are preventing this national and Christian solution are not the Governor Faubuses and the Governor Wallaces in Arkansas and Alabama. The people responsible for the stalemate are *we*—white Christians who have isolated our bodies from the realities of the city by living in the suburbs or by having doormen in high-rise apartments, and our minds from the realities of the injustice our laws and social patterns impose upon Negroes by forgetting all about them whenever they become quiet and patient. We have a national crisis which may lead to all sorts of violence, and even to revolution, if we do not now decide to throw our persons and our influence into changing the segregated pattern of American life. The Negro community is tired of being patient under a century of excessively slow progress. They have seen what less qualified peoples of their own race have done in Africa to become free, and they don't intend to wait any longer. If there is increasing violence in the United States it will not be the fault of Negroes striving for fairness and justice; it will be the fault of all of us who, in apathy and ignorance, let that injustice continue. I might say here that if any of you are worried at the lack of popularity of our American way of life in Asia, Africa, and even in Europe, you could do more to make "the free world" strong by helping establish justice and dignity in our land for the colored people in it than in any other way I know. Communism makes worldwide progress with each headline of violence in Alabama, Mississippi, New York, or Illinois.

That is merely the national crisis. The second reason why you and I must act now to establish justice (and this second reason is of first importance for any Christian) is that there is an equally grave crisis in the Christian church to which up until now Negroes have been amazingly loyal.

There is a greater crisis yet in the church. It would be my estimate that there are at least 5,000 Presbyterian pastors who have a bad conscience about what they are doing and failing to do to help right Negro wrongs. This is because they are fearful that their congregations would not support them if they simply obeyed the gospel and led their people to take the lead in this contest for human dignity for all men for whom Christ died.

I estimate that 5,000 Presbyterian ministers hesitate to lead in this effort because they are afraid for their jobs. And they have good reason. Again and again congregations all over this land have made it clear that they do not want their pastors to be "controversial" even when that controversial position is clearly based upon the gospel of Jesus Christ. And I do not believe my denomination lags behind the others in this battle.

This leads us to a further crisis in the ministry of the church. I am sure you know by now that the recruitment of the ablest young men for the pastorate has fallen off in recent years. I am sure that one of the chief reasons why the ablest of our dedicated young men do not look forward with joy and enthusiasm to becoming pastors is that they do not want ever to find themselves in the embarrassing position in which too many sincere and conscientious pastors are today. Despite all the attractiveness of the pastorate and its daily opportunity to serve Jesus Christ, these young men do not see enough congregations willing to follow truly Christian leadership.

I dare not estimate how many of the 3,250,000 United Presbyterian members or the 40,000,000 Protestants have bad consciences too. You know that we all have allowed our own comfort, our own prosperity, our own fears, and our own conscious and unconscious prejudices to guide us in our actions (and equally in our lack of action) rather than our professed Christian faith.

Frankly, the Christian church in America does not look much like a Christian church as far as race is concerned. Even an advanced congregation like this has only reached the "token" stage of integration. We look like religious clubs for our own kinds of people, the religious holy embroidery on a secular culture which is essentially more and more selfish and fearful the wealthier and more comfortable we become. I say then that the reason people like you and me should stand with our Negro brethren in their effort

114

to achieve equality is that if we do not we shall reveal ourselves at last as hypocritical and we shall fail in our day to witness to Jesus Christ whom we proclaim to be the Savior of the world.

One of my correspondents since July 4 wrote me to inquire if I thought Jesus Christ would ever demonstrate and cause violence. I wrote him that that was entirely too simple a way to put the question. I am sure that the white and Negro school children who have gathered in churches all over the South and then have gone out to "sit in" in physical danger in protests at lunch counters are nearer to the Kingdom than most of us.

What then can you do? May I conclude this sermon by suggesting some very concrete actions:

1. You can try to get Congress to pass stronger civil rights legislation. If you believe in upholding the law will you not do your part to get the laws in this matter strengthened?

Write your two Senators and your Congressman today. Tell them that you believe civil rights to be a moral matter, that you want good legislation passed, and that you do not want your representatives to make this a partisan issue—nor will you countenance their allowing a filibuster to prevent this needed legislation. This effort will cost you fifteen cents and an hour's time to write good letters. This is vital now in fifty states.

Begin to demonstrate. No segregated marches any more. The invitation is to you. Unless people like you begin to demonstrate it is now freely predicted that no civil rights legislation will pass, and if the Congress is unable or unwilling to legislate it is freely predicted that a new and more violent phase in civil rights demonstration will then begin.

2. Tomorrow join the NAACP and make a whopping big contribution to its legal and defense fund. Again let me appeal here to any of you who really would uphold the law. The NAACP has for a quarter of a century and more pressed in court after court trying to honor the law by seeking justice and equality for all under the Constitution.

Join the Urban League which is a national organization that has been working for years to make a break for Negroes in getting jobs and being advanced according to merit. Make a contribution to the Urban League, and add to your charities (all, by the way, are not deductible), the Southern Christian Leadership Conference of Martin Luther King, Jr.; the Congress of Racial Equality, headed by James L. Farmer; and the Student Nonviolent Coordinating Committee. These are the organizations that are leading the effort for justice and equality now. If you are unwilling to give to them give then to the National Council of Churches and earmark the funds for its Commission on Religion and Race.

What else can you do besides writing letters and joining organizations and supporting them?

3. You can make it your project where you work to see that jobs are open to Negroes who are qualified and that your business will train unqualified Negroes the same way you train and upgrade presently unqualified white people. If you don't work but are a stockholder, write the management and tell them, or the owner, that you want your company to be a leader in enlightened employment policies as to race. You may lose a bit of your popularity if you really take this seriously, but you must begin wherever you have influence.

4. You can pray each night for the Negro community and its leaders; you can pray for the people who are in Mississippi jails under excessive bond and have been there for weeks and months. You can pray for any of us who day by day have to make hard decisions, realizing that we may be wrong in them, but must nevertheless try to make them as Christians.

5. You can begin an effort to make it possible for anybody who has the money to buy and rent in your own town, your apartment, your community. I know I am moving into a touchy subject here. I do not speak only to you. I speak to myself as a resident of a lovely spot of suburban isolation and retreat. Ah, but that is the place that I have found for my own family's peace and development. "Don't make us ruin our hometown!" "Suburban living" by the power structure of our society is one of the causes of the racial

crisis. I have driven from New York to Connecticut off and on for thirty years. I noticed that recent racial disturbances on the Boston Post Road in the Bronx are in a part of the city I used to drive through. But I have not been on Fordham Road for fifteen years. We have thruways and expressways now which make it possible to isolate ourselves almost completely from any ugliness. In these years more and more Americans are driven from rural to urban life —and those who are poor live in increasingly crowded cities.

You will find that you will not increase your popularity in your town, or your white community, if you really mean to back the open housing program already begun by many churches.

6. You can protest everytime you hear any one blaming Negroes for agitation or saying they ask too much. Some, of course, do ask too much, and some ask for the wrong things; but the cause of extremism is justice delayed, and we, not they, are responsible for that.

What you can do is to begin to act your faith even if it may lead you to arrest, ridicule, poverty, or even physical danger. The widely publicized demonstrations in Mississippi and New York and the August 28, 1963, March on Washington will not be important unless they symbolize and encourage the members of our churches to act in a new pattern of witness to Jesus Christ with regard to racial equality and justice. If this happens widely, not only among a few ministers and a few members, it will go far to mark the very renewal of the church by the Holy Spirit of God in faith and in hope and in love. It is time for us all to stand up and be counted.

"We must obey God rather than men" said Peter and the apostles, and that simple decision became the foundation of the Church of Jesus Christ and the reason for its winning the world to him. It is not easy always to know how to obey God. But no one who is failing to try to find the way to change the racially segregated pattern of American life can claim these days to be trying very hard to obey God. And then when we have done our best, we will still be sinners, as the gospel reminds us, and we will need each others' fellowship and prayers as sinners who are forgiven freely when they do repent of evil and turn to God through Jesus Christ.

The Christian gospel is a power for reconciliation, of sinners to God, and of all men to all men. In worship here or in any Christian sanctuary we need to be helped to be agents of that divine reconciliation, loving one another even when we deeply disagree, loving the enemies we make and those too who make us their enemies. Thus the Church of Jesus Christ will be his church. Thus will the church witness to its Lord.

# 12. who is my neighbor?

JOHN R. BODO

*Born in Budapest, Hungary, in 1920, John Bodo received his early education in Europe before coming to this country in 1941. He graduated from Union Theological Seminary, New York (B.D.) and received his Th.M. and Th.D. degrees from Princeton Theological Seminary.*

*For eight years Dr. Bodo was pastor of the First Presbyterian Church in Princeton, New Jersey, and is now the chairman of the Department of Practical Theology at San Francisco Theological Seminary. A number of his sermons and articles have been published in leading journals, and he is a frequent lecturer throughout the country.*

*The sermon, "Who Is My Neighbor?" has a special history. It was preached in Princeton in 1957 a day or two before a "Covenant of Open Occupancy" mailing was to be received by the members of the church. Along with a copy of the covenant was a request from the church's board of elders, which earlier had adopted the covenant, that all adult members whose conscience so inclined them sign and return the covenant to the church. Dr. Bodo's church received signed covenants from nearly one third of its members and at the same time experienced no significant loss in its membership.*

the pulpit speaks on race

Who is my neighbor? (Luke 10:29.)

Tomorrow or the next day you will receive from the Session
a little document giving you an opportunity as members of this
church and citizens of this community to go on record, individually,
in favor of equal opportunity in housing. It is no secret that every
tenth Princeton resident is forced to live in a strictly defined area
just because of his complexion. The Session, following the action
of the 1956 General Assembly of the Presbyterian Church, has
studied the problem from the standpoint of both civic and Christian
concern and is now laying it upon your conscience.

To be sure, segregation is not peculiar to Princeton. It is still
the prevailing pattern, South and North. In the North great progress
has been made in many phases of the problem, especially since
World War II. Princeton has shared in this progress by gradually
equalizing opportunities in education, in public accommodations,
in employment. But the housing barrier—patterned on the ghetto
system of the Middle Ages—stands fast.

Against this local background it may be worthwhile to explore
some of the reasons why the ancient question, "Who is my neighbor?" should receive our renewed attention, and why the implied
question, "Who may be my neighbor?" should be raised in the
oldest church of Princeton.

I

What guidance do we find in the Bible on this problem?
All our lives we have been hearing and repeating the Ten Commandments and their summary, enthroned by Jesus as the supreme
commandment, "You shall love the Lord your God. . . . And . . .
your neighbor as yourself." If we were asked who is meant by the
word neighbor we would probably answer that in the Christian
perspective all our fellow men are our neighbors, especially in this
shrunken world of ours. But the biblical meaning of neighbor was
primarily geographic. In the context of Palestinian society neighbor
meant the man next door or a few doors up or down, because vil-

lages were very small, and common defense and other interest demanded physical nearness. There were other laws for the conduct of the Jews toward strangers and foreigners, but the law of neighborly love was God's law for a neighborhood—literally.

A good neighbor was a great asset. In Prov. 27:10 we are reminded,

> "Better is a neighbor who is near
> than a brother who is far away"

which is like saying, "a friend in need is a friend indeed"—if he is near enough when I need him! On the other hand, the temptations of a neighborhood are realistically admitted in the Old Testament. What could be more candid as well as contemporary than "You shall not covet your neighbor's house, you shall not covet your neighbor's wife, or his power mower or his station wagon, or anything that is your neighbor's"? We dare not push away from us the homely edge of God's neighborhood law. The Bible shows that the awareness of human brotherhood under a common heavenly Father was born, nurtured, and refined in neighborhood situation, complete with front lawns, back fences, and children playing together.

It is on this foundation that Christ's law of love is built. The story of the good Samaritan assumes all the rich meaning of the word neighbor and then enlarges it to include others to whose presence we might not be accustomed, and whom, in our ignorance, we might fear or scorn. The real point of the story is not that we should help our fellow men when they are down, but that a fellow man we may have been excluding from our fellowship—from our "neighborhood" —might prove to be a more genuine neighbor than even some of the most distinguished members of our own in-group, club, or race —whatever that word means.

## II

Now residential segregation in Princeton has received considerable official and public recognition in recent months. It would not be proper for me to comment—at this time and in this place—on the efforts of the Borough Housing Authority and the subsequent discussion between the Borough Council and a citizens' committee from the affected area. It is my understanding, however, that the Mayor's Advisory Committee on Housing, in its latest report, makes it unequivocally clear that there can be no permanent solution to the problem of the Witherspoon-John Street area until all parts of our community become open to all persons, subject only to such economic limitation as apply to all of us.

But Christian concern with any public issue is always personal rather than technical. Technical considerations are important and cannot be lightly dismissed in the name of abstract principle, but for the citizen who strives to think and act primarily as a Christian the question must always be, "What is the human side of this issue? What is happening to people as a result of this state of things?"

It is on this personal level that the deepest psychological and spiritual damage is being inflicted on Negro Princetonians. No one can fully develop his God-given potential as a person unless he is free—as free as the next person—to take a responsible part in the life of his community according to his individual ability and inclination. The issue is not integration per se. The issue is freedom. As long as we actively perpetuate or passively condone a system which makes it impossible for an otherwise fully qualified Negro family to live on our street we are accessories to robbery. We are robbing fellow citizens and fellow Christians of their freedom just as effectively as if those "ghetto" walls were real walls, with the doors left open during certain hours and under certain conditions, but in this respect, tightly shut and bolted on our side.

Oh, it would do some of us a great deal of good to change places —if only for one week—with a Negro Princetonian in search of a house or building lot! Our purpose would not be to prove an abstract point. It would be as simple as finding a better place to live, with a spacious yard for the children and an environment more adequately reflecting our economic, cultural, and social level. What an eye-opener it would be for us, in our dark disguise, to make the rounds and get the "runaround"—to be told by agents that they have nothing to suit our needs when the newspapers scream with their "for sale" ads, to hit snag after snag in conversations with well-meaning but uninformed, conventionalized people! With what shame and indignation would we come back to resume our fair skin and to take our stand with the forces that will not rest until Princeton becomes at last one community, "indivisible, with liberty and justice for all"!

## III

If the effects of residential segregation on Negro Princetonians are damaging as well as obvious the effects upon us are equally damaging though more subtle.

For one thing, segregation keeps us in a state of uneasiness and apprehension. The day of "white supremacy" is done throughout the world. The nonwhite majority of mankind has caught up with our technological advantage, or is catching up fast. Millions of hands—yellow, brown, and black—are reaching for the abundant life. Through our foreign aid program we endeavor to grasp these hands in friendship and to work out a partnership in the defense of freedom and peace. But our hands are sticky—sticky with nearly a hundred years of unfulfilled promises—and the Russians, whose hands are sticky with blood of millions, still manage to pose as the friends and saviors of the colored peoples of the world by making sure that they know all about Emmett Till and Autherine Lucy and the so-called "code of ethics" of America's real estate brokers.

So we fear the march of history in a vague, haunting way, but paradoxically, we fear our friends even more. The unforgivable sin in our day seems to be nonconformity. A pamphlet published by the American Friends Service Committee has the significant title *They Say That You Say*. Its thesis is that continued residential segregation cannot be blamed on the real estate brokers or anyone else—except on ourselves. We worry about what our friends might

123

say if we stepped out of line, and they worry about what we might say if they stepped out of line, until we are all trapped in a strange ghetto of our own—a spiritual ghetto—whose walls are made of unexamined assumptions and within whose bounds we live like carbon copies of one another, outdoing one another in that most un-American trait—conformity.

But the spot where residential segregation hurts us most is our conscience. As Americans in general and Princetonians in particular we are committed to the ideals of John Witherspoon, Woodrow Wilson, and many others like them. This heritage of Christian and democratic ideals weighs on our hearts with an aching weight. The more we cherish our past the more painful becomes the present with its big words and small deeds. Negro Americans and Negro Princetonians are the only ones whose conscience need not and does not hurt at this crucial point. They did not ask to come here in the first place; our ancestors brought their ancestors over by force. They did not ask to be cheated of the fruits of their freedom once freedom became the law of the land; our great-grandfathers, South and North, made sure that their freedom should remain largely on the books. Even now, a century after the Emancipation Proclamation, they are asking only that we begin at last to keep our own laws—that we become what we say we are—and they are pleading their case with all the dignity and power of a clear conscience, while all of us—whether we are pro or con—must live with a corroding sense of guilt, for no other reason than that we are free, white, and over twenty-one!

## IV

Now what is the Christian potential of equal opportunity in housing? What would happen, specifically from the Christian point of view, if through your witness and friendly endeavors Princeton should become what you have long desired it to be—an effective, unself-conscious showcase of American democracy at its best?

For one thing, the opening of all of Princeton to all residents on the basis of individual merit alone would strike at the roots of one of our gravest sins as Christians—the sin of pride. I do not mean being proud of worthwhile accomplishments and cherished possessions. I mean pride in the biblical sense—the arrogant, unwarranted exalting of ourselves at the expense of others. Just remember one ironic fact: Princeton is a residentially integrated community right now, because Negroes can and do live everywhere—right in our homes—as servants. They may live under the same roof with us, minister to our most basic needs, share our life at the closest range —as long as they do not forget their "place," their inferior status which our infantile craving for superiority demands. I ask you: If this be not sin, what is sin?

Again, the opening of all of Princeton to all residents on the basis of individual merit alone would help our churches become what God designed them to be and what they actually claim to be. If there is one fellowship in a community where persons should be together regardless of all incidental differences, the churches should be that fellowship. Unfortunately this is usually not the case. At a conference I attended, D. T. Niles of Ceylon reminded us that "fellowship" in the New Testament is always a noun, because it is conceived as God's gift through Jesus Christ, in whom we have a unity more fundamental than any of our divisions. But, he went on to say, in this country we have made "fellowship" into a verb, to indicate how little we care for our God-given unity in Christ and how much we prefer to associate with one another on the basis of superficial likeness, until our churches become little more than mutual admiration societies.

The shoe fits. We dare not deny that the churches of Princeton —and this church in particular—have not been in the vanguard. As Christians we can ill afford to point any fingers, for the finger we point always turns around to point at us. Right here, in the sanctuary, we are still—not by law, not by direct intention, but in lame statistical fact—a segregated church. And my conviction is that our broken fellowship will never be restored at all unless you as Christian citizens help to take down the wall which is the main cause of our continued division as Christians—the wall of the ghetto by which our impulse to Christian togetherness has been effectively contained and well-nigh stifled.

May I close with a little personal confession, quite typical and quite damning. I have not always said or even known the things I have said today. Rather, I knew them in theory but did not feel them in my flesh and bones. I got through five years in a church in Newark without ever discovering the problem, because the nearest Negro lived a mile away and might as well have lived on another continent. But even in this church—half a block from Witherspoon Street and three blocks from our sister church—I got through two years without really facing the problem, so high and strong are the walls of the ghetto. Even to the most "broadminded" among us something special must happen to awaken him and to help him discover his brothers on the other side of the wall.

How did it happen to me? I wish I knew. I am reminded of a science fiction story in which there was a whole fascinating world enveloping New York in another dimension, impinging on the city at all points but unknown to New Yorkers except when one of them inadvertently fell through the hole. I forget where the hole was supposed to be or what it was supposed to symbolize in the story. But, speaking of my pilgrimage through Princeton, I humbly thank God for that unremembered day when he caused me to fall through the hole. For in my discovery of that other Princeton—among the missing ten per cent—my experience of the potential glory of America and the fullness of the church of Jesus Christ has been deepened and enlarged far beyond my deserving.

So tomorrow or the next day, when you receive your "covenant of open occupancy" from our Session, remember it may be your road map to the hole—to the hole in your private ghetto wall—through which God may guide you into a fresh dimension of love and fellowship and into a more faithful obedience to his commandment, "You shall love your neighbor as yourself."

126

# 13. a new resource

ARCHIBALD JAMES CAREY, JR.

*Archibald James Carey, Jr. is a man who has mastered at least two professions, the law and the ministry. He received his theological training from Garrett Biblical Institute (B.D.) and his legal training from Chicago-Kent College of Law (LL.B.). For nineteen years he served as minister of Chicago's Woodlawn African Methodist Episcopal Church, where the Congress of Racial Equality (CORE) was formed, and for the past fifteen years he has been pastor of the Quinn Memorial Chapel, the first Negro American congregation established in Chicago. During this same period he has maintained an active partnership in a well-known law firm in Chicago's Loop and has gained wide recognition as an alderman from Chicago's populous Third Ward. He also teaches legal ethics at John Marshall Law School.*

*In 1953 Dr. Carey was a delegate to the Eighth General Assembly of the United Nations, and in 1957 President Eisenhower appointed him chairman of the President's Committee on Government Employment Policy, he being the first Negro American ever appointed chairman of a White House committee. In 1961 he was a speaker at the Tenth World Methodist Conference in Oslo, Norway. Dr. Carey has been active in politics and recognized frequently for his work in human relations.*

127

*Both the Doctor of Divinity and the Doctor of Law degrees have been conferred upon this man of diverse and unusual talent.*

> You shall not see my face, unless your brother is
> with you.                                    (Gen. 43:3.)

The Negro American today represents the greatest paradox on earth. He is, at once, the symbol of liberty and of limitation. He is a native son of the greatest democracy in the world. His liberties have been proclaimed by amendments to our Constitution and specially delineated by Executive Orders from Presidents Lincoln, Roosevelt, Truman, Eisenhower, and Kennedy. Exhibits have been organized on massive scale to display his achievements and progress, and all over the land special observances are hailing one hundred years of his freedom. Nevertheless, eminent ministers are jailed for attempting to use public facilities and an honored soldier of our armed forces needed 23,000 federal troops to register for advanced studies. Listen to three observers of the American scene. One is Lerone Bennett in his fine volume *Before the Mayflower.* "Today, one hundred years after the Emancipation Proclamation, American Negroes are still permanent exceptions to the melting pot theory. Not only are they not melting, one writer says, but most white Americans are determined that they shall not get in the pot." Another is Abraham Heschel, eminent Jewish scholar. Speaking to the National Conference on Religion and Race, January 14, 1963, he said, "It was easier for the children of Israel to cross the Red Sea than for a Negro to cross certain university campuses." And James Baldwin in his book *The Fire Next Time,* wrote, "The country is celebrating one hundred years of freedom, one hundred years too soon."

A few years ago George Washington Carver was selected as the "Man of the Year" for having made the outstanding contribution to Southern agriculture. Is it not a strange commentary on any society that a man can be named the "Man of the Year" for having made the outstanding contribution to the basic occupation of his

often by their white brethren and sisters, some eminent and some nameless of both races, have converged in a multiplicity of gallant assaults upon the ramparts of race discrimination. They have ridden buses, sat at lunch counters, waded at beaches, registered at polling places, applied at universities, kneeled in churches, and instituted proliferate litigation in the most virile and protracted attack upon inequality of opportunity our century, if not history, has seen. With Spartan fortitude they have braced themselves to withstand any torture the mob may invoke, and they have announced the unwavering quality of their commitment by the unfaltering chant, "We shall overcome."

For generations the Negro American's aspirations could be stifled by the tactics of terror, but not any more. Today he can be brutalized, but not browbeaten. His head may be struck with truncheons, but not his heart with terror. Like a waking giant he is rising to his feet and bursting his bonds, and he is determined not to stop until he stands full erect.

This surging revolt is not limited to the master plan of one supreme council or a torch lifted by one leader. It is a prairie fire. Among Negro Americans today the excitement for freedom is everywhere. A speaker in Chattanooga said publicly, "Kill a Negro leader today and a thousand will rise where he fell." A reporter of the metropolitan press asked, with obvious skepticism, "Do you really believe that?" A few days later Medgar Evers was shot, and 2,000 Negroes, without his leadership, marched from his funeral on City Hall. The ferment for freedom has leavened the whole loaf.

In Birmingham I walked among the ruins of the bombed homes and businesses and heard some of the 3,000 Negroes who went to jail and somehow found 400,000 dollars bail money to get out, declare they were ready to go again at any time. In Jackson, Mississippi, I viewed in dismay the stockade strung with wire, reminiscent of Hitler's concentration camps, devised to contain the thousands of Negroes and whites who demonstrated and were jammed into that compound under a merciless sun and amid abominable conditions of sanitation. In Jackson, too, I watched the three small children of Medgar Evers (who led the NAACP in Mississippi and was slain by a sniper) play about in their home under the round hole in the wall above them, made by the bullet which killed their father. As the husband and father got out of his car that fateful night in the carport driveway the sniper hiding in the bushes shot him in the back. It tore through his insides, fatally, came out through his stomach, continued into the living room of his home, pierced the wall, and dropped, spent, on the other side. I listened to the widow, calm and serene, tell of her plans not to flee, but to continue living in that very house and to increase rather than diminish the tempo of her own activities in her husband's work. Then in the mass meeting at Masonic Temple I heard the young Negroes of Jackson sing, in resolute defiance:

> If you don't see us in the city jail
> And you can't find us no more,
> Come on over to the county jail,
> We'll crowd it to the door.

Prime Minister Nehru spoke at the Chicago Council on Foreign Relations dinner in the fall of 1949. Telling the story of India's achievement of freedom by Gandhi's nonviolent techniques, he said, "If you aren't afraid, they can't put you down. They may threaten you and injure you—but they can't put you down. They may try to kill you, and even succeed, but—if you aren't afraid, they can't put you down."

The Negro American has comprehended and embraced this truth, and he has added to the resources of the nation the shining qualities of a new determination which is massive and a new courage which is audacious.

Today the Negro American has a new spirit of impatience with second-class citizenship. He feels he has waited long enough—and so do a host of people who are not Negro. He will become more restive as the days pass with his dreams and aspirations unfulfilled. He will no longer be content with exclusion. He will not accept segregated schools, segregated housing, segregated rights, or in-community—and in that same community be denied the right to eat in a restaurant, sleep in a hotel, ride in a first class seat, or even to cast the vote of his citizenship?

This list itemizes the long indulged practice of race discrimination, sanctioned by statute and condoned by custom—but much more, it dramatizes the tragic waste of the nation's resources.

The fact is that the Negro American has become, of material things and cultural values, a rich resource of the nation. The public image of the Negro is otherwise. It is that of an untrained, impecunious, often tortured, but easily victimized character. This distorted public image has framed him as the illegitimate child of his own indolence or limited equipment of mind and morals and has ignored the fact that he has been the helpless victim of mob rule, shackled opportunity, and throttled aspirations. When, by the Emancipation Proclamation on January 1, 1863, 4,000,000 bondsmen were suddenly freed they were woefully untrained, pitifully impoverished, and desperately demoralized. Suddenly they stood forth in a new world, unarmed for defense and ill-equipped for survival. Though nurtured and sustained by the compassion of some former slave owners and that assistance which came from the North, they were yet the picture of pathos, able only to rejoice that they were free. Any people who have the poorest education, or none, the poorest jobs, or none, the least incentive, or none, will find it difficult to produce and achieve like others. Color has nothing to do with it.

But in the moment of his greatest desperation the Negro was sustained by a support he had found under the weight of chains. It was his faith in God. Eleanor Wembridge once said in the *American Mercury* that only the Negro among the elegists of literature have presumed to begin with the plaint "Nobody knows the trouble I see" and end on the triumphant note "Glory, glory, Hallelujah." In short, the Negro looked at the heavens and reached out to God, and with a help which was as sure as it was unseen he began to make his way through the wilderness.

Even before emancipation, however, the Negro had made his contribution in spite of limited opportunity and inspiration. The first Negro to come to these shores was not one of the twenty Africans brought to the Virginia Colony as indentured servants in 1619 (a year before the Mayflower), but a discoverer of the New World. Alonzo Pietro, a Spanish Negro, helped pilot one of the ships under the command of Christopher Columbus. The toil of the Negro, very largely, developed the wealth of the New World, although little of it fell into his hands. He tilled its fields, laid its highways, constructed its buildings, built its railroads, and helped produce the chief export crops and products which caused the new nation to rise as a commercial power of the world. In national defense he became the first to shed his blood for America's freedom, when Crispus Attucks fell on March 5, 1770, in Boston, and in every crisis of the nation's history he proved himself a hero from Lexington to Lebanon.

But the Negro American of today is a new resource. In numbers he has become 1,000,000 residents of New York City, 55 per cent of the population of the nation's capital, every fourth man in Chicago, and one of every nine Americans. In purchasing power he has increased his annual income to 21,900,000,000 dollars. This is more than the combined income of the entire population of the Dominion of Canada and is estimated by the *Wall Street Journal* to be further growing at the rate of nearly a billion dollars per year. In education there are 250,000 Negroes in colleges and professional schools today, producing 15,000 graduates each year. They have scintillated on the athletic field, the concert stage, in the science laboratory, and at the negotiating table. They now sit in high places of government, education, and commerce, and nearly 200 have crowded into the diadem of Who's Who in America.

But the newest resource lies in the Negro American's new purpose and new courage. He has lost his fear. In his quest for freedom, in revolt against second-class citizenship, the Negro American is probably making his greatest contribution to America and to democracy in his astonishing drive to widen the strictured channels defined by race discrimination. Uncounted Negroes, joined very like Buchenwald. A few days after the liberation some of us went to the camp, taking with us some of the leading citizens of that little German city, including the burgomeister. They had told us that they had no knowledge of what had been going on inside the walls of that camp. Yes, they had used the labor of some of the people in the fields, a few of them had worked in the factories from time to time, but they really didn't know anything about the conditions under which the prisoners lived—and as it turned out, died. On this particular morning, seeing the shock and revulsion on their faces, I had to believe that they spoke the truth when they had said they didn't know. A couple of days after that, the burgomeister, confessing his failure as a Christian and as a citizen, took his life.

This was a long time ago, and in a foreign country. I remember wondering how it was that good people—basically decent people—could not know, and how a nation, a city, could allow such things to happen in its midst. I remember wondering how a Christian-oriented people could be the agent of so much death, suffering, and persecution directed to those of a different race; how the Church of Jesus Christ with only a few exceptions could keep silent in such a time. I also remember, now with quite vivid guilt, how critical some of us were of the church in Germany because of her silence, and how critical we were of the solid mass of the German people who through their silence and their indifference seemed really not to care about the persecutions. That was a long time ago, and in a foreign country.

On October 30, 1963, I spent the late afternoon and evening in Plaquemine, Louisiana. This, you will remember, is the city where James Farmer, the National Director of CORE, was imprisoned the end of August, at the time of the March on Washington. I had gone there with five others, staff and directors of the Board for Homeland Ministries of the United Church of Christ, which was meeting in New Orleans. We had been asked by the board to go to this beleaguered community as evidence that we knew and cared about what was happening there. In that little city the Negroes hadn't been able to hold a public meeting for some time because there had been too much violence and bloodshed on the past two occasions when they had gotten together. Because we were coming, however, that night seemed to be a good time to try it again. They got out some handbills around the town, and in other ways spread the word that some Christians from outside were coming to be with them. So we gathered in the Plymouth Rock Baptist Church. The last time folk had gathered there to talk about freedom and their civil rights and to confess their faith in the Lord of Creation, the local police had ridden horses up into the vestibule, and indeed, one of them into the church, and had fired tear gas into the building. The medical repair bill for that little exercise in freedom had been over 800 dollars. It included the repair of very serious second-degree burns from tear gas fired at point blank range and repairs to flesh and bone and muscle injured by iron shoes on the hooves of the horses ridden by the sheriff's men. Most of these injuries were on feet and ankles and lower legs, but at least one of them was on the chest of a man. This bill also included treatment to injuries of vital and sensitive parts of the human anatomy inflicted by the cruel and abusive use of cattle prods.

What was it like in Plaquemine, Louisiana, in this year of grace? The overpowering sense that one got was that of being in a foreign land. There was really nothing familiar, and the dependable things that you and I have unconsciously based our lives upon were all absent—the verities, the principles which structure all solid communities—they just weren't there. In communities like this one the police are not your protector; they can be your enemy, the specific instrument of your torture. The community is not your friend; it becomes a kind of battleground. The six of us rode together in a rented car the sixty miles from New Orleans. Because Archie Hargreaves, a Negro, was with us, we were followed many of those miles. The law there is not that majestic protector of the rights of citizens which we like to believe it to be; it becomes one of the instruments for persecution in the hands of a few. It is twisted and distorted to suit the desires of one group. Ideas like justice and freedom and decency—these cornerstones of any community where ferior status at any point. More than other citizens enjoy he does not ask, but with less he will not be content.

In Gen. 43:3 there is a significant message for today. There it is recorded that one said, "You shall not see my face, unless your brother is with you."

These words were spoken by Joseph. He had become the ruler of Egypt, and under his administration the corn, which was harvested during the seven fat years, had been stored for the seven lean. Now there was famine in the land of Canaan, and Joseph's father, Jacob, sent his other sons down to Egypt to buy corn. When these men came to Joseph they did not recognize him. Years before they had sold him to the Ishmaelites, and it never occurred to them that the rich and powerful ruler before whom they stood humbly was their own brother. Joseph did not make himself known. But when he saw his brothers Joseph's eyes searched the group for his youngest brother, Benjamin, whom he dearly loved, and whom he did not see. So Joseph, in order to see Benjamin, accused them of being spies and required that they bring Benjamin with them the next time they came. He concluded his remarks with the words which form the text of this message. "You shall not see my face, unless your brother is with you."

The Negro American has been revealed as a treasure of talent and capacity. He remains an untapped reservoir. Wise men will not squander the gifts a bountiful God has provided. They will incorporate them into united effort to achieve the utmost for the common weal.

The unfulfilled dreams of mankind—peace, prosperity, progress —they all stand before us to say, "You shall not see my face, unless your brother is with you."

# 14. as if in a foreign country

### DAVID G. COLWELL

*David Colwell is pastor of the First Congregational United Church of Christ in Washington, D. C. Following study at Yale (B.A.) and Harvard (M.B.A.), he took his theological training at Yale Divinity School (B.D.). Following a tour of duty as a U. S. Army chaplain in World War II, he served churches in both Massachusetts and Colorado before coming to Washington. He is recognized both in Washington and throughout the United Church of Christ as a leader in ecumenical and interracial concerns.*

*His sermon was preached on the occasion of receiving a special offering for his denomination's "Racial Justice Now" project.*

We must obey God rather than men. (Acts 5:29.)

In the late winter of 1945—it must have been in Lent—I found myself at a concentration camp outside the little German city of Ohrdruf. A few days earlier American troops had first entered the area, and the concentration camp had been liberated. This was a kind of minor-league concentration camp, not one of the big ones the authorities and charged to keep silent—this is revolutionary teaching, this Gospel. But Peter and the apostles answered, "We must [there is no option here] obey God rather than men."

In the providence of God the time has again come for the Church and for Christian men and women to face precisely the same question of obedience. In some places the risks again are jail and violence. For most of us, however, it is not jail and violence, but a kind of social ostracizing and uncomfortable stares. For some maybe this is worse than going to jail, but it doesn't make any difference. The question still is being pressed upon us by the Lord of the church.

What are some of the things that you and I can do in the midst of the revolution? First, I think, we can recognize that we are in a revolution. Whether we like it or not is immaterial. This is where we are. As in any revolution the great, uncommitted, neutral middle ground is the most irrelevant piece of real estate in the United States. I mean by this that in this revolution we are called to stand on one side or the other. God does not call his people in this day to silence; God does not permit us to sit by silently and uncommittedly pretending that it is really none of our concern. Mark this well! In this day and generation the silent man is really on the side of injustice, of persecution, of segregation; whether he wants it that way, once again, is immaterial here. This is the nature of our time.

Secondly, we cannot all go into the crucial areas to testify. But we can thank God that we are called into membership in a denomination that has committed itself to real and faithful involvement. But, it can't do this unless we give the kind of support, financial and otherwise, to make it possible for the United Church of Christ not only to maintain its commitments, but also to penetrate new fields of testimony with the truth of Jesus Christ. In short, we can give generously in the special offering for Racial Justice Now.

Thirdly, we as persons who have confessed that Jesus Christ is Lord can take steps to become members of the "Fellowship of the Committed" (which is a denominational project to bring together people who are willing to take a stand for racial justice now). This is not an easy commitment to make, nor an easy one to live up to. No man should do it lightly and without due counting of the possible sacrifices that might be demanded of him. But insofar as I can see these matters, in our time this is the call to Christian discipleship and obedience. You will note that a part of this commitment is to press for civil rights legislation. I should earnestly hope that each member of this church would today write to his representatives in the Congress. If he doesn't have a representative—if he is one of the disenfranchized residents of the District—he should write to the leaders of both the House and the Senate. In these letters I trust that you will confess your commitment to justice, to the American principle of democracy, to your faith as confessing Christians who are called to speak that Word which God gives you to speak. I hope also that in some of these letters the idea will get through to the respected members of the Congress that the people are tired of their stalling; and that they are becoming failures through their refusal to overhaul their structures.

Finally, I trust, that God will give to each one of us the grace to join the great company of Peter and the apostles that we may testify to the nature of our obedience in clear-cut language, "We must obey God rather than men."

I have ever lived—are gone. They just aren't visible when the white community meets the Negro.

But above all was the incredible silence—that massive, depressing, awful silence in which so few white voices are raised to cry out against brutality, against discrimination, against persecution. The deadening pall over all of this, however, is the incredible silence of the Church of Jesus Christ. If one really wants to express himself on the issue of obedience to God's will in this racial struggle the only place he can safely do it in this town of 8,000 people is in one little Negro church, and even there, there is no safety. There is no place else. Massive intimidation against those who stand for racial justice is so great that it takes great courage and real faith to serve the Lord obediently in that place.

In war-torn Germany most of the people were not cruel persecutors; they just didn't want to know what was happening. When Nazism began its rise it played upon little prejudices, and the people said, "This is all right. I really don't like the Jews anyhow." Then the monster began to devour and to destroy, and they couldn't stop it; they just sat silently in their fear. Now, most of us are not cruel persecutors either. We have our little prejudices, and we try to tell ourselves that it really doesn't make any difference. But we have in this country police states like those we so hated in Nazi Germany and in some places in the Soviet Union today. They exist because we just sit silently.

"But Peter and the apostles answered, 'We must obey God rather than men.' "

For America, it seems to me, the crisis is very clear. Can democracy—this cherished form of government—give justice to the oppressed, the persecuted? Can the national government act to protect its citizens from brutality, from injustice delivered at the hands of elected and appointed officials of the states, counties, and towns. Documented evidence of brutality has been forwarded to the Department of Justice over and over again, but somehow it seems powerless to act in the protection of citizens of this land who are only seeking their Constitutional rights. Can the federal govern-

137

ment prevent state and local governments from persistently keeping certain citizens from voting through the exercise of various means of intimidation, beginning with outright violence and running through various more subtle forms of persecution and discrimination, and down to a failure to apply impartially the voting registration rules? Can the whole people do something about a school system in which the Negro school has no equipment for its laboratory, no maps on the walls, and miserably few textbooks that are hopelessly out-of-date? This last happens to apply also to the District of Columbia, you know.

These are not academic questions. These are the crucial questions which face this nation—our future hangs in the balance. Can this nation, can American democracy, act for justice?

Can the Congress of the United States rid itself of the unreality and the ritual that keep it bound to dead traditions and act to give justice to the whole people?

What about the Church of Jesus Christ? Can it overcome its sin and its sloth and resolutely and courageously speak the word of truth to this generation? Some time ago I placed a large poster on the bulletin board near the Chapel entrance. The text on the poster asks, "Shall we betray our Lord?" And then it says, "Racial Justice now." During the past days someone has crossed out the "Now" and scrawled in the word "Never." I have left it just that way. It is still there, a proper, poignant reminder to all of us that the church is called to obedience. This is not just pious language. It means enough that someone feels so threatened that he has to fight back. At least that unknown person was startled into action—betrayal action though it was—and left the great morass of neutrality into which most of us comfortably sink and prepare to die. The question of course is: "Is the Church of Jesus Christ on the side of Racial Justice Now?" Or is it content to keep its mind and its energies directed toward safe and inconsequential things? God calls for a decision.

Peter and the apostles had been jailed for preaching the word about Jesus Christ. Now out of jail, they were again hauled before great flood tide of history breaking through many fearful and selfish souls are saying, "Wait! Don't move so fast and so wrecklessly. Don't try to change things overnight." In all too many instances ministers and churches have joined in this chorus. They fail to understand that there comes a time when you can't wait. There are epochs in history when your "face is set towards Jerusalem," and no pleading for patience and better timing can minimize your ardor, courage, determination, and sense of destiny.

"The cancer of segregation can never be cured by the sedative of gradualism; our society has lingered too long with the cancerous disease of segregation; it must now have a radical operation, nothing short of a radical operation will save it." These words were spoken by retired Federal District Judge J. Waites Waring a few years ago. He spoke them in the turbulent period in our American life following immediately after the school desegregation order of the Supreme Court. He spoke prophetically. But, before this brave man spoke these words to a vast audience in New York City he had already used the power of his office in South Carolina to doom to oblivion the white primary and had already forced the equalization of salaries for public school teachers in the same state. With the spirit of an Amos of old, he established the principle that where there is undue recalcitrance, lethargy, and stubbornness in complying with the law of the land, force must be used to save the body politic. He knew that a radical operation would be accompanied by severe pains, but he also knew that these pains in their severity would not be nearly as damaging to our national life as the malignant growth that would ultimately destroy us all. His words did not catch fire as suddenly as they should have, but thank God, we are now in the midst of that operation. The patient is still alive; the skilled surgeons still have steady hands; the nurses are alert in providing the instruments; and there is strong hope that the patient is soon going to be fully well. But during and after the operation the patient will need the proper care and the proper nourishment. I seriously ponder this question, How ready are the ministers and churches to care for this patient?

*143*

## I

In accepting seriously the urgency of his earthly ministry, Jesus said, "[I] must work the works of him who sent me, while it is day; night comes, when no one can work." In challenging you and me to know our worth and to possess the proper sense of destiny, he said, "You are the salt of the earth . . . you are the light of the world." The powerful, compelling urgency which Jesus felt burning in his bosom, and the forthright, dynamic, and positive assertion that he proclaimed to his followers, speak as well to us now as to the problems he faced in his earthly ministry. If the Christian ministers and churches are to face squarely the problems of segregation and discrimination—if we are to make our mission relevant to the needs of the times, we must feel the urgency of Jesus as he says, "*I must work now.*" We must also believe him when he says that we have access to saving power and that we can transmit a great light. Therefore, in a society where there are so many decadent areas and where so many lights have gone out we must hasten to apply the healing salt where it is needed, and we must turn on the light of truth with no uncertainty. Here is our challenge. What are the steps ahead?

## II

There is no moral justification for segregation, and segregation based on color cast has neither legs of history nor religion to stand on. In the long-range time perspective color prejudice and segregation in the Western world are rather new. In fact, this practice goes back a scant third of a thousand years. It was only about 350 years ago that the unholy alliance was formed between greedy and unscrupulous kings of some West African empires, mercenary Portuguese and Spanish shipping companies, and unprincipled British and American slave traders and exploiters. Then for almost two and a half centuries this country built a large share of her economy on the free labor of slaves, while building a religious system that

144

# 15. segregation, discrimination, and the christian church

THOMAS KILGORE, JR.

*Thomas Kilgore has been a minister in the American Baptist Convention since 1935. After spending his early ministry in North Carolina, he began in 1947 a long and meaningful ministry at the Friendship Baptist Church in New York City, which ended in October, 1963, when he became pastor of the Second Baptist Church in Los Angeles. As a leader in the racial struggle, he has served as the Executive Director of the Southern Christian Leadership Conference, New York office, and was one who helped organize the historic March on Washington.*

*He was educated at Morehouse College (A.B.) and Union Theological Seminary, New York (B.D.) and has been honored with two Doctor of Divinity degrees.*

We must work the works of him who sent
me, while it is day; night comes, when
no one can work.          (John 9:4.)

The most disturbing moral issue before America today is the fact of segregation and discrimination based upon color cast and race. It is a reflection on American democracy that it is utterly impossible for a thinking Negro child or adult to salute the flag without partially, or wholly, choking on the phrase, "with liberty and justice for all." With no uncertainty and no hesitancy, Christian ministers and Christian churches must sound the warning that the fabric of our American society is wearing thin, and unless rewoven now with new threads of justice and equality for all, the entire garment will soon give way to rot and decay.

Time moves on—and changes take place. Blindness and stupidity seem to have short-circuited the vision of political, educational, and religious leaders of white America. They fail to recognize the law of growth. They cannot see that the capacity, the quality, the purpose, and the aspirations of the American Negro have changed, grown, and expanded. It is no longer true (in fact, it has never been true) that the Negro is contented with his lot. The lie has been given to the oft repeated contention that he can only be stirred by outside "meddling Northerners." The Negro, in the South and North, has moved in hundreds of demonstrations and exposed our country's traditional capacity for unreality. More recently the "Bull of Birmingham," who so deftly manipulated and frustrated the lives of Negroes, has been himself manipulated out of office and properly but unceremoniously put out to pasture.

Christian ministers and churches must not be insensitive to a peculiar tragedy of our times which reveals that much of white America, in her position of advantage has become a victim of disinterest, stupidity, and a false sense of superiority; and thereby, has displayed a woeful inability to come to grips with the very practical problems and the deep-seated moral issues posed by the second-class citizenship status given to Negroes. Negroes are no longer supplicants—they are now standing at the door of freedom knocking, saying, "We belong inside, and we are coming inside, and nothing will stop us."

In the midst of a revolution that is so definitely symptomatic of a

142

family's choice. The only gradualism that he should be subjected to is the God-imposed gradual process of development. For this to be thwarted today, tomorrow, or anytime in the future is a sin against humanity and an insult to God.

The term "gradualism" is in bad repute—it is in common parlance synonymous with the status quo. In our fight proper terms are important and words must be employed to mean what we say and to direct our activities positively. Words and terms like "progressive improvement," "with deliberate speed," and "with good *faith*" must be substituted.

The spirit of a developing and growing America has never been a spirit of gradualism. We have never been satisfied in this great country with snail's pace progress. When Great Britain attempted to strangle our initiative and keep us in a subservient position we declared ourselves independent and engaged in a powerful arms struggle in the late eighteenth century to certify our rights to move on unhampered.

We were not gradualists in embracing the tools of the Industrial Revolution. We moved with almost lightning-like speed from an agrarian economy to the most powerful industrial complex in the world. In scientific research we have startled the world with our discoveries and inventions, and in transportation we have few peers. *Gradualism! Status quo! Wait! The time is not ripe!* These are not American expressions. We have always been ready to move ahead. Why, then, the cry for gradualism as the American Negro emerges in his fight for first-class citizenship? Why ask him to be gradual? Why ask him to wait? Crispus Attucks did not wait at the Boston Common. He rushed forth with courage and with love of country to be the first to spill blood in the American Revolution. The thousands of Negro soldiers who fought in the Civil War did not wait. As Frederick Douglass prodded the government and traveled from one section of the nation to another, men of color rallied to the call of the Union and fought bravely to save the integrity of America. In subsequent years they have done the same at San Juan

Hill, at Okinawa, on Normandy Beach, and at Heart Break Ridge.

In the proper assessment of the developing American culture these denied and neglected citizens have not been reluctant to add to the fabric. Let America truly sing and you will hear tones, cords, and melodies born of the suffering and deprivation, but at the same time, the hope of slaves and the descendants of slaves. You will hear songs of joy, sorrow, pathos, and longing. Let America sing, and the clearest and most clarion voice heard will be that of her dark sons and daughters.

Let America boast of her great scientists and her many miraculous achievements in the field of science and this boast will have to include the names of Benjamin Benneker, George Washington Carver, Percy Julian, and many others. On thousands of farms, in the building trades, in the classrooms, and in industry the vitality of American life has been greatly enhanced by the dedicated services of the American Negro.

For a long time the Negroes' religious expressions were looked upon as primitive. He was thought of as religiously childish. And even today in some areas his practices of religious worship are looked upon as entertainment. It is not remiss to say that there is some justification for this image in some parts. As we view the total image of the Negro church, however, we see a picture that is far different from that of a semiliterate group playing church. The picture is shocking and challenging to the total American culture, for it bears faint, but unmistakable, glimpses of that church of the first and second centuries that turned the world upside down! This segment of the church seems now to be the one great hope in our land for the preservation of a way of life that is worth living. In some strange way this part of the church has been spared the curse of total conformity to the prevailing cult of materialism. Thank God, it can still provide the wellsprings of creative worship, vital witness, and uncompromising Christian social action. Her persistence in this area of dynamic Christian service is now arousing from lethargy and indifference other areas of American church life. It is gave approval to this travesty of decency and justice. In the seventh decade of the nineteenth century we engaged in a terrible war to rid ourselves of the scourge of slavery. The shackles of bodily slavery were broken, but subsequent developments tended to fasten chains around the minds and spirits of former slaves, and the end result was a slavery more intolerable than bodily imprisonment. This new slavery was imposed in the form of segregation laws passed by many states in the late 1880's, 1890's, and early 1900's. Extra-legal enforcement powers for these new slavery laws grew up in the form of the Ku Klux Klan and other night-riding and intimidating groups. This terrible period from the end of the Civil War to the rendering of the Supreme Court decision which established the "equal but separate" principle in the mid-1890's, robbed the freed slave of his dignity, his citizenship status, and much of his spirit of aspiration. The high quality of culture and dignity of the descendants of kingdoms like Benin and Ashanti of Central West Africa, accentuated by their mixture with the great European cultures and the culture of the American Indian, produced a new American that yearned for freedom and longed to make his contribution to our society. But unfortunately, those who brought the African to America against his will could not stand to see him emerge from a slave to the status of a free man. Hence, we have had this nationwide development of a system of segregation and discrimination. This diabolical system has given birth to, and nurture for, the widespread concept of *a place* for the American Negro. Our ears have burned and our spirits have revolted as white America has talked about and referred to the Negro church, Negro school, Negro society, and Negro culture—and, always a reference with a condescending air and an implication of inferiority. Not only did these paternalistic "benefactors" of the Negro "set his place," but they also undergirded their action by the false ideas of the Negro's biological difference, mental incapacity, proneness to loudness, and quick addiction to immorality. True religion has always given the lie to these false and perverted concepts, and in these late years science has vindicated these true religious beliefs. The great

145

American tragedy is that some white Americans and some Negro Americans are still trying to foist these concepts upon us. But they must know the truth. The sun is too high now on freedom's horizon for lies to prevail. There is no waiting any longer, and there is no turning back.

## III

We hear the cry of the gradualist as he cautions patience and forbearance. He says the time is not right and too many are not ready for freedom. Unfortunately, this cry is color-blind. It comes from Negroes and whites. Even at this late date there are many Negroes in America who are still brainwashed and who live under the spell of a slave psychology. There is an injunction resting on the conscience of every committed Christian to proclaim the truth that every person is ready to be free when he is born. This fact was recognized by the framers of our Declaration of Independence, "All men are created equal . . . they are endowed by their Creator with certain inalienable Rights, . . . among these are Life, Liberty and the pursuit of Happiness." These lofty words must find their place in every city, town, hamlet, and village. They must find their place on the mountaintops and in the valleys—on the lakes and on the seashores. The very spirit and practice of all citizens in this great country must be to induce by law, to mold by custom, to instill by education, and to inspire by religion a society that will not permit the inhibition of the God-given potentialities of any individual. The Christian church must keep herself in the vanguard of leadership in the fight for freedom of all God's children. With Christian love we must put to fight the demagogues, the rabble-rousers, the crackpots, and the bigots who turn their freedom into license to peddle a spleen of racial division and racial hate based on color.

Every child born should be free to cry in freedom, play in freedom, be educated in a free society, practice his religion in a free church, work on a job that he is best fitted for, live where he is able to buy a home, and die and be buried in a cemetery of his

# 16. the new american revolution

ROBERT BOYD MUNGER

*Robert Munger is the minister of the University Presbyterian Church at Seattle, Washington, following pastorates in Hollywood and Berkeley, California, his native state. He received his education at the University of California and at Princeton Theological Seminary. Whitworth College has honored him with a Doctor of Divinity degree. The author of one book and many articles, Dr. Munger has traveled abroad extensively for the church and is a speaker in great demand on university campuses. He is known also for the many young people he has led into church-related service.*

> There cannot be Greek and Jew, circumcised and
> uncircumcised, barbarian, Scythian, slave, free man,
> but Christ is all, and in all.           (Col. 3:11.)

The lead article of *Time* magazine, June 7, 1963, began as follows:

Spring 1963 will long be remembered as the time when the U. S. Negro's revolution for equality exploded on all fronts.

Negroes faced snarling police dogs. They went to jail by the thousands. They risked beatings as they sat on lunch-counter stools. They were bombed in their homes. They were clubbed down by cops. They sent out their children to battle men. In the weeks, months and even years to come, there will be lulls in the revolution. But it will revive—for, after the spring of 1963, there can be no turning back.

The revolutionary struggle of the underprivileged for basic human rights, which has been convulsing many of the countries of the world in recent years, is now convulsing our own. We are involved in a national crisis of deep gravity. To most of us it comes as a shock. We didn't really think it could happen here. Our national life seemed so well ordered and mature. We were so oblivious of the injustices under which others were suffering, so insensitive to the resentments and frustrations of those in our midst, that the ugly scenes in Birmingham, Jackson, and Philadelphia seem like nightmares unrelated to the world in which we live. We stand bewildered at the intensity of feeling which has erupted out from the seething tensions beneath the surface. A real revolution is going on. What we have read about in other lands is occurring in our own. Nor is it limited to the Deep South or the large metropolitan areas with sizeable minority groups. What happened in Birmingham yesterday and in Philadelphia this morning may very well occur in Seattle tomorrow. All the same elements are here—the same injustices and the same intensity of feelings. Because we have had no mass demonstrations, no sit-ins or parades, does not mean that we do not have tensions. We do, but perhaps not yet with the same intensity which has wracked and torn other cities. Therefore, it is most urgent that Christian citizens understand what is happening and act responsibly.

Benjamin Muse in his book *Virginia's Massive Resistance* records that after the Supreme Court's verdict of 1954 ordering the integration of schools the citizens of Virginia for the most part were open to integration. They did not want it, but they felt it was inevitable. Many of them agreed that it was just. Even if they did not rejoice possible that this very period may be the period of redemption of church life in America. If it is so that credit must go to the Negro church in special movements for freedom and justice for all.

## IV

On one occasion the disciples found some men casting out devils and asked the Lord to permit them to stop the others because they were not in their band. Jesus chided them for their shallow insights and bade them not to interfere with anyone doing good. "He that is not against us is for us." The church must realize that she is not alone in the battle for freedom. Segregation and discrimination are not only enemies to the church, they are enemies to all segments of life. The various social and civil rights organizations and movements must always be able to find a friend in the church. Their finely developed methods, techniques, and procedures must clasp a friendly hand with the deep spiritual and moral motivation of the church. Then down the road toward freedom all must march together placing truth above earthly gain, service over popularity, and lasting values above those that are transitory.

When Jesus was proclaimed the Son of God in the Jordan River and the Holy Spirit affirmed the proclamation of God he walked boldly away from the baptism experience and in a lonely wilderness settled the problem of value judgments. Thus, turning his back on the mighty offerings of the world, he went home to the little synagogue in Nazareth and before a semi-hostile audience proclaimed:

> The Spirit of the Lord is upon me,
> because he has anointed me to preach good
> news to the poor.
> He has sent me to proclaim release to the captives
> and recovering of sight to the blind,
> to set at liberty those who are oppressed,
> to proclaim the acceptable year of the Lord.
> . . . . . . . . . .
> Today this scripture has been fulfilled in your hearing.

This was not gradualism. This was immediacy.

The church must proclaim now that the day is here to:

> Let justice roll down like waters,
> and righteousness like an everflowing stream.

The church must proclaim now that the day is here: when God says "Woe to them who call evil good and good evil, who put darkness for light, and light for darkness."

The church must proclaim now that the day is here: "When the tongue of fire devours the stubble and the dry grass sinks deep down in the flame."

The church must proclaim now that the day is here: "When the Lord is riding on a swift cloud . . . and the idols of the world will tumble at his presence."

The church must proclaim now that the day is here: "When the Lord will arise against the house of evil doers, and against the helpers of those who work iniquity."

The day is here when we must listen to the bursting thunders of freedom resounding all about us and proclaim to the world, "You will know the truth, and the truth will make you free."

You must defeat segregation in Chicago because the "de-facto" segregation of Chicago is as bad as the "de jure" segregation of Birmingham. We're through with tokenism and gradualism and see-how-far-you've-come-ism; we're through with we've-done-more-for-your-people-than-anyone-else-ism. We can't wait any longer. Now is the time.

You see, the American Negro has come of age. He has matured. He has broken out of the inferiority complex which was handed him by the past. A very strange and remarkable transformation of feeling is occurring among many Negroes. Instead of feeling inferior before their white brethren, they feel morally and personally superior. The Negro is convinced that he is on the side of righteousness and justice. He is willing to sacrifice and suffer for freedom and principle. He views the white man as morally irresponsible, cowardly, and compromised before clear moral issues. Increasingly he senses his moral worth. So far the Negro has chosen moral and spiritual weapons, for which we should thank God. He senses the moral rightness of his cause, the strength of his convictions, and the power of united action by 16,000,000 Negroes in our land. He knows who he is.

Singularly, the church has become the staging base of operation for this new crusade. Even those who in recent years have been alienated from the Negro church or have no religious faith are looking to the church as the organizing center of action. It's significant, is it not, that preparation for participation in action for civil rights generally begins by praying together, by singing the hymns of praise together, and then in a disciplined purpose not to retaliate in violence they move out to take action together? To be sure, there are extremes, excesses, irrational and unreasonable acts and attitudes. But these are not limited to the Negroes, as we are painfully aware. In Amsterdam, Zurich, Beirut, and Teheran, I had opportunity to catch something of the reaction of non-Americans to what is happening in the United States. Viewed from the outside, the Negro is seen to be behaving with amazing courage and self-control in a crusade which seems obviously right. The

155

opposition the Negro faces appears to them grotesque, irrational, and immoral.

## II

The demand of the American Negro is a simple one—social justice. He has learned about this from our own American tradition. He has been taught that every man is endowed with "certain inalienable Rights," that "all men are created equal." He learned these things in our own public schools. Before the American flag he has stood and repeated the pledge of allegiance, "with liberty and justice for all." E. Stanley Jones relates that while he was visiting a classroom in which there was a predominance of Negro students they gave the pledge of allegiance to the flag. Afterwards he remarked to the teacher, "How can they say this, coming from the kind of segregated communities they do?" "Well," she replied, "they repeat 'with liberty and justice for all,' and then add under their breath, 'for all but me.'"

## III

The points of conflict have moved beyond the segregated classroom and the segregated church to discrimination wherever it is encountered, exploding beyond classrooms, courts, and the church into the streets. The Negro is insisting that the walls of segregation must go. He will no longer be regarded as a second-class citizen without rights to join in public groups wherever public groups gather. He demands that the walls of the real estate ghetto must go, insisting that he has a right, along with every other citizen, to own property according to his ability to purchase property and his responsibility to behave in a manner acceptable to the community. He stands before the walls of employment discrimination and says, "These barriers must go." It's interesting that the president of the United States Chamber of Commerce has issued a special appeal to all business concerns of the nation to eliminate discrimination in it they were acquiescent. Then, largely through the activity of certain political leaders, the mood changed from one of acquiescence and acceptance to one of ugly defiance. The author summarized the situation in a significant sentence: "Then the golden moment of common sense passed; there was a polarization of feeling and of attitude, a breakdown of communication, and a widening gulf in the problem."

There are still a few days in Seattle in which "the golden moment of reason" may operate. But the margin is narrowing with every tick of the clock. Today it is ours to use. If entered properly we may be delivered from the bitterness and conflict engulfing many areas of our nation. Recently I enjoyed reading, over a period of time, Carl Sandburg's biography of Abraham Lincoln, *The Prairie Years* and *The War Years*. As I traced the development of the conflict which finally consummated in the Civil War and considered the power of pride and self-interest which clouded the thinking of men and of prejudice which blinded their judgment, finally flaming out in unreasoning passion to engulf a nation in an agony of blood and tears, again and again I found myself putting the book down and staring into space. How incredible that intelligent, well-meaning men could let a situation drift into a conflict which would result in a million casualties on the field of battle, desolate the South, and erect a gulf of bitterness which remains to this day!

It was with strong feelings, therefore, that I read Vice President Lyndon Johnson's Memorial Day address at Gettysburg. He said:

One hundred years ago the slave was freed. One hundred years later the Negro remains in bondage to the color of his skin. Our nation found its soul in honor on these fields of Gettysburg one hundred years ago. We must not lose that soul in dishonor on the fields of hate. The Negro today asks justice. We do not answer him. We do not answer those who lie beneath this soil when we reply to the Negro by asking patience. It is empty to plead that the solution to the dilemma of the present rests upon the hands of the clock. The solution is in our hands. Unless we are willing to yield up our destiny of greatness among the civilizations of history, Americans, white and black together, must be about the business of resolving the challenge which now confronts us. To ask patience of the Negro is to ask him to give more of what he has already given enough. But to fail to ask of him and of all Americans perseverance within the processes of a free and responsible society would be to fail to ask what the national interest requires of all its citizens.

I

You see, an entirely new situation confronts us. We must not approach the racial problem with the same categories of judgment we used ten years ago or think that we can meet the present crisis the same way in which we might have responded even one year ago. Since 1945 the main effort to rectify the restrictions against minority groups has been through education and the due processes of the courts of law. It was felt that time would prevail and enable us to come to solutions. Time has leaped ahead of us, however. Time will not wait for us. It demands giant strides and radical measures. Time did not wait in the Congo. Time did not wait in Algeria. Time will not wait anywhere in the world where under-privileged people are struggling for justice against the insensitivity of privileged people.

Elder Hawkins, addressing the United Presbyterian General Assembly in Des Moines, noted three signs of the changed mood, the deeper mood among the American Negroes. He said:

Negroes have accepted primary responsibility in their push for freedom rather than delegating responsibility to others. They are now speaking with an honesty and integrity unknown in the past—even though they offend some of their friends. They are willing to stake their lives on the outcome of the issue, recognizing that a freedom so necessary is also one for which they must suffer and possibly die.

Speaking in Chicago the Reverend Martin Luther King, Jr., was more blunt. Addressing some 5,000 cheering Negroes, he cried:

has made a statement about the necessity of an integrated church in an integrated community. This year it went beyond mere pronouncement to send down to the Presbyteries a resolution which would require every Presbyterian congregation to accept into membership those who truly believe in Jesus Christ as Savior and Lord, regardless of color, origin, or worldly condition. The Session of this church has had spread on its minutes, dated September 10, 1957: "Resolved that race or color shall not be a qualification for attendance, participation, membership, office, teaching, ministry, preaching or employment in the University Presbyterian Church or any of its sponsored activities." Again at our general assembly they did something significant when there was set aside a fund of 500,000 dollars to establish a commission on religion and race to assist the local churches, pastors, and people in eliminating prejudice and segregation from congregational and community life.

Yet on the whole our performance is rather poor. Gayraud S. Wilmore, Jr., brilliant Negro scholar, wrote an article entitled "The New Negro and the Church" for *The Christian Century*, February 6, 1963. He stated that the new Negro is becoming disillusioned with Christianity and desires forthright action.

Rather, they want a church which has divested itself of moralistic complacency about the status quo and become a revolutionary force revealing the true religious significance of human life in a world where naked power is rampant.

For many Negro intellectuals a more serious indictment of the church than segregation in pew and pulpit is what seems to them to be white Christians' timid acquiescence to, if not active participation in, discriminatory patterns of social and economic life in America and elsewhere. This is not only the primary reason for the black intellectual's growing tendency to reject Christianity; it is also the cause of the increasing estrangement of the whole Negro Christian community from the white Christian community. If the white Protestant church does not more speedily enter the struggle in which the Negro is engaged, the psychological and ideological distance between the two communities may become so great as to prevent authentic integration for years after the merely spatial distance has been closed.

In my judgment the Negro Christian community and the white Christian community is farther apart today than they were ten years ago. It is more difficult for us to understand each other, to feel at ease in each other's presence, or to communicate our deepest feelings, largely because we, the white Christians, have not clearly identified ourselves with them in that which is, in their view, a dominant moral and spiritual crusade for basic rights.

## VI

I cannot answer for you specifically what should be done. I can only speak for myself.

1. *I will ask God to forgive my own pride and prejudice.* I dare not judge those in Birmingham, Jackson, or Chicago, or any other place, whether they be white or black. I am too keenly aware of the remnants of prejudice I still retain and of my personal involvement in a society in which these sins exist. I acknowledge, under God, the need of forgiveness, confessing that I am a sinner among sinful men. I will pray that God will grant grace that I may be reconciled to my brother in truth.

2. *I will endeavor to know the facts and to share them,* to explode the myth of racial supremacy which drifts in an amorphous mass about the minds of the prejudiced, enlarged by unreasonable fears. I will seek to dispel the misapprehensions and misconceptions which distort the truth and foster anxieties. I refer to such things as fear of decreasing property values. When studied factually one will often find that property values deteriorate most rapidly in communities which are striving with most determination to maintain lines of segregation. Fears produce the facts of decreasing property values. A freer, more natural distribution of minority groups in a community may actually be a better way to meet the problem. We also need to know the facts about the fear of marriage between

in employment, if only out of self-interest. Of course, the establishment of full rights of citizenship brings problems, penalties, and costs to some people, but the costs to citizens not to give full rights to fellow citizens are greater than the penalties we may incur in pursuing the course of justice.

The Negro is seeing these objectives as far more than a means of personal improvement. Not to understand this is to miss the modern mood of the civil rights movement. To them this is a crusade in a cause of righteousness. As our forefathers left the plows and took guns to fight for freedom, they are increasingly willing to suffer to accomplish a cause which, to them, is essentially right. The challenge to the Negro in turn is to act responsibly. Full acceptance by a community cannot be won by court action. It cannot be achieved by enforcing laws. It can be won only by the kind of behavior which will win acceptance. But until the fundamental rights of full citizenship are granted the Negro does not have the opportunity to win acceptance. He labors under an impossible disadvantage.

## IV

The retiring moderator of our denomination, the Reverend Marshal Scott, addressing what is now being called "The Race Assembly" of the United Presbyterian Church at Des Moines, gave the keynote when he said, "The core of the racial situation in the United States lies in the all-white residential communities that circle our cities. It is precisely in those neighborhoods where Presbyterianism flourishes that the center of the evil lies." That is to say, you and I are in the front line of conflict. The revolution is not occurring somewhere in the South merely, or somewhere in Chicago, or in another district of Seattle. You and I are at the focal point of it. Whether we like it or not we are being called to take a stand. Tomorrow when we go to work, tomorrow in a dozen ways the issue will confront us—in real estate sales, in bank loans, in employment policies, in labor union councils, and in our own emotional reaction in conversation with other people. Not to take a stand is to take a position for the status quo. We cannot avoid taking a stand. Do not think for a moment that I am saying it is easy to know what to do. Neither do I profess to have all the answers, but I am sure as responsible and intelligent Christians we must understand that we are involved in the struggle, and therefore, under God, we must move courageously in the light he gives to us. Our convictions may involve a real cost to us personally. (So far the cost to white communities is really insignificant.) It will involve a cost. But tell me, did Jesus Christ ever say that to follow him would not be costly?

## V

The crisis involves the church of Christ as well as the country and nation. Fundamental to the Christian faith is the revelation of a God who so loved the world that he gave his only begotten Son, who loved "the world of people." The gospel is offered to *all* men everywhere, not just to the righteous but to the unrighteous, not just to the religious but to the irreligious, not just to the privileged Jew but to the underprivileged Gentile—to all men everywhere who will hear, repent, and respond. Jesus Christ breaks through all the barriers which separate man from his brother. Moreover the concept of the church as the Body of Christ means that the church is more than a gathering of fellow citizens of the kingdom of God, more than colleagues in a common cause, more than children of the Heavenly Father. We are brought together in Jesus Christ as a living organism which is his Body. We are members one of another, sharing the same Lord, the same Savior, the same Holy Spirit, the same common life. We are one body. Paul wrote, "Here there cannot be Greek and Jew, circumcised and uncircumcised, barbarian, Scythian, slave, free man, but Christ is all, and in all." (Col. 3:11.)

This has been the position of Christians from the beginning, and repeatedly this biblical position has been uttered in pronouncements of the church. Our general assembly every year for years

races. Coming from the city of Berkeley, where nearly 30 per cent of all children enrolled in the public school system is Negro, and where the schools have been integrated for some time, intermarriage has not been found to be a problem. When studied factually it simply does not hold together. Thus we need to know the facts and to help dispel the clouds of misunderstanding and explode the misrepresentation of myths.

3. *I will strive to keep this congregation truly interracial*, to let it be known that we genuinely welcome those of all races in the name of Jesus Christ. I will pray and work to the end that our Christian fellowship may be a clear demonstration of real oneness of life and love among all those who name the name of Jesus Christ.

4. *I will endeavor to reach out my hand in friendship to those of other races*, not out of condescension, as a gesture, but out of conviction of my own personal need of my brother. I need them for what they will teach me and what they will bring to me. I want them as my friend. I want them in my home. I want them by my side in the work of church and community. Therefore, I am going to reach out my hand in warmhearted friendship.

5. *I will endeavor to stand for social justice wherever possible.* Perhaps you have read Sargent Shriver's Memorial Day appeal to the American people. He suggested specific steps. What is needed, he declared, is not more laws, but "the self-organization of society on a large scale to solve the problem which, more than any other, threatens the integrity of America."

Specifically, he suggested the following:

That citizens organize groups "to finance and support those who are in the front lines of the struggle."

That businessmen make clear that "investments and commerce will not be safe in areas of racial strife, and lend their weight to peaceful solutions, as did the negotiators of Birmingham."

That homeowners "band together in societies for the integration of housing, seeking out Negro homeowners for their neighborhoods, helping to break down the awful housing ghettos which disgrace the North."

That church congregations and ministers "actively recruit Negro members for their congregations, admitting them to their fellowship of God and the society of their members."

That individuals form volunteer groups to "do social welfare work, job training and the many tasks which are necessary to give the Negro the social and economic tools to achieve equal opportunity."

6. *I will seek grace from God to love all men, even those who disagree with me.* Some years ago the Reverend Martin Luther King, Jr., when he was undergoing a prison term in Montgomery, Alabama, wrote these words in a pastoral letter to the members of his church:

If we are arrested every day, if we are exploited every day, if we are trampled over every day, don't let anyone pull you so low as to hate him. We must use weapons of love. We must have compassion and understanding for those who hate us. We must realize that many people are taught to hate so that they are not responsible for their hatred. We stand as lights at midnight, but we are on the threshold of dawn.

7. *Finally, I will glory in the Gospel of Jesus Christ* as the means of reconciling men to God and to one another. Let us understand that the issue is bigger than Birmingham. An editorial in *Christianity Today*, May 24, 1963, is to the point:

The issue is bigger than Birmingham, as big as all America; it is deeper than color, as deep as evil in the human heart. In Birmingham's riots, men saw themselves. They saw how thin is the veneer of their everyday decency, how dark the hatred and how raw the violence in the deeper chasms of the human soul. Christians saw that personal regeneration is not enough to solve our social evils, for not all the guilty were non-Christians. And any man not blinded by twisted prejudice could see that Nazi Germans were not special sinners, for morally nothing distinguishes anti-Semitism from Birmingham's racism. In the ugly clash of American against American, one could see the common human nature we all share, and the common judgment under which we all stand. He who looked hard at the social ugliness in

Birmingham saw not special sinners who fight for state's rights but trample on human rights; he saw the human nature we all share. He saw a time to weep, to repent, to remember—"inasmuch as ye have done it unto these ye have done it unto me."

Indeed the issue is bigger than Birmingham, larger than the crowds upon the street, penetrating as deep as the sickness in the soul of man. It stems from the perversion of self-centeredness and self-interest which is the mark of the fallen sinner. The glory of the gospel of Jesus Christ is that it produces the new heart and the motivation to act as the new man in love and forgiveness. If in certain areas of the church Christians have not responded in reconciling love to others it may be because we have need of a second conversion. The first conversion must be to Jesus Christ as Savior and Lord. The second conversion is to the world for which Christ died, calling us to respond obediently and lovingly, with the everlasting gospel upon our lips expressed in the concrete acts of our lives.

William Stringfellow, young Episcopal lawyer who entered into the heart of Harlem to share his legal experience with those who had no recourse to such legal counsel, and who became so intimately involved in the inner struggles of Harlem, concluded an article in *The Christian Century*, February 14, 1963, with this striking witness—he calls it, "An Apocalyptic Episode":

On one of those steaming, stinking, stifling nights that each summer brings to Harlem tenements, I had a dream:

I was walking in Harlem on 125th Street in broad daylight. I seemed to be the only white man in sight. The passersby stared at me balefully. Then two Negroes stopped me and asked for a light. While I searched my pockets for a match, one of them sank a knife into my belly. I fell. I bled. After a while, I died.

I woke quickly. I felt my stomach: there wasn't any blood. I smoked a cigarette and I thought about the dream:

The assault in the dream seemed unprovoked and vicious. The death in the dream seemed useless and, therefore, all the more expensive.

163

The victim in the dream seemed innocent of offense to those who murdered him.

Except for the fact that the victim was a white man. The victim was murdered by the black man because he was a white man. The murder was retribution. The motive was revenge.

No white man is innocent.

I am not innocent.

Then I cried.

# 17. that you may have integrity

### ROBERT B. MCNEILL

*Robert B. McNeill is pastor of the Bream Memorial Presbyterian Church in Charleston, West Virginia. A native of Alabama, he received his education from Birmingham-Southern (A.B.), Union Theological Seminary, Richmond (B.D.), and the University of Kentucky (M.A.). He has written several books and articles.*

*Prior to his coming to Bream Memorial, Mr. McNeill was pastor of the First Presbyterian Church, Columbus, Georgia. As a result of the 1957 Look magazine article which he wrote, entitled "A Georgia Minister Offers a Solution for the South," he was subjected to a campaign of harassment by a hard-core minority within his church. This, together with other civil rights activities, led to his dismissal in 1959. He was discharged not by the congregation but by a judicial commission of the Presbytery because "the good of religion imperatively demanded it." His sermon "That You May Have Integrity" was the last he delivered to his congregation.*

I had not planned that my farewell message to you should be tonight. But my severance from you, the congregation of this

165

church, came so abruptly that I have not had the time to prepare my words as carefully as I should. Neither had I planned to be autobiographical—ever—but the circumstances seem to require that I explain to you why I am like I am. I have been called stubborn and uncompromising concerning the race issue and all the many side issues that have sprung from it. I have been called so because it has been brought to light from time to time that I have persistently identified myself with this cause of justice instead of dropping it in favor of the more important business of the church. And I should know by now that my unyielding attitude on this issue is a constant source of antagonism to those who ought to be appeased. I do know this and I confess to the charge of stubbornness, but I must explain why it is necessary to be so.

When I entered the ministry it was vague to me why I should accept this calling. Now, on this day of my dismissal, when fifteen minutes from now I shall pronounce my last benediction here not knowing where or whether I shall serve another congregation, I have greater assurance than ever before as to why and how I should serve the church.

In the early years of my ministry I was nagged by a subconscious feeling that I was not fully committed. When this feeling reached the conscious level I tried everything to dissolve it—more prayer, more Bible reading, more "expository" sermons, more frenzied pastoral calling, more mysticism. Much of this was good, but none of it brought the relief I sought. Slowly it dawned on me that there was one pressing human problem that I never faced without first preparing for myself some escape routes. I could not commit myself completely to the doctrine of the brotherhood of man without reservation, the reason being that a substantial minority of mankind living in my area was colored, and I had to make some allowance for the double standard of brotherhood I had always practiced. I wore myself out rationalizing. I came to despise the clichés I was mouthing. Worse still, I learned the bitter lesson that you cannot segregate the problem from all the other phases of the ministry or personal religious living.

You cannot pray as you ought because invariably you will begin with "Our Father" and God is the kind of father who has but one standard for his sons and daughters. Dare we then have more?

You cannot practice the virtue of humility if at any time you must assume a counter attitude toward another people. George Mason, himself a slaveholder, confessed that the ownership of slaves makes petty tyrants of us all. Either we are humble at all times and before all people or we cannot be humble at all. Humility must be our nature, not our technique.

You cannot honestly extol freedom or democracy if you are not as willing to confer them as to enjoy them. And freedom and democracy brook no exceptions. Free men become slaves once they abridge another's freedom. Democracy means that *all* are rulers and *all* are subjects to their own rule. And I need only to suggest that you review your own aspirations to remind you that shackles to freedom can at once be extremely subtle and painfully strong. Silken cords are as binding as chains of iron.

You cannot read your Bible, even devotionally, without sensing that our long-standing tradition of enforced racial separation is contrary to a way of life given us several thousand years ago. Can we shut our ears to the voice of Amos who cried, "Are you not like the Ethiopians to me, O people of Israel, says the Lord." Have we forgotten that the man who so tenderly lifted Jeremiah out of a muck-filled cistern, even padding the ropes that went under his arms, was an Ethiopian? There were people of several nations and degrees of color in Israel. These wanted to become naturalized and counted as citizens of their covenant. Their great anxiety was that they should not be allowed to become assimilated. Their concern prompted these words:

> Let not the foreigner who has joined himself to the Lord, say,
> "The Lord will surely separate me from his people."
>
> .  .  .  .  .  .  .  .  .  .  .  .
>
> And the foreigners who join themselves to the Lord,
> to minister to him, to love the name of the Lord,
> and to be his servants,

.   .   .   .   .   .   .   .   .

these I will bring to my holy mountain,
    and make them joyful in my house of prayer;

.   .   .   .   .   .   .   .   .   .

for my house shall be called a house of prayer
    for *all* peoples. (Italics mine.)

What was your reaction to the incident in which Peter began eating with the Gentiles only to move over to a separated table for the Jews when certain important Jewish churchmen arrived? Was he right or was Paul, who challenged this deportment to his face, right? With whom did you side when you read it? Remember that an integrated meal was more difficult for the Jew because of ceremonial and dietary differences in addition to his tradition that Gentiles were unworthy of his company.

We have been taught that we cannot compose a standard by which we achieve salvation. By the same token, we cannot frame one by which one person determines that he is of more value than another. Did not Christ reverse every standard of importance man on his own ever set up? Therefore, I can never again look upon any person as being inferior to me. Nor can I ever again require my conscience to consent to a system, legal or traditional, that enforces separation that is in effect subordination and which leads inevitably to alienation. Am I ahead of my time in saying this? Am I not late? The Bible in its present form has been with us at least 1,500 years and God has been with us always.

So we cannot pray, become humble, proclaim freedom, refine democracy, read our Bibles; nor can we extend the church, honestly evangelize, practice community charity, rise to face the issues of each day, without our racial attitude's coloring our every thought and act.

This I had to discover for myself, though the lonely prophets of a previous generation patiently warned me that this would be so. At last I have found the integrity of my calling. Would you deprive me of it in order that your consciences be given a temporary reprieve and a fitful rest? Is this what you mean by the peace and unity of the church? Peace and unity are linked to and dependent upon a third quality—purity. Without the purity of the church our peace is but an armistice and our unity is but an uneasy coalition. If I have found the integrity of my calling could I not serve you better by moving you to throw off this final reservation to your total Christian commitment?

But it is argued that this uncompromising attitude promotes discord that cannot be dispelled as long as it is maintained, that the church suffers irreparable damage from it. We had better ask ourselves which church we mean—the church as an institution or as that intimate fellowship of the concerned which aspires always to live up to its designation as the Body of Christ? Are we jealous of the structure of the church, or its function? In short, what image do we see, Organization Church or Proclaiming Church?

Organization Church is but the lengthened shadow of Organization Man. A church like a single individual can fall for the lures of the present generation. It can prefer security to venturesomeness, group thinking to personal conviction, community concensus to biblical authority, popular mediocrity to contested excellence. The Organization Church has a manager for minister, promoter for pastor, reporter for preacher. Its measurement of success is in terms of enrollment and budget. The caliber of its gospel depends upon the satisfaction of its clientele, and this gospel, though verbally honored, must become subordinate to the institution that holds it in trust. Was this not what the Reformation was about? Any kind of revolutionary spirit which is essential to the pristine church is entirely absent from Organization Church. It could not revolutionize life because it would have to revolutionize itself, and that is the very thing it is organized against. Is this the kind of church you want, or is it not so agreeable to your fearful, immature self as to become a depressant to your soul? Is there not a deep yearning in you for the Proclaiming Church, that church that above all else speaks forthrightly the whole gospel and in quiet courage structures its corporate life about it?

If my spirit has been uncompromising it has been so not only

169

for the sake of my fellow child of God in dark skin, but also for the integrity of the church itself. In our day it must become the agency through which God redeems the time, and it must become the ground upon which humanity becomes reconciled to itself. So if I have been stubborn, uncompromising, relentless, it is not that I should have my way but that you should have your integrity. Loving you as the people I serve, I knew no greater gift to offer.

# 18. on reviving a doctrine

### WARREN TYREE CARR

*Warren Carr, a Southern Baptist, served a long pastorate at the Watts Street Baptist Church, Durham, North Carolina, until September, 1964, when he became pastor of the Wake Forest Baptist Church, Winston-Salem. He was educated at Transylvania College (A.B.) and the Southern Baptist Seminary (Th.M.) and has been a leader in Durham's efforts at desegregation. He is the author of the recently published book,* Baptism: Clue and Conscience for the Church. *"On Reviving a Doctrine" was first delivered from his pulpit, and later repeated before the student body at North Carolina College.*

> Thus, sinning against your brethren and wounding their conscience when it is weak, you sin against Christ.            (I Cor. 8:12.)

The yoke of oppression and second-class citizenship cannot forever chafe upon the desperately powerful shoulders of suppressed people. Wherever they are in the world—Far East, Middle East,

*171*

Near East, Africa, India, and the Americas—they are exploding from the ocean deeps of their oppression. Like flotsam these people appear on the surface of history, a level of life to which they have never been accustomed. This new found freedom; this unobstructed view of the world is fraught with numerous ironies. The tone of free novitiates is different from that once used. No longer do they bow and scrape while whining for condescension. No longer do we hear their timid scratching upon the window panes of power and influence, like shaggy-haired shrubbery, frozen stiff, begging for sanctuary from the wintry blasts of impoverishment and disfranchisement. Theirs is no longer request, but demand. The casual listener can easily detect the notes of confidence and assurance. And honesty requires reporting that the more strident sounds of resentment, arrogance—even hatred—issue from the throats of the common man on his way out and up.

A more careful ear will uncover other and more telling noises. The voice of aggressive assurance is so often a cover for fear and lack of confidence. It is, when revealed, a pitifully inept endeavor to appear assured when assurance is so very much to be desired because it is lacking. Then it is that the truth is most apparent. The free man, in so many instances, is not yet equal to the awful challenge of this very freedom which he has literally pulled from life and holds within his trembling hands. This is the picturesque spectacle which the church must look at soberly and responsibly. Presently this is crucial to the saga of freedom, and Christians must seek the revival of a wonderful and powerful doctrine of their faith. That is the doctrine of brotherhood. It is the singular witness of the church to the world, and it must not fail.

I

That the newly emergent man cannot play his part on freedom's stage is hardly worth the argument. Free states everywhere are proving this point conclusively. And when we become more specific with a view to the plight of the Negro, the same general opinion seems both relevant and accurate. Coming from a segregated society in which he has been at great disadvantage the Negro cannot compete in the world in which he wishes to engage in freely. When he enters the previously all white school he discovers that his education is deficient. When he asks for job opportunity he realizes that he is not adequately trained and does not have the skills which could have brought him many job opportunities. Educationally, socially, economically, politically, and culturally, the Negro does not show to good advantage in a society in which his freedom is quickly and abruptly secured.

There are a number of sentimentalists among us, both white and colored, who try very hard to prove to the contrary. Their efforts meet with little success. It matters little in the exegencies of the present crisis that Negroes are not inferior by nature and inheritance so much as by virtue of their environmental history and circumstances. The man who likes his society the way it is—segregated, ripe for his exploitation, and providing the means by which he works his own advantage—pays no attention to these subtleties as he proclaims his unyielding opposition to the Negro's right to freedom and equal privilege. It is this person who can contend with great piosity that he loves the colored man and wants very much the best for him. At the same time, under the guise of justice he insists that man must earn equality. He insists that this does not fall into the category of gifts. It is a right which must be won.

I would be forced to agree with so much of this argument if I could first accept the major premise. This premise is chiefly characterized by the word equality. Equality in a democratic society, grounded in justice without being informed or tempered by love, is a doctrine for human relationships which at once may be simply stated and simply practiced. In this setting we treat those on our level as equals. Those beneath us are to be treated as inferiors. Those above us must then be treated as superiors. Equality does, therefore, become a figment of our imagination. We, at whatever station we live, find ourselves incapable of catching up with those ahead of us and unwilling to pull those below us up to our level.

For this reason I am unable to accept equality as the basic principle of human relationships. It is also evident that those qualitarian concepts which have been written into the literature of our free and constitutional United States is not the doctrinaire equality which the oppressor of the Negro brings to the support of his own position. John Dewey writing in his "Democracy and Educational Administration" in 1937 had this to say:

Belief in equality is an element of the democratic credo. It is not, however, belief in equality of natural endowments. Those who proclaimed the idea of equality did not suppose they were enunciating a psychological doctrine, but a legal and political one. . . . While what we call intelligence (may) be distributed in unequal amounts, it is the democratic faith that it is sufficiently general so that each individual has something to contribute, whose value can be assessed only as (it) enters into the final pooled intelligence constituted by the contributions of all. . . . The democratic faith in equality is the faith that each individual shall have the chance and opportunity to contribute whatever he is capable of contributing and that the value of his contribution be decided by its place and function in the organized total of similar contributions, not on the basis of prior status of any kind whatever.

Equal before God, equal before the law, and equal with respect to opportunity—this is implicit in the democratic process.

But let us come to the crux of the matter. Kyle Haselden, in *The Racial Problem in Christian Perspective*, reminds us that the Christian answers to the myriad questions which spring from the tragedy of racism are not easily concentrated. "The answers to these questions," he observed, "cannot be given in a single and comprehensive pronouncement but must be set forth in three distinct forms which meet the needs of three separate yet overlapping areas of human relationships: what all men owe to all men, what all Christians owe to all men, what all Christians owe to all Christians."

Christians must surely be aware of the "oneness" of all men. To think otherwise is a disclaimer that we belong to the uniqueness of the human race. This is at least a first principle, but it by no means exhausts the Christian responsibility. Man, according to our faith, is made in God's image. Our primary view of him is not with reference to equality, but with respect to his sacredness because God has made him. This is why the gospel is not noticeably explicit about equality. It deals with different value judgments. "This means," Haselden wrote, "that we cannot acclaim the sacredness of any man until we acknowledge the sacredness of all men; for the dignity and the holiness are not in man the created except as they are in God the Creator. Cancel that innate worth of man anywhere and it is canceled everywhere; deny it to one and it is denied to all."

It is ironic that the gospel relieves us of the secular legalism demanding man's equal treatment of other men. I quote almost brutally what I have heard in many rooms and on numerous street corners: "I cannot treat an illiterate, immoral, unwanted, crude, and unclean Negro as my equal." I hasten to condemn this unfair caricature of the Negro. But the real point is clear. Not only would it be unwise and ridiculous to attempt equal treatment to such a person, it could be extremely cruel and insensitive. Furthermore, such treatment is impossible in any practical sense. Hear then what the gospel declares: "You should not treat your inferior as your equal. You must treat him as your brother. For indeed, under God and in the spirit and mission of Christ, you can do no other."

The fact that a brother is weaker than we are, that he is indeed our inferior, is all the more reason that we should accept him as our brother. This will recognize and support his right to every possible equality and intercede for him in his inequalities.

The words of Paul, set in different context to be sure, are no less germane: "Only take care lest this liberty of yours somehow become a stumbling-block to the weak. . . . And so by your knowledge this weak man is destroyed, the brother for whom Christ died. Thus, sinning against your brethren and wounding their conscience when it is weak, you sin against Christ."

*175*

## II

I am well aware of the unfortunate connotations of the doctrine of brotherhood. It is incontestably so that when the average white Christian hears that he need not treat the Negro as his equal, but as his brother, his unspoken response will probably be, "Well, I am glad to know this. It helps. It means I can leave the Negro exactly where he is." In consequence, the Negro retorts, "Brotherhood—this is poorly disguised paternalism! I can expect nothing from this."

This is a reaction to a doctrine of brotherhood which has been gutted of two of its basic elements. The first element is that of responsibility. We are responsible for our brother without the condition of paternalism. Paternalistic responsibility is concerned protection for one whose immaturity and inadequacy militates against freedom. The responsibility of a brother for a brother means responsibility for him in freedom.

It is not within the province of a brother to limit the freedom of another no matter how inadequate for liberty he may be. A greater responsibility is here implied, since it means that one's freedom is defended while his limitations are the object of concerned and helpful treatment.

The second element is that we cannot love God without loving our brother. We can try to treat him as equal without loving God. We may even love him without loving God. But when our point of reference is our relationship with God, then love for all men is not only indicated but demanded.

As Christians it may be that we cannot make all men our equal. But we can make all men our brothers, and this we must do!

# 19. we seek a city

### KELLY MILLER SMITH

*Kelly Miller Smith is the pastor of the First Baptist Church in Nashville, Tennessee. He is a former president of the Nashville branch of the NAACP and was the organizer and former president of the Nashville affiliate of the Southern Christian Leadership Conference. He received his education from Morehouse College (A.B.) and Howard University (B.D.).*

They shall ask the way to Zion. (Jer. 50:5.)

The enslaved Israelites never lost sight of the city of their dreams—Zion. They could not help contrasting the ecstasy of the Holy City with the painful inconveniences of their Babylonian captivity. As they sat by the waters of Babylon they thought of the smoking altars, the solemn pageantry, and the antiphonal singing of the city called Zion. They remembered that the city of their dreams was one where each man sat under his own vine and fig tree—it was the city of freedom. And every time these slaves thought about it they wept.

177

When bidden to sing they refused, for they would not fill the air of a city of bondage with the songs of freedom. Their instruments of music were left hanging on the swaying branches of the willow trees. They yearned for freedom but their fare was slavery. They could not reach their maximum potential under such conditions. This drab existence was a far cry from the life God intended for them. They longed to travel to the holy city of freedom, but they could only beat a path down to the river side where they mingled their tears of sadness with the murky Babylonian waters.

Then there came a light that penetrated their darkness, a message of hope which displaced their despair. The message was that God had issued an "Emancipation Proclamation."

> Babylon is taken,
> Bel is put to shame,
> Merodach is dismayed.

The slaves are free! Now they could retrieve their harps from the willow trees and begin rehearsing the songs of freedom; they could pack up their slave clothes and put on their marching shoes.

What jubilation there must have been! What exhuberant joy! It was a dream come true before their very eyes. What could keep them from joining the colorful procession of those who march in and out of the Holy City? They had now the legal right to go to the city of freedom. The shackles of bondage no longer bound their limbs. God had made it clear that they were free, and yet, proclamation was one thing and direction was another. These captives were a second generation of slaves. They had never really been to Zion, but had learned of its glories from their fathers. Although it was the city of their dreams they needed direction. How do they get there? "They shall ask the way to Zion."

Like the ancient Israelites we too seek a city. It is a city which shall be illumined by the holy light of freedom and where all citizens shall be called brothers. We seek a city where the relationship between men will be regulated more by something internal—

a renewed spirit—than by something external known as law. To be sure, just laws must exist. There must be no stopping short of this. But the Christian is called to go beyond the mere external regulation of behavior between people. There must be that "something within that holdeth the reins." Where this is is found the city which we seek.

And it has been made crystal clear that we may go there. The legal barriers which once enslaved are now being removed. Men are becoming more aware of the grievous wrongs that have been involved in our human relations activities. But how do we get to that city? Many have gotten on the wrong roads because they have not known the way. In the great tradition of the church there are directions. The timeless words of Jesus tell us the name of the route which leads us to the City of Freedom. It is Truth. "You will know the truth, and the truth will make you free." Any solution which fails to recognize man for what he truly is can only be said to be a false route. This whole problem of man's freedom must be seen within the context of reality; it must be viewed from the perspective of truth. Men have not always been willing to stay on the road of truth, even though they were in quest of the City of Freedom. Sometimes it is a hard road to travel, but there are no alternate routes.

I

A side road called "fear" has proven attractive to far too many travelers. It is a road that seems so broad and inviting that many have felt that it was perfectly natural for them to take it rather than the sometimes difficult, narrow, and rocky main road. The dangers on it are not easily seen, for fear does not always announce its presence. It wears many masks. A little boy was sent to the store by his mother. Upon returning, a dog about twice the size of the boy growled at him in tones that were anything but playful. The little boy ran home as fast as he possibly could. His mother, seeing him from the window as he left the dog far behind, said to him, "You weren't really afraid of that dog, were you Tommy?" Little Tommy was still panting when he said, "No, Mother, I wasn't afraid of him. I just wanted to see how fast I could run." So fear does not always admit that it is fear. In Nashville, Tennessee, an interracial ministers' organization was sponsoring joint pre-Christmas services. In order to accommodate the large crowd the group erroneously expected a very large downtown church was secured. A few days before the services were to be held, however, the minister of the host church suddenly "remembered" that he had to take an out-of-town trip which would prevent him from attending the interracial services. The organist and most of the members of the church had something else "more important" to do. One cannot resist applying the words of little Tommy here: "No, I wasn't afraid. I just wanted to see how fast I could run." Harry and Bonaro Overstreet, in their book *Understanding Fear,* point out the significant fact that fear very often makes us do what we ought not do and leave undone what we ought to do. How true this is! If human freedom, for example, were kept in proper perspective and balance, Christians, and especially ministers, would be afraid *not* to do certain things.

Fear sometimes disguises itself as dignity, or as patience or even as courage. While we recognize that there are fears that are necessary and that cause us to be alert and appropriately cautious, we also must face the fact that we would be much nearer the City of Freedom if so many persons in high church and government positions had not chosen to travel the road of fear.

The church has in its sacred tradition that which serves as the antidote to fear. It is perfect love which casts out fear. When the tenant of love moves in the tenant of fear moves out. This is what the church has been talking about through the ages. It is what sustained the early Christians during the times of great peril and danger. The pre-Christian psalmist sums up the proper attitude of those who are truly Christian and who will not be deflecting in the pilgrimage to the City of Freedom:

*180*

The Lord is my light and my salvation;
whom shall I fear?
The Lord is the stronghold of my life;
of whom shall I be afraid?

## II

While marching down this road of truth we must pass along the way of the mountaintops of intermediary victories. Here is where many come to a grinding halt, thinking the journey is ended. A few minor victories and tents are pitched. Put one Negro on a municipal board and the feeling is that the battle has been fought and the victory is won. This is how tokenism gets a foothold and, all too often, blocks real progress.

Token progress is, in a very real sense, painfully crippling, for it has the tendency to give us a false sense of accomplishment. It sometimes causes us to forget about the job yet to be done, suggesting we rest contentedly on what has been accomplished instead of impatiently on what yet remains. It often causes us to examine critically the practices of others while ignoring our own shortcomings. This is why no amount of "progress" is really satisfactory, unless it presses on until there is no more progress to be made. Progress suggests process, and process, all too often, means "piecemeal" or tokenism. We must work for complete integration and complete freedom. No way station is sufficient. No civil rights bill, for instance, is satisfactory if it does not provide for *all* the blemishes to be removed.

C. Eric Lincoln has suggested that avoidance is a technique used by some people in their effort to deal with the problem of racial discrimination. These are the people who attempt to avoid, through various means, a confrontation with the problem. Once when I was speaking to a group in Cleveland, Ohio, I mentioned that our children, who had recently moved from Nashville, Tennessee, were attending segregated schools for the first time. And incidentally, this was the first time they had attended school in the North! During

*181*

the discussion period one of the persons in attendance asked why we didn't simply move to a predominantly white neighborhood and avoid the problem. It took some effort to explain that this does not really solve the problem. The existence of de facto segregation anywhere is a threat to everybody. Staying away from it does not suddenly usher one into the City of Freedom. It is short of the proper goal.

Even complete desegregation is not the ultimate goal, but, rather, it is integration. Desegregation tears down something that is undesirable while integration builds up something that is desirable. The goal for Christians can never be mere desegregation, because this is mainly external and structural while integration is internal and spiritual.

## III

We are likely to search more diligently than ever for an alternate route when we discover that the road of truth to the City of Freedom leads us directly through the valley of sacrifice. Perhaps it would be better, we think, if we could know what would happen to us in it, but we cannot know. The way through is dark and dismal, and the fear of not knowing what lurks ahead is quite as painful as the experience which awaits us. Yet, if we would reach the City, we must travel this way.

Why must it be this way? It is because the thesis and the antithesis are conjoined and there must be conflict. It is because righteousness and unrighteousness, by virtue of their very natures, must be in mortal conflict with each other. We do not know all the answers to why men who are identified with the right side of an issue must suffer. God does not provide us with the complete answer, but he does equip us with that which will enable us to endure even though we do not know. And this is what is important.

Going into the valley we discover there are relics which provide inspiration and, indeed, direction, for us. There we behold the bars of a Bedford jail wherein John Bunyan languished. There are the bomb fragments that have torn asunder homes and church buildings and have taken the lives of Sunday-school children. There we find the charred remains of a burned bus which once held freedom riders. And towering above all of the relics of the valley we see a crude, rugged cross. If we listen with our soul, we can hear a voice coming from that cross saying, "I am the way, and the truth, and the life," and we see a light—the Light of the world, beckoning us to walk in that light so that we shall surely reach the city.

We are pilgrims to the City of Freedom, and if we travel on the road of Truth with quiet dignity, calm persistence, and with courageous spirits we shall reach our destination.

# 20. some comments on race hate

GARDNER TAYLOR

*Gardner Taylor is a Baptist who was born in Louisiana in 1918. Educated at Leland College (A.B.) and the Oberlin Graduate School of Theology (B.D.), and the recipient of two honorary Doctor of Divinity degrees, he is the pastor now of the Concord Baptist Church in Brooklyn, having served earlier in Elyria, Ohio, and in New Orleans and Baton Rouge, Louisiana.*

*Dr. Taylor has a worldwide reputation as a preacher. Three times he has been the preacher at the Baptist World Alliance, in 1947 in Copenhagen, in 1950 in Cleveland, and in 1955 in London. In 1958 he preached throughout the Australian Commonwealth, and in 1961 was an exchange preacher in England and Scotland.*

*A leader in the civil rights movement, he has spoken at rallies throughout the United States. When integration was first implemented in New York City he was a member of the Board of Education. Also, he has been a member of the New York City Commission on Human Relations. In July, 1963, he was arrested for demonstrating against job discrimination in the building industry in Brooklyn.*

Then saith the woman of Samaria unto him, How is it that thou, being a Jew, askest drink of me,

184

which am a woman of Samaria? for the Jews have
no dealings with the Samaritans. (John 4:9 KJV.)

Race hate is an old and persistent disease in the bloodstream of
society. It has divided Jew and Samaritan, Greek and barbarian,
black American and white American. Race hate is not a one-way
street. It infects the hater and the hated, since the hated learns to
hate the hater. Prejudice and bigotry produce prejudice and bigotry.
The church's supreme consideration must be that such hatred of
people, for whatever reason, and most especially on the basis that
they are physically different from us, offends heaven and shuts
so many out from God. This is the ultimate danger in any sin and
makes race hate eligible for consideration and concern by the
church. It may, rather it does, shut men from God.

This nearly happened in the well-known meeting of Jesus with
the Samaritan woman. A long and bitter enmity had existed between Jews and Samaritans who, in truth, had a common ancestry.
The basis of the ancient rift had been religious, but was also compounded with difference of race. When Jesus appeared at Jacob's
well with Mount Gerizim in the background the woman of Samaria of whom he asked water was blinded by her prejudice.
Now, let us leave out of the matter the divinity of our Lord. Even
then we must say that there was force and thrust in his words of
wisdom and insight, but race hatred blinded this woman to that
wisdom and insight. He was full of compassion, and an infinite
sympathy for people rested like a holy light upon his countenance.
Again and again it is said in the New Testament by those who
watched as he dealt with the people, "He was moved with compassion." Bigotry blinded this Samaritan woman to the sight of
that deep and pervasive sympathy which beamed forth from his
face. There were in his voice the accents of conviction and tones of
authority, so that people hearing him went away saying, "No man
ever spoke like this man." Race hatred deafened this woman's ears
to those notes of blessed assurance that sounded forth when he
spoke. She said to him, "How is it that thou, being a Jew, askest

185

drink of me which am a woman of Samaria?" Bias of race blinded this woman's eyes and deafened her ears. Such prejudice can prove fatal.

The pulpits of this land must point out that this hatred—this deep, angry, bitter animosity which we call racial prejudice—warps our thinking in this country and is a cancer eating at this nation's vitals and dooming it to failure. In addition to the acts of hatred aimed at black men, there are depths of hatred and bitterness in the Negro community toward white America which would shock and shake this land if they could be plumbed and beheld.

The Church of Jesus Christ might well bow its head in America, for it, North and South, led in promoting the ceremonies and rituals which institutionalized and shaped the contours of this evil. Kyle Haselden in *The Racial Problem in Christian Perspective* has pointed out that segregation in public facilities in this country goes back only to the 1870's and in many places only to the early 1900's, even in the South. This is true as far as the secular institutions are concerned, but in 1795 in New York City, in the John Street Methodist Church, free black men found so much embarrassment because of race that Peter Williams, a former slave who had purchased his freedom, led the Negro members of that church forth to form the African Methodist Episcopal Zion Church. In Philadelphia at the turn of the century, Richard Allen who started the A.M.E. Church was pulled from his knees while praying in old St. George's Church. In reality the church set the pace, established the pattern, and provided for segregation in this country. For this the church must bow its head in shame.

At the same time, the gospel of Jesus Christ agitated and prodded and disturbed and distressed some Christians so much that they, black and white, made their protest, some in their own blood, against the evils of racism that existed and still exist in this country. John Brown whose raid on Harper's Ferry helped light the fires of civil conflict was religiously motivated. On the side of the slaves, the gospel of Christ helped to motivate the uprisings of Denmark Vesey in Charleston, South Carolina, in 1822 and Nat Turner in Southhampton County, Virginia, in 1831. It is to the credit of the gospel and its releasing power for freedom that these incidents led the Virginia legislature to decree that "No slave, free Negro, or mulatto shall preach, or hold any meeting for religious purposes day or night." The prohibition is a badge of honor for the gospel. For where Christ truly is, man must and will be free.

There are those who constantly assert that morality cannot be legislated, and that people's acceptance of one another must be a matter of religion and not of law. This is palmed off as religious insight. But this is only a half truth. Our Christian faith recognizes the place which law must hold if man will not obey grace. Paul Tillich, the theologian, has put it aright: "If law is not internalized in conscience, then conscience must be externalized in law." Christians must press for laws that restrain the wild, primitive, savage lunges of race hatred and bigotry. Paul speaks of the law as a schoolmaster who brings men along, trains them, and restrains them until the power of Christ can go to work.

We must dismiss the idea of a Christian faith that is all sweetness and light and patience and niceness. There is judgment with God, swift and awful. A cry is heard in the midnight chill, "Behold, the bridegroom cometh," and the wise are by that sudden summons divided in judgment from the foolish. Every man's work is judged. Every nation's work is judged. We mourn in this country the necessity for the long bitter campaign that goes forward to make the deeds of the land fit its words. We lament the traumas and shocks and pains and deaths suffered in the cause of liberating the nation. But we would have reason to wonder and to doubt God if this season of trouble and tension, hatred and violence had not come upon the nation. This country could have solved this problem with double ease a hundred years ago. It is doubly hard a hundred years later. It will continue to be hard because hatred and suspicion and bitterness are all through the land. This is the judgment of one who has said, "Whatsoever a man soweth, that shall he also reap." In our lifetime we shall not know peace between the blacks and whites in this country. It is because not enough blacks are so dedicated to liberty that they are ready to confront the nation in love with every resource at their command, including their own death. It is because not enough whites believe sufficiently in the Christian religion, the Jewish faith, or the Constitution to make them living reality.

This matter of men disliking each other because of color is basically, like everything else in life, a religious problem. False gods cannot finally save us for they cannot solve our problems. Elijah Muhammed, the Black Muslim, and his followers are understandably angry, and it must be said that he has given to his disciples a sense of identity and dignity. But the doctrine of separation has already failed when sponsored in the white community. It is doomed to the same failure when sponsored by the black community. We, black and white, have irrevocably and indelibly influenced each other and cannot be separated in this land, as James Baldwin has pointed out with classic eloquence.

List the cures and they are all partial. Nonviolence is an attractive, but only a partial answer to the problem of race, since it must be attended by the force of boycott in a situation where boycott will hurt. In addition, it presupposes a goodness in man which may be alien to our true nature. Many speak of amalgamation as the full and sufficient answer to the problem of race in this country. This is to think in terms of centuries rather than years, since the rate of amalgamation in this country is perhaps slower today than ever before. The new status of personhood makes Negro women less vulnerable to the clandestine trespasses of the white male, and the Negro male is better equipped to defend his hearth against the sexual adventures of the white man. In addition, interracial marriages face the severe strains of a society grievously sick at this point of race. In my own fifteen years in Brooklyn, I have performed more than a thousand weddings. Fewer than fifty of them have been interracial.

No, the problem of people accepting one another is religious. James Baldwin, honest, bitter spokesman of the current American scene, has stated the religious consideration, though he doubtless would not admit the religious nature of his thesis. "It is not a question," he said, "of whether the white man can love me, it is a question of whether he can love himself." The same may be said of the black man as he faces the white man. I can accept other people only as I have accepted myself. I must first identify myself before I can tell who you are. I must first be delivered from self-loathing before I can regard you with reverence and respect. I must first have my own center of loyalty established before I am eligible to offer loyalty to you.

The reason I owe respect and reverence for every human person is ultimately religious, and roots in my faith about my origin, status, and destiny and, in turn, about every man's. What is it that gives preciousness to every human soul, never mind the color, the creed, the previous condition of servitude, as we like to say? It is our origin, our worth, and our destiny that we find the price tag which belongs upon every man. There is no satisfying word about when and how we started other than that contained in the Hebrew-Christian Bible. God! Our beginnings are no meaner, no more parochial than that! The psalmist, looking back upon the high, brave assumptions of his fathers, exclaimed with a gasp in his voice, "It is he that hath made us, and not we ourselves; we are his people, and the sheep of his pasture." There lies our origin, in the words "It is he that hath made us." So! Every man is kin to God. However much we may differ from him there is something in us of him. However defaced the likeness there is in every man the image of God himself. This is every man's origin, and the nature of his beginning marks every man as authentic nobility.

There is in every man a worth attested by God. Again, the psalmist looks at man and remembers admiringly that God is mindful of him in the face of the vast stretches of his creation and his divine prerogatives and responsibilities. Never was a more extravagant paean of praise sung to man under God than by this ancient Theist, "What is man, that thou art mindful of him? and the son of man, that thou visitest him? For thou has made him a little lower than the angels, and hast crowned him with glory and honor." This is the biography of every human soul.

The New Testament contains a still sublimer proof of worth. There is the act at Calvary and the vast mysterious transaction which occurred there involving us men. All that God means by that hill and that Cross and that man on it we cannot pretend to know. But this one thing we do know: There God placed his price tag, his estimate of value, on every human soul who walks the face of the earth. And if God so assesses, so gages worth, then I have an obligation to every man who means as much to God as Calvary.

There is a third element in the constitution of the human spirit which mandates my respect and enlists my regard. There is some august destiny within and beyond this time sphere which belongs to every human being. I sense that awareness in myself and in other men. Wordsworth was spokesmen for all men, black and white, when he wrote:

> Though inland far we be,
> Our Souls have sight of that immortal sea
> Which brought us hither.

I hear that same cadence of destiny in the mysteriously compelling words of the music of my fathers. Black backs glisten with sweat in the moonlight after a long and cruel day of unrequited toil. If ever there was a dead-end street this is it. They have been snatched from Mother Africa and planted in a cold and hostile land. Their customs have been wrenched from their lives by the alien culture with which they are surrounded. Maybe 30,000,000 of their people died in the iniquitous Middle Passage. They were "motherless children a long ways from home," and yet there is in their music that theme of a high and lofty destiny.

> Before I'd be a slave
> I'd be buried in my grave

And go home to my Lord
And be free.

I looked over Jordan
And what did I see?

.    .    .    .    .

A band of angels coming after me.

That sense of destiny in every man, given body and substance by
the New Testament, demands in me respect and regard for every
man. It is in this sense that religion, alone, is the answer to our
deep chasms of tension and mutual hate which afflict white and
black people in this land. God grant us his grace that we may be
equal to this issue with which our lives are met.